GET YOUR
RELATIONSHIPS
RIGHT

Inside and Out

GET YOUR
RELATIONSHIPS
RIGHT
Inside and Out

Birgitta Gregory, Ph.D.

Library of Congress Control Number: 2007902939
ISBN: Hardcover   978-1-4257-6125-7
                 Softcover   978-1-4257-6110-3

To order additional copies of this book, contact:
Xlibris Corporation
1-888-795-4274
www.Xlibris.com
Orders@Xlibris.com
37100

CONTENTS

TABLE OF FIGURES

To Bruce,
who so lovingly and generously
continues to challenge and stimulates me to grow

Acknowledgments

So many people have been instrumental in the process of writing and publishing this book.

I want to express my gratitude to all my clients and students who have encouraged me to put my teachings into a book format. Their courage and commitment to growth, shown by their personal example, have been a great source of inspiration.

I appreciate all the support from my editors Jeanine LaFrance, Kristina Tabon y Suñer, Kathrina Garcia, Lisa Fernandez and Elmer Mangubat for their diligent editing, removing any distractions that would otherwise take away the essence of the book, while still managing to keep the integrity of my words.

I thank Tony Medina for transforming my sketches and ideas into creative illustrations inside the book, and Annika Magnusson for providing the perfect photo for the front cover.

I extend my gratitude to Gina Gregory, Paige Jacobs, Dr. Steven Glass, Deborah Green, and Anna Olsson for so tirelessly and diligently reading the manuscript at various stages of development and providing valuable feedback and suggestions.

I owe special thanks to my exceptional friend Paige Jacobs and to Mark Waxman for creating the title *Get Your Relationships Right: Inside and Out* that so clearly captures my vision.

I extend a heartfelt thank you to my long-term friend Lena Adolfsson for her enthusiastic and unconditional support.

I thank Fredrik Wall for his commitment to follow through and accountability that directly influenced the writing process.

I want to convey special appreciation to my Mom, Barbro Lindberg for giving me the strength and courage to follow my heart and my dreams, and to my dad, Widar Lindberg for teaching me that as human beings we are all equal regardless of age, sex, race, education, status in society, or money.

I extend my deepest thanks and admiration to my daughter Gina for her extensive review of the final manuscript and her thorough assistance in helping me complete this book.

Most of all, I want to express my profound appreciation and gratitude to my husband and creative partner, Dr. Bruce Gregory, for his daily support, continued feedback, invaluable suggestions, and endless patience—without which I could not have written this book.

Finally, thank you to all of you who I've had, am having, or will have a relationship with in the future. You have taught me priceless lessons about communication and relationship dynamics and I look forward to continuing to learn more for the rest of my life.

It is Worth the Investment

Without oxygen, we won't survive very long! Without healthy interactions, we will starve and eventually we will reach emotional death. We may be there physically but emotionally we are unfulfilled, wasting away. We will engage in communication and behaviors that only lead to further alienation from others but more importantly from ourselves.

It is time to stop, to take a moment and discover the hidden dynamics that we weren't taught in school; uncover the secrets and differences between a happy and fulfilling interaction versus a mediocre and unsatisfactory one.

What do you want? What is your vision?

It starts with you *and it ends with you.* How well you know yourself, your needs, your fears, your desires, your feelings, your thoughts, will greatly determine how well you will know someone else. The more real you are with yourself the more real you can be in relationship with someone else. When you have a real relationship, you don't get to avoid unpleasant feelings or experiences, you get to experience depth, and reach peace as you work them through and get closure. You build your self-esteem, realize your self-worth, and you get to experience a richness that doesn't occur in superficial and unreal relationships.

When we think about relationships, we so often look outside of ourselves. We are not happy with a spouse, a friend, a parent, or a child. We fall victims of our emotions and fail to recognize that our expectations are unrealistic. How can we possibly be content and at peace in relationships with others if we haven't developed healthy, supportive relationships with all the forces within ourselves first? Isn't that like putting the cart before the horse?

If I am afraid of my anger, how can I expect that I will be comfortable with yours? If I am not comfortable with your anger, then how can I expect that I will be able to deal effectively with my own responses to you when you are angry? If I am not able to deal with my own responses or you effectively when you are angry, how can I expect that I will have a healthy, real relationship with you? *I can't.* If I do, I am setting us up for failure. I may never be comfortable with anger. However, if I don't develop a relationship with anger and discomfort I will become a victim of it, whether it is my own or yours, and I will react in various ways. I may avoid it. I may suppress it and act it out later. I may overcompensate for it by being extra nice. I may act cowardly and give in and resent you later. I will not experience having choices and I will most definitively not be making proactive, conscious choices since the driving force behind my behavior will be my desire to avoid the anger.

This book is about consciousness. It is about a desire and a need to learn, to continue to grow and expand in our relationships so that we truly can be the best we can possibly be, feel the best we can possibly feel, and create the most fulfilling relationships we can possibly create inside and out.

There are tools, questions, suggestions, and examples to learn from real life experiences. You may recognize yourself or a friend and feel as though I have written about you. I have, and I haven't. I have, since we are all human beings and the examples are about human experiences. I have not, since I have changed names, genders, and situations to maintain the integrity of and the respect for the people that I know and work with.

This is where it begins and you will decide where it will end.

1

Relationships

A relationship *can be described as a state of being related to or connected to.*

For you to love someone else you must first love yourself.

Have you ever heard someone say that and wondered what they really mean? To love yourself, what do you do with yourself? What is required to love yourself? Is it enough to say I love myself? How do you come to love yourself? Are you born loving yourself? Or, do your parents teach you to love yourself? Where does the love for yourself come from? The purpose of this book is not to delve into philosophical questions. The main purpose is to provide some insight and clarity, so that you can find answers for yourself, and be empowered in your relationships.

Let's say that it is true that you first must love yourself to be able to love someone else. Is it not also true that you must first have a healthy relationship with yourself before you can have healthy relationships outside of yourself? What is a healthy relationship with yourself? What does that look like? How do you get it? You probably picked up this book because you want answers, not a barrage of questions.

The purpose of the questions is to stimulate and support your
curiosity so you can access your inner resources.
That is where the power lies, within each and every one of us!

When you look at this picture, you'll see a place inside that houses your resources. In an ideal world you would be able to tap into your resources, without interference, on an as-needed basis. A thought would come up and before you would respond, you would access your place inside and find the right resource. The easy access between your need and your resource would make it simple to relate. Thus, your interactions would be filled with joy and curiosity and you would see the world with clarity. Unfortunately, that is not how it works; life happens and things become complicated.

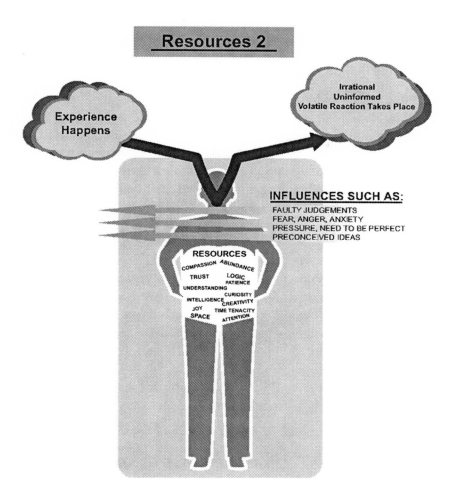

What you see in this drawing is how a variety of *influences*[1] enter into our lives. Those influences will challenge us, as they tend to interfere with our abilities to access our resources. The first step is to understand and recognize the force those influences have on our interactions and experiences. The second step is to develop healthy relationships with each influence.

---

[1] An influence is something that manipulates, affects, impacts, or controls or has power over us, examples used herein: anger, disappointment, frustration, hostility, pressure, faulty judgments, rigidity, pressure, etc. An influence when supported correctly can become a resource and as such an asset in our interactions.

Influence of Anger

A healthy relationship with the influence of anger can look like this:

1. You know what your anger feels like.
2. You recognize what triggers your anger. Different situations and behaviors (e.g., Someone cuts you off when you are driving. Someone interrupts you while you are talking). You experience the thoughts (Who does that person think he is? What gives him the right to be rude?) and feelings (Anger when someone doesn't listen to you. Pain when someone says something that hurts you.)
3. You become aware of your anger as it happens in the moment. "I am really angry."
4. You recognize the level of the anger you feel in response to the situation, behavior, thought, or feeling. Is your anger a 10 on a scale from 1-10, 10 being very strong and 1 barely being present?
5. You *experience having choices* when your anger is attempting to cut you off from accessing your internal resources. You can be confronted with the following:

   a. Choose to allow your anger to dominate and act it out. You can, for example, lash out, withdraw, say something hurtful back, or interrupt. Hence, allow your anger to cut you off from your internal resources.
   b. Choose to add a *faulty judgment*[2] about being angry and decide that anger is "bad." Dismiss and suppress your anger because you don't want to be a "bad" person. Thus, not access your internal resources.
   c. Choose to become scared of your anger. Take the position that you can't handle it. Consequently, ignore your internal resources.
   d. Choose to accept your anger. See it as a signal that something in your life or in the situation needs to be changed. Be *proactive*[3] and look in your resources and see what kind of support you need when

---

[2] Faulty judgment is the kind that is made carelessly, irresponsibly, without sufficient information or knowledge, in fear or used to compensate for fears or unaccepted or unrecognized needs.

[3] Proactive means taking the initiative.

you get angry. Do you need *time to* calm down? *Attention? Contact?* Do you need to *vent*[4]? *Find a resolution?*

Once you have increased your awareness about the various influences you can reach an acceptance about their presence and develop tools to deal with them more effectively. Instead of fighting the anger, or the disappointment, attempting to alienate the experience from your life, pretending that the anger or disappointment don't exist, or trying to destroy the experience, you can take charge and decide what kind of relationships you will have with those influences. How much power are you willing to give up to the anger? How much of the time are you going to be a victim of the disappointment?

You already have relationships with each and every one of those influences right now. *The question is do you want to redefine the structure of those relationships or not?*

You probably have an avoidant type of relationship with anger if you don't recognize your anger. Before you get a chance to recognize feeling angry you may be suppressing your anger. Then all of a sudden when the pressure becomes too much you may "blow up" to the surprise of other people in your life. You may withdraw and become depressed when you get angry or when someone gets angry at you.

If you avoid conflict, you may have a fear-based relationship with conflict. That will determine how you will interact with others. Most likely, you'll be "putting up" with behaviors you don't like, develop *resentment*[5] over time, and act it out later. You'll probably be more *passive-aggressive*[6] in your relationships with others.

Depending on what kind of relationships we develop with those influences, we will either become their victims or grow stronger from learning about them. Some of the influences have been internalized from our parents, peers, and society. Some come from conclusions we have made after encountering experiences that produced pain or disappointment.

If we don't develop healthy relationships with each of the influences, our access between our experiences and our internal resources will be

---

[4] To vent is to relieve or unburden emotions/feelings via verbal expression.

[5] Resentment is a feeling of displeasure and indignation from a sense of being injured or offended.

[6] Passive-aggressive translates to indirect expressions of anger, disappointment, frustration, or resentment.

compromised. When that happens, we become victims of the influence that cuts off the access. We react instead of responding appropriately. We get derailed and off-centered in our communication and relationships.

Andrew and Julia

Andrew is tired of Julia's *constant nagging*. If it is not one thing it is another. She is dissatisfied *all the time*. Here she goes again:

"Andrew, *what's wrong with you* why don't you put the dishes in the dishwasher?"

Andrew knows it is not really a question, so *he ignores it*.

"Stop *hounding me*. I *just* got home from work. *Can't I get any peace around here, and you wonder why I don't like coming home?*"

Andrew's response is not a question either, so *Julia ignores it*.

"*I don't ask for much from you. The least you can do* is put your dirty, *disgusting* dishes away!"

Julia *storms out* of the kitchen.

Andrew *grabs a drink, and goes and turns on the TV.*

Neither Andrew nor Julia is accessing their curiosity and inner resources in their interaction. They ask questions that aren't really questions. They use exaggerated and inflammatory language. They ignore each others communication as if it doesn't matter, isn't important, and doesn't have any value. Both of them are unconsciously acting out their frustration, disappointment, discouragement, anger, and resentment. They get no closure, and they don't get closer to each other.

Their interaction has been derailed by a *lack of perspective*. Julia cannot possibly nag *constantly*. Maybe she does it often, even too often; *constantly*, probably not. Julia may be *dissatisfied* often, maybe even too often; *all the time, 100 percent* of the time, probably not.

They *act out*[7] their anger and resentment. They are using inflammatory words that are intended to hurt the other and to create doubt in the other person. *What's wrong with you? Stop hounding me! You wonder why I don't like coming home. I don't ask for much from you! The least you can do! Disgusting!*

---

[7]   To act out is to behave in a way that unconsciously expresses (often repressed) feelings, thoughts, fears, or needs.

They behave as if the other person doesn't exist, doesn't have any value, and doesn't need to be respected. They pay no attention to each other's questions. *Julia storms out. Andrew turns on the TV.* They accept that their questions aren't being taken seriously because they know that they don't really care about the answers. The intent behind the question is not to get an answer. It is to recklessly vent their frustration, anger, and lack of tolerance. It is a blatant example of disrespecting themselves and one another. Julia and Andrew's situation is out of control.

What we sometimes forget is that our communication speaks volumes about how we feel and think about ourselves. It shows what kind of self-esteem we have. What kind of morals and values we believe in and what our standards are.

*Our self-esteem is greatly dependent on how well or poorly
we deal with the influences and the force behind them.*

Our communication and ability to interact also shows the following:

1. What kind of relationships we have with the influences and our resources; how well we know ourselves, our needs, our fears, our feelings, our thoughts
2. How severe or mild the cut off is to our internal resources
3. What kind of support we need to stay centered and balanced
4. What we do when the influences cut off our access
5. If we experience having choices

*How could Andrew and Julia's interaction been different if they
would have accessed their internal resources?*

First of all, the interaction would not have happened the way it happened. They would have dealt with their anger and addressed and resolved the issue of "nagging" and "dishes in the sink," long before they would have had a chance to build up resentment.

Secondly, they would be able to vent their feelings in a constructive and direct way. Andrew and Julia would differentiate between making a statement to vent and asking a relevant nonhostile question. They would not disregard the other person's question. Instead, they would respond directly with a reasonable and logical answer.

They would maintain perspective and realize that once in a while they would disappoint and anger each other. They would acknowledge that those feelings are part of any relationship. Their behaviors and feelings would be understood, respected, and dealt with accordingly. Therefore, they would be forgiving and compassionate toward each other. They would make an agreement of how the "nagging" and keeping the "dishes in the sink" would be dealt with in the future.

They would not use inflammatory language. Instead, they would try to describe their feelings, thoughts, and behavior as clearly and objectively as possible. They would be curious to explore any *underlying issues*[8] that may be causing the behaviors to persist, and look for a solution.

To have a relationship with anger, you need to be connected to it. That means that you need to experience, understand, and accept the anger. When you are so uncomfortable with anger that you try to discard it without even knowing that it is there, you'll become a victim of it. An influence can be used as an asset. The following is an example of using an influence as an asset:

Peter and His Mother, Sara

Peter went to his mother to discuss a small loan to start a business. Peter's mother, Sara, thought the idea was great. The potential to make a lot of money was there. Sara's main concern was that Peter hadn't been in business for himself before. Sara didn't have a lot of money and had no experience herself as an entrepreneur. She wasn't sure Peter had worked long enough yet. After serious consideration Sara finally decided against lending Peter the money he needed to get started. In Sara's eyes, Peter was still her "little boy" whom she wanted to protect. Sara wasn't able to recognize Peter's abilities as an adult entrepreneur. She wasn't able to work through her own fears of failure.

Peter became very disappointed in his mom for refusing to invest in the business. Other people had expressed an interest in his idea, yet his own mother didn't believe in him. Peter had some choices to make:

1. He could choose to allow his disappointment to derail him from his goals and vision and give up his idea.
2. Peter could choose to let his mother's inability to believe in his abilities affect his own trust in himself and give up his idea.
3. He could choose to acknowledge his disappointment and seek out other sources that could lend him the start-up funds instead of giving up.

---

[8]   An underlying issue is one that is not easily seen or noticed.

Peter chose the third option. It took him a few years to become successful. When he did he became hugely profitable and he continued throughout the years to get involved in one endeavor after another that brought him great financial security. Peter had used his disappointment as the fuel to keep him going when he encountered let downs and hard times. His disappointment turned into anger and it led him to thoughts like: "I'll show her. I'll show everyone. I will never fail. I will make it with or without her help!" which spurred him along. Time went on and, eventually, Peter's anger and disappointment dissipated. Instead, he felt proud of himself and his accomplishments. It didn't take Sara long to recognize her son's skills and hard work. Forgotten was the time when Sara hadn't been able to give Peter the support he needed. On some deeper level, Peter recognized that he had been able to take the feelings that became triggered inside him when Sara said no and used them to his advantage. He used the feelings as a resource, instead of allowing his disappointment to cut him off from his internal resources. He had chosen not to become a victim of his own feelings and his mom's inability to support him.

It is a fantasy to believe that we won't have to deal with influences from our experiences in life. That is why it pays to invest the time up-front and take an inventory of ourselves to create a foundation for successful relationships.

Priorities

In business, we set priorities. If we didn't, we would be unfocused and ineffective. Priorities guide our choices. When our priorities are clear and well defined it is easier to set and reinforce *boundaries*[9]. As aware as we are of the value of using priorities as tools in business, we often seem to forget them in our personal relationships.

Rachel, Adam, and their two children, Evan and Ashley, decided to go on a family outing. As Rachel was backing up Adam's new car, she could hear the sound of the left, rear passenger side scraping against something. She had looked in the rear mirror before she backed up and she had seen nothing that was in her way. Rachel knew as soon as she heard it that she would be in trouble. Adam already thought of her as careless, now he would get really angry. She thought to herself, "What could it possibly have been?"

Adam burst out, "Rachel, what are you doing? I knew I shouldn't have let you drive my car! Get out! I want to switch seats right now." Rachel could understand

---

[9]   Boundaries are lines or things marking a limit or a border.

that Adam was upset but she didn't like the way he was talking to her. It was only a car. It wasn't as though she had harmed him or their kids. Rachel felt her anger surge through her body and she yelled back, "Adam, calm down you are scaring the kids. I am not getting out of the car. You are being ridiculous. An accident can happen to anyone. I am an adult and I can drive." Rachel's reaction only fueled Adam's anger further and he yelled even louder;

"I'm scaring the kids? I'm not the one who doesn't care about anything but myself. How about, for once, you listen to me?" Rachel couldn't believe what she was hearing. She remembered not too long ago when he had accidentally opened his car door too wide and scratched it against the wall. As Rachel and Adam continued their argument Evan and Ashley started fighting and crying in the back seat.

What were Adam's and Rachel's priorities during this interaction?

1. They didn't have any clear priorities.
2. Their priorities were in the background and inaccessible.
3. Adam's priority was to switch seats with Rachel and drive his car.
4. Rachel's priority was to remain in the driver's seat and continue to drive Adam's car.
5. Their priority was to react to the event and vent their anger unto each other.

If their priority would have been their children's welfare, then their interaction would have had to change. How would the children benefit from Adam and Rachel yelling at each other and making comments that were hurtful? *They wouldn't have.* So right from the beginning, having had the priority of the children's welfare in the foreground would have guided both Rachel and Adam to think before they reacted.

The clearer the priority is the more support we can receive from it. Focusing on the priority will actually help reduce the intensity of the feeling, which will make it possible to experience having a choice, which will, in turn, empower us and positively impact our actions.

It is predictable that Adam would react to his car being damaged. There is nothing wrong with his experience. The problem lies in how he behaves after he has had the experience and feeling. Adam can choose to focus on the anger he is feeling, and make that be his priority, or he can focus on his priority: his children's welfare. Once he has made a choice on which priority he will focus on, some actions will automatically be excluded from his response; the same applies to Rachel.

Shifting to a mind-set that is committed to keeping the focus on the priority can almost instantaneously shift dynamics:

> *I have feelings, thoughts, and reactions but I am not willing to have those feelings, thoughts, and reactions run my life or exclude me from having choices. Making my relationships, whether it is my relationship with priorities, or anger conscious, is the first step to achieve the freedom to make choices.*

2

Back to Basics

Without water we will die! Without communication our lives break down. Without enlightened, effective communication our existence will be imbalanced and deprived of potential fulfillment.

Communication *is* the most powerful way to develop, learn, and grow. It is a way to express feelings, share thoughts, exchange experiences, information, and knowledge. It is a way to get close or create distance: to feel good or bad, empowered or powerless. In our communication we can be useful or useless, happy or sad, stressed or peaceful. It can be joyful or dreadful.

Communication is like a diamond in the rough, full of potential and beauty, but it can be shapeless and unclear until properly cut and polished. Enlightened, effective communication is the finished diamond, crystal clear and ready to enjoy. Whether you are looking to grow spiritually, emotionally, psychologically, or intellectually, communication is an essential tool for your successful journey.

We spend 80 percent or more of our time awake[10], communicating in one form or another. Yet communication seems to be an area that we are "supposed" to know how to do, without being taught the subtle nuances of the hidden dynamics that so profoundly affect our success or failure.

Granted, throughout school we are taught the mechanics of communication. We learn grammar, spelling, and how sentences are to be structured. We learn to understand the difference between a verb, adverb, adjective, noun, and pronoun. We often even learn a second and a third language. Still, unless we are subjected to special training later in life, we are not given a map, or clear instructions, of how to avoid misunderstandings or how to identify and deal with the vast variety of obstacles involved when we send or receive a message. We are not given the secrets of how to achieve effective and satisfactory communication between each other. We use trial and error as we move through life.

From the beginning of time, there have been communication breakdowns. There are numerous reasons communication is misunderstood. Sometimes

---

[10] Chris Roebuck, *Effective Communication* (New York: AMACOM, 1998).

it is because we don't speak the same language. Other times we don't use the right words to convey a feeling or a thought. The result is that we spend hours wasting time being frustrated, irritated, aggravated, and disappointed in ourselves and in others when we interact and communicate.

Effective communication can be translated to: *Desired result gained from the act of giving or exchanging information signals or messages via talk gestures or writing.*

When we drive through a city, the signs of how to get from one place to another can be very helpful. If the signs are clear, easy to understand, and simple to follow, they may help reduce stress and frustration.

Verbal communication that is done well can also reduce stress and frustration. Likewise, when communication breaks down it can have a long lasting negative effect on our relationships.

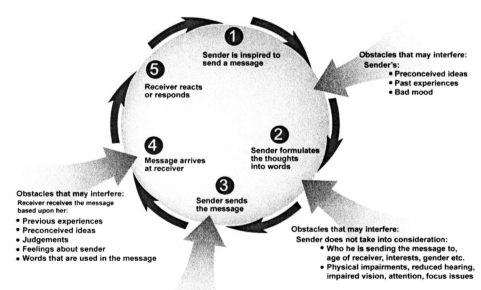

Communication Circle

Receiver SWITCHES ROLES WITH SENDER
• The communication Circles starts all over

1. Sender is inspired to send a message

Obstacles that may interfere:
Sender's:
• Preconceived ideas
• Past experiences
• Bad mood

5. Receiver reacts or responds

4. Message arrives at receiver

2. Sender formulates the thoughts into words

3. Sender sends the message

Obstacles that may interfere:
Receiver receives the message based upon her:
• Previous experiences
• Preconceived ideas
• Judgements
• Feelings about sender
• Words that are used in the message

Obstacles that may interfere:
Sender does not take into consideration:
• Who he is sending the message to, age of receiver, interests, gender etc.
• Physical impairments, reduced hearing, impaired vision, attention, focus issues

Obstacles that may interfere:
Sender does not know if:
• The email or fax will be received
• The noise factor is a problem
• The receiver is preoccupied with other tasks

How the Communication Circle works:

- Sender = Susan who sends the message
- Receiver = Rebecca who receives the message
- Obstacles = factors that may interfere with or inaccurately color the message that is being sent

Step 1

An idea is born. Susan decides she wants to send a message to Rebecca. Susan is irritated with Rebecca and wants to let her know.

First mistake: Susan doesn't distinguish between what seems so clear to her in her own mind and the possibility that Rebecca may see the situation completely differently.

Step 2

Susan chooses the words she will use to convey her message.

Second mistake: She doesn't take into consideration that Rebecca is hard of hearing, and doesn't adjust her volume. Susan chooses the location for their get-together to take place in the park where a class of preschool children is playing, further aggravating Rebecca's hearing problem.

Step 3

Susan sends the message.

> *"Rebecca I have something important I need to talk to you about. When you question whether I understand you it makes me angry because I feel like you think I am stupid. If I don't understand I'll tell you. Will you stop asking me after every other sentence if I understand what you said?"*

Third mistake: Susan is hostile in her tone and delivery. Her irritation is overpowering the essence of her message.

Step 4

Obstacles that may interfere with the clarity and understanding of the message:

- Background noise or other distractions
- Place that is chosen when sending the message
- Susan's assumption that as a result of her message her request should have been obvious to Rebecca
- Susan's and Rebecca's

  o Previous experiences
  o Preconceived judgments
  o Emotional frame of mind

- Rebecca's preoccupation of thoughts, receptivity, and interest
- Rebecca's physical impairment
- Susan's tone, volume, rate, pitch, and articulation of speech
- Susan's choice of words

Step 5

Arriving at Rebecca

Reality: Rebecca is preoccupied thinking about an upsetting interaction that she had had earlier that day with another coworker. Rebecca's hearing is reduced in her left ear, the kids are loud, and she has a difficult time hearing Susan, which frustrates her. Having to ask Susan to repeat herself infuriates Rebecca further. Finally, she gives up trying and reacts to Susan's message, as she understood it.

Step 6

Rebecca has a reaction to Susan's message. Without having heard every word, her response is based on emotional triggers. Rebecca switches roles with Susan and starts Step 1 again by saying,

> *"How dare you call me stupid, Susan, just because I can't hear you at times doesn't mean that I don't understand."*

An enlightened, effective form of communication has taken place when the message that was sent and received is one and the same[11]. This example demonstrates how easy a message can be misunderstood.

---

[11]   Ibid.

Various Forms of Communication

There are so many forms of communication. Sometimes we may choose to communicate verbally if the issue is time sensitive and we need an immediate response. On the other hand, we may choose to use a written method like a note, memo, or letter if we would like to have a record of the interaction; or if we need to process our feelings before we convey the message to the other person. We may use the telephone instead of an in-person meeting if the distance between the parties involved prevents face-to-face verbal communication. A group meeting may be the choice if we think that it would be more time efficient in reaching a large number of people at the same time. In today's world of technology, an e-mail or a fax may be the most appropriate method of instant communication. The method of communication one chooses is critical toward overcoming the obstacles described in the communication circle.

Direct or Indirect Communication

Direct communication can be translated to communication that is straight to the point. Indirect communication can be translated to communication that is not taking a direct course.

The choice of when to use one form versus the other may depend on the following:

- How comfortable you are with conflict
- How safe you feel within yourself and in your interaction
- How you, yourself respond to direct communication versus indirect communication
- Whether you determine one form of communication is presenting more of a risk than the other
- If you are willing to face possible rejection more directly
- What you have learned from role models in your life
- The sensitivity of the subject
- If time is of the essence
- If clarity is a priority
- Your own personality style

Direct communication can help prevent misunderstandings and confusion. However, there are also situations where indirect communication will work better. For example:

- If you are dealing with a person who prefers indirect communication and therefore relates to and understands that form of communication better
- If you have been told often that you are abrasive and insensitive
- If you determine that there is a better chance you will achieve the goal using indirect communication
- If it seems to be important to the other person that he or she came up with the idea in order to reach a common goal, and that aspect is not important to you or the cause
- If you use indirect communication as a tool to distract a person to ward off danger without alarming the person

By being alert to your style of communication, you become more aware of the process and thus, create more choices. Some good questions to ask yourself can start with these:

- *Why* . . . is it important that I talk about my concerns?
- *When* . . . is the best time to discuss my concerns?
- *How* . . . should I formulate my concerns?
- *Who* . . . is it that I need to address my concerns with?
- *Where* . . . should we meet so that our meeting can be as productive as possible?
- *What* . . . is my intent with discussing my concerns with X?

(The above words were used in the riddle by Rudyard Kipling: "I keep six honest serving men. They taught me all I knew. Their names are What and Why and When and How and Where and Who.")[12]

When you are exploring your communication style, ask some questions:

- *Is the form of communication you use working well for you, or is it causing you unnecessary aggravation?*
- *Have people in your life often complained about the form of communication you use?*
- *Do you feel that you have chosen the form of communication for reasons that support you, or reasons that help you avoid something uncomfortable?*

---

[12]   Ibid.

- *What benefits could you imagine would happen if you tried using the opposite form of communication?*
- *Knowing what you know now, how will you use this information in your future interactions with others?*

The Listening Process: Active or Passive

An important part in the communication process is the ability to listen. You can listen passively or actively. Some signs of active listening may be a nod, a verbal acknowledgement, a question, steady eye contact, or a statement that repeats back what was said confirming that you understood the message correctly.

Hearing

Hearing is not necessarily the same as listening. Hearing someone may mean that you more fully understand or relate to what is said. When a person feels heard, communication is generally more effective and satisfactory. A person may feel that you have listened, but not heard what he wants to convey. To hear someone involves validation and at times reassurance. It doesn't mean you have to agree, only convey that you have heard the words that have been spoken.

An example may look like this:

Jane is having a difficult day at work and comes to you to talk. Jane says, *"I am so upset! My boss is too demanding. I never seem to be able to satisfy him. He always makes me feel that I am not fast enough, that I don't pay close enough attention to his instructions and that I make too many mistakes. I'm fed up!"*

A sensitive and validating response may sound like this: *"I am so sorry you're upset. It sounds like you are going through a really difficult time right now. I can understand that you are fed up."*

It is important to listen and hear what Jane needs.

- Does she need to vent, express her fears, and feelings?
- Or is she looking to you to solve a problem and create a strategy to resolve her issues?

Jane will most likely experience not being heard by you if you move to the problem-solving stage of the process when she wants to vent.

A problem-solving response may sound like this: *Have you reality tested[13] your experience with your boss? Does he, in fact, think that you are not fast enough, don't pay close enough attention to his instructions and that you make too many mistakes? Or, are you being too hard on yourself? If he, in fact, thinks those things and you agree, what kind of support do you need from me, from him, from other people at work to improve in those areas?*

The purpose of allowing space for Jane to vent is so she can experience being heard. If you skip over that stage in the communication process and move directly into the problem-solving stage, Jane will most likely not be receptive, or be available to receive your support, and listen to your suggestions to solve the problem. To hear the difference between a need to vent and a need to solve the problem can be the difference between listening and hearing.

Some people vent and are ready to start solving the problem almost at the same time, others need more time to make the transition to problem solve. It helps to ask some questions to clarify what the person's needs are if you are unsure.

Here are some of the probable questions:

- Are you venting right now?
- Do you want me to help you problem solve now?
- How can I best support you right now?
- What do you need from me now?

When you listen, hear, and pay attention, you are giving the other person an opportunity to communicate effectively with you. When you interrupt, you prevent the person from having that experience. Likewise, if you skip a stage or jump ahead before the other person is ready to receive your input, enlightened communication becomes more difficult to achieve. It can be tricky to identify when the need to be heard is not being met. It is not like the need for food that is conscious and can readily be recognized, *"I'm hungry, I need to eat!"*

It is interesting that the need to be heard although mostly unconscious is a need that expects to be met. That means that I have the need to be heard and that I expect that you will hear me. When it is not met, we tend to get

---

[13]   To reality test is to verify one's experience by asking questions when unsure, repeat back information and ask the other person to verify or correct what one's interpretation of what the intent of the communication is.

flooded or overwhelmed by emotions, such as anger, rage, disappointment, hopelessness, and helplessness, and react accordingly. These may be some behaviors that may be acted out when we don't feel heard:

- We may repeat ourselves over and over again.
- We may stop communicating and withdraw from the interaction.
- We may give up and feel hopeless.
- We may punish the other person by not answering, or answer in an abusive fashion.
- We may lash out indirectly.
- We may make accusations such as you're not listening.

The following are some strategies that may be helpful to identify the need to be heard when we start feeling frustrated and are inclined to engage in the behaviors described above:

- Ask questions.
- Ask for feedback.
- Explore other creative ways to change the communication.
- Slow down the process.
- Become proactive instead of withdrawing.
- Move to the next step and look for different ways to be heard, like asking the other person to repeat back to us what he heard us say so we can determine whether he did hear us or not.

The goal to reach enlightened communication can be achieved by starting to raise our awareness. Have you noticed that the *characteristics* of the people you think are *effective listeners*[14] often are the following?

- Interested
- Patient
- Alert
- *Doesn't Interrupt*
- Caring
- Loving
- Sensitive

---

[14]   Robert W. Lucas, *Effective Interpersonal Relationships* (New York: McGraw-Hill, 1994).

- Not reactive to emotions
- Compassionate
- Other centered
- Uses nonverbal communication to reinforce verbal responses
- Responsive
- Nonjudgmental
- Focused
- Empathetic
- Effective evaluators

Similarly, have you found that the following are often the *characteristics* of the people you think are *ineffective listeners*[15]?

- Self-centered
- Insensitive
- Easily distracted
- Reactive
- Defensive
- Disinterested
- Judgmental
- Interrupts frequently
- Impatient
- Condescending
- Patronizing

Interpreting, Evaluating, Assessing, and Responding

After listening and hearing the other person's position, having checked back to ensure that you have understood what was said without interrupting, it is time to *interpret*[16] what you have heard so that you can gain an understanding of the message. Based upon your interpretation you evaluate and assess the message according to your belief system, and choose an appropriate way to *respond*[17].

---

[15]   Ibid.

[16]   Interpret means to explain the meaning of something by making it understandable.

[17]   To respond is when logic is used with the absence of emotionalism followed by a constructive choice to act responsibly. Logic takes priority over the need for the emotion to be acted out in the moment.

Factors that may affect your interpretation may be your previous experiences, background, biases, knowledge, and *projections*[18]. Other aspects may be circumstances in your current situation and your emotional state of mind at the time you are receiving the message.

When you respond it is important to consider a number of elements:

- Is the content of the message time sensitive?
- Will it make a difference if you respond now or next week? If so, how?
- Is it a sensitive subject?
- Are you emotionally invested in the message?
- Avoid inflammatory and provocative language such as *you are always, you never, that's stupid, you can't, you never will.*
- What is the person's intent?
- How can you best convey that you have understood the issue at hand and give an appropriate response that will reflect that appropriately?
- Is there any of your own issues that are interfering right now?
- What kind of support do you need to be *nonreactive*[19]?
- Postpone the response if you are emotionally unprepared.

The listening process can be summarized in five steps:

1. Listen
2. Hear
3. Interpret
4. Evaluate/Assess
5. Respond

Changing the way you listen, takes effort, practice, dedication to not interrupt, and a commitment to excellence. Be aware of your own agenda, personal views, and faulty judgments that may interfere in the listening process.

---

[18] Projections are the unconscious act or process of ascribing to others your own ideas, impulses, or emotions that are undesirable or cause you anxiety.

[19] Nonreactive means to not be affected by some influence and act out.

Nonverbal Communication

A large percentage of communication is nonverbal. Some say that 93 percent of our communication is nonverbal[20]. The power of this form of communication is astounding and well worth paying attention to.

A researcher, let's call him Tom, did a study by asking various people on the street the same question while engaging in a peculiar nonverbal activity at the same time. Tom was an average man in his forties. He was dressed in typical pants, a shirt, and a jacket, similar to other pedestrians in the area where he conducted his study. By looking at Tom, one would think he was just another person from the neighborhood, nonthreatening and friendly.

The scenario was that Tom claimed he needed help with directions to get to the closest subway station. He was about three blocks away. Tom's verbal communication was in the form of the following question, *"Excuse me, can you tell me how to get to the closest subway station from here?"*

Tom added the following nonverbal communication shortly after he had posed his verbal question. With his right arm and hand, Tom pointed to the side of his head with his index finger and made repeated circular motions while waiting for the person to answer. (This is a motion often used to indicate that the person is crazy.)

What Tom found was that most of the people he asked directions from were polite and started out being really helpful; but once Tom added his nonverbal behavior, they became confused and reacted in various ways:

1. They left immediately without answering, avoided looking at Tom at all.
2. They stared at him for a while, without answering then shook their heads and left.
3. They started to answer Tom's question, and then when Tom's nonverbal behavior was added, tried to complete their information as quickly as possible and then rushed away, or stopped in midsentence and left before finishing giving the directions.
4. They showed signs of agitation, looked at Tom's face, and tried to disregard Tom's nonverbal actions but remained speechless with a bewildered facial expression.

---

[20] Gordon R. Wainwright, *Teach Yourself Body Language*, 2nd ed. (Illinois: NTC/ Contemporary Publishing, 1999).

5. If there were two people that appeared to be friends whom Tom had stopped, they would look curiously at each other and laugh nervously before leaving without providing directions, shaking their heads as they quickly walked away.

It became clear early on in the study that the majority of the people would respond stronger toward the nonverbal message than toward the verbal message. More often than not, they would completely disregard the verbal request.

By choosing appropriate nonverbal signs you can improve the effectiveness of your communication. Likewise, by choosing inappropriate nonverbal signs you can confuse or distort the verbal message you want to send.

Nonverbal signs often accompany each other. When you greet somebody, you may smile and extend your hand. If you want to interrupt somebody, you may make a motion with your hand or finger, raise your head up, and seek eye contact. When you are tired, you may place your head in your hand and give out a sigh. You may massage your temples if you have a headache, or cross your arms and raise your shoulders upward if you are cold or scared.

Most of the time nonverbal signs are quick and; therefore, easily ignored. Sometimes they are misinterpreted because they are taken out of context. In either event, if you learn to pay attention to, recognize, and understand nonverbal signs you have a better chance of becoming an enlightened communicator.

If you are confused, hesitant, or have trouble understanding the message due to conflicting verbal and nonverbal communication, ask the person some questions. There may be a number of reasons why a person may deliver a verbal message that is accompanied by an inconsistent nonverbal sign or motion.

The person may be in any of these conditions:

- Preoccupied
- Unaware of the inconsistency
- Thinking of something and feeling something different
- Running late and feeling anxious
- Having had an unsettling interaction previously
- Being scared or intimidated by you
- Feeling sick or being in pain and trying to cover it up

- Be lying and trying to hide it
- Deliberately wanting to throw you off balance

The key to understanding nonverbal communication and making it work for you is to put it in the *context*[21] of what else is going on. Raising your awareness and sensitivity to understanding nonverbal communication can become very disruptive and counter productive if it is interpreted in isolation.

By asking questions, you can avoid misinterpretations and get clarification[22]. By identifying nonverbal communication as you see and understand it, and sharing your experience with the person who delivers the messages you can give that person a chance to raise his awareness level and understanding of what, otherwise, often is automatic behaviors. Your feedback allows the person to recognize his nonverbal signals and it may help him to use those signals more effectively or appropriately. Simultaneously, feedback will help raise your own awareness and help you better assess how you read and use body language. This can greatly improve the communication between the two of you.

Nonverbal communication can be divided into several categories[23]:

1. Eye movements
2. Facial expressions
3. Head movements
4. Gestures and postures
5. Proximity and space
6. Bodily contact and touch
7. Timing and synchronization

1. Eye Movements

Increased eye contact is generally experienced as a positive behavior. A person who has good eye contact is often seen as trustworthy, dependable, and interested. Staring should be avoided since it is often interpreted

---

[21] Context refers to the whole situation, background, or environment relevant to a particular event or personality.

[22] Lucas, *Effective Interpersonal Relationships*, 29 (see chap. 2, n.14).

[23] Wainwright, *Teach Yourself Body Language*, 31 (see chap. 2, n.20).

as rude. Eye movements are different in children than in adults. Many eye behaviors that are accepted, but not liked from a child, are seen as reprehensible, if engaged in by an adult. Shifty eyes may reflect a shifty character.

How do you use your eyes to make your
communication more enlightened and effective?

2. Facial Expressions

Facial expressions are often very telling. Emotions such as anger, joy, happiness, sadness, disgust, contempt, and fear can often be detected easily in your face. Interest is often looked for in the face by observing a smile. By observing facial expressions when you first meet a new person, you often unconsciously make judgments about the person's disposition, intelligence, and suitability.

Do you more often than not present a facial expression that is
congruent with your verbal communication?

3. Head Movements

Head movements are especially powerful when you are listening. A nod in the appropriate place when someone is talking is often experienced as supportive and reassuring. You appear interested in what the person has to say when you nod either in agreement or to acknowledge that you heard what was said. The absence of nods can sometimes be very disturbing for a speaker, and at times may make the speaker stop talking or lose his place.

How are you affected when head nods
are absent in the interaction?

4. Gestures and Postures

Expressive gestures that are enhancing your verbal communication are often seen as supportive, open, warm, and friendly. Postures that are friendly like leaning forward when communicating can also enhance the communication. A slumped posture can indicate a lack of care, disregard, disrespect, or be seen as *oppositional defiant behavior*[24].

> *Do you prefer a person who uses more or*
> *less gestures in her communication?*

5. Proximity and Space

In body language, the term proxemics was coined by Edward Hall[25]. He describes four zones as follows:

1. Intimate zone (0-0.5 meters)
2. Personal zone (0.5-1.2 meters)
3. Social-consultive zone (1.2-3 meters)
4. Public zone (3 meters and on)

The distance within each zone for each person may differ slightly as seen by the given measurements above. Each person responds differently when he feels his space has been invaded. More often than not, these zones or spaces are not discussed verbally. Instead, they are adhered to and respected on an unconscious level among people and are reinforced by nonverbal behaviors.

> *What do you do when you feel that your personal*
> *zone or space has been violated or invaded?*

6. Bodily Contact and Touch

Bodily contact may be referred to as unintentional when your body touches another in passing. Touch may be referred to as a deliberate and intentional act, using your hand to direct someone, show concern, or show you care for them.

---

[24]   Oppositional defiant behavior may be taken to mean as an actively hostile and disobedient attitude toward something or someone or a resistant stance against something or someone.

[25]   Wainwright, *Teach Yourself Body Language*, 31 (see chap. 2, n.20).

There are certain places where you may be more forgiving when a stranger has bodily contact with you; for example, when you are in a crowded subway, elevator, or at a concert. However, if the same bodily contact would occur on an empty street you would most likely respond negatively. Touching can be experienced as a warm and friendly act, or by some as an intrusion of their personal space and a violation of a boundary.

*Do you see yourself as a "touchy feely" person? If so,
how does that enhance your communication?*

7. Timing and Synchronization

When timing and synchronization is working it is like an effortless dance between people. This area consists of fine nuances that make the difference between good communication and enlightened communication. An area well worth exploring!

*Do you have a person or persons in your life where the timing
and synchronization between you seem to work effortlessly?*

Nonverbal Cultural Differences

Culture is another important factor impacting nonverbal signals and communication. Different cultures and social groups establish meaning to nonverbal communication in accordance with their value system. Unless you have an internal understanding of various groups' and cultures' value systems it is wise to attribute less importance to the nonverbal messages. Instead, ask more questions for clarification if you are unsure about the message. Don't personalize or jump to conclusions without first verifying your observations.

3

Barriers to Enlightened Effective Communication

Some barriers to enlightened and effective communication are easily identified, and it is simple to understand how they may affect the message:

- If you speak a different language, communicating can be difficult
- If you try to send a fax and the fax machine is broken, communication will fail
- If you are distracted, you may have a hard time listening and therefore miss valuable information
- If you are experiencing hearing loss due to a physical impairment and your hearing aid is malfunctioning, it may make the communication more difficult and time consuming

Use of Language

The use of language as a barrier could refer to the specific language that is spoken. English is a barrier if you speak English and the rest of the people in the group only speak Swedish and can't understand you. On the other hand, when referring to the use of language as a barrier, it may mean the use of words in the language, not whether it is English, Swedish, or Russian.

There are many ways of saying similar things using different words. Likewise, there are many ways of saying different things using similar words. Some words will be more effective than others and some will be provocative or hurtful. The choice of words that you use or how you structure a sentence can change an entire interaction.

If you read the following sentences aloud, putting the stress on the italicized word, you will find that the exact same words in the same sentence can deliver a very different message[26].

"*I* cannot believe you did that."
"I *cannot* believe you did that."
"I cannot *believe* you did that."
"I cannot believe *you* did that."
"I cannot believe you *did* that."
"I cannot believe you did *that.*"

As you can see depending on what word you emphasized, what volume you used, the rate in which you spoke, and the tone you applied, the sentence could be interpreted quite differently.

The power and responsibility lies with you to ensure you convey the intended message. People are often unaware of the tone they use and many times resist taking responsibility for it when they are approached. When you add nonverbal communication such as expressions and gestures or remove appropriate and supportive body language you will find that the dynamics of the interaction changes significantly.

Here is an example of an interaction:

Joe was angry with Greta. She had been insensitive to him during dinner, and as usual, she had flirted with the waiter. Greta knew Joe abhorred her behavior and during numerous discussions that they've had over this issue, she continued to dismiss his irritation and invalidated his feelings. She would say, "Oh, Joe, don't be silly, you know how I am. I don't mean anything by it."

Joe would tell her he realized that, but it still bothered him, and could she please stop. Greta, would brush his comment off, teasing him that he didn't need to be insecure, she only loved him.

Joe would fume and feel helpless, believing it didn't seem to matter what he said. Greta did not understand his feelings and he certainly didn't achieve his goal to make her stop her behavior.

This evening Joe had had it. He wanted to hurt Greta as much as she hurt him so he said, "Greta I'm telling you not because I'm hurt but because you're making an ass out of yourself. You're too old and you look stupid. I'm embarrassed for

---

[26] Lucas, *Effective Interpersonal Relationships*, 29 (see chap. 2, n.14).

you." Greta's smile disappeared and her eyes filled up with tears. She immediately excused herself and left for the restroom.

Joe, who had felt great as he spoke the words, felt instantaneous pain in his stomach as Greta left. He knew he had used the words that would trigger Greta.

1. *Making an ass out of yourself . . .* was intended to humiliate Greta
2. *You're too old . . .* was intended to hurt Greta since he knew she was sensitive about her age
3. *You look stupid . . .* was intended to feed Greta's self-doubt
4. *I'm embarrassed for you . . .* was intended to patronize and shame Greta

Joe's use of the language had a profound effect on Greta. It had helped him achieve his goal, Greta stopped her behavior, but at what price? When Greta came back from the restroom, she barely looked at Joe. When Joe tried to communicate with Greta, he hardly got a response. He soon gave up and they continued the evening in silence.

Who is at fault: Greta for having acted disrespectfully toward Joe or Joe for having used cruel language that hurt Greta? It is simple they are both at fault: Greta, for continuing a behavior that was self-serving, hurtful, disrespectful, and insensitive to Joe; Joe for retaliating. The question is how does continuing the cycle of acting out support enlightened communication? The answer is, it doesn't. Therefore, the choices could become either of these:

1. Continue to feed the cycle of acting out; Greta acting out her need for attention and lack of impulse control; Joe acting out his hostility and need for revenge
2. Change to enlightened communication

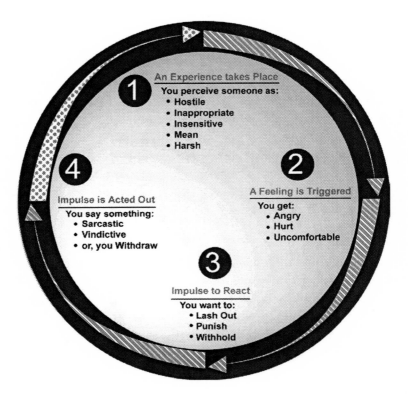

If Joe would use enlightened communication, he would be doing the following:

- Protecting his own needs and feelings and simultaneously be holding Greta accountable for her behavior in a constructive way
- Achieving his goal to be treated with respect and sensitivity by reaching an agreement with Greta about future interactions
- Avoiding building up resentment by taking responsibility for setting appropriate boundaries
- Stopping himself from acting out despite Greta's actions

Inconsistency between Verbal
and Nonverbal Messages

When there is inconsistency, there is a lack of harmony between the verbal and nonverbal communication.

If your spoken message and body language differ significantly from each other, it can become very confusing. Confusion frequently creates discomfort and uncertainty that lead to misunderstandings and mistrust. This barrier in your communication significantly influences trust-building processes.

- If there are two vastly different messages delivered by the same person in the same moment, which one should you choose to trust?
- Why choose to trust either?
- What if you choose to trust the wrong one?
- How will the inconsistent message and your interpretation influence your trust in yourself?
- If the person who delivers the message is unaware of her contradictory behavior, how else does that affect her and more importantly how will that affect your future interactions with her?

The ability to separate preconceived ideas or inappropriate faulty judgments from incongruent messages will not only impact the trust building you do with another person, *it is instrumental in building trust within you*. It is a good idea to reality test by asking some questions when you are experiencing inconsistencies:

- I am confused. I hear two things, is that correct?
- I am not sure I understand what you are saying. Can you clarify what it is that you would like from me?
- I am getting two very different messages as you speak. Can you help me understand what you mean?
- Repeat back what you understand when the message seems to be inconsistent.

By addressing the inconsistency, you generate an opportunity for yourself to reality test and for the other person to reflect on his behavior as well. When you ignore the inconsistency, it becomes a barrier and can create an array of future problems such as these:

- Misunderstandings
- Inefficiency
- Disappointment
- Frustration
- Conflict
- Retaliation
- Imbalance in the relationship
- Ending of the relationship
- Breaking of agreements
- Poor follow-through

Culture

Depending on what part of the world you are from, there may be certain words and phrases or nonverbal communication cues that allow you to relate to some cultures better than others. At times, it is confusing for a foreigner to come to a different country and adjust to new traditions and habits. There is so much to learn and there are so many situations where misunderstandings can take place. Therefore, it is helpful to identify some cultural differences that enhance yours and other people's lives, and others that you see as potential or actual barriers in your communication.

The power lies within you to be interested and curious about cultural differences and the effect they have on communication so that you can use the differences as a guide to communicate more effectively.

Emotions

An emotion can be described as a state of consciousness having to do with the arousal of feelings, like a strong surge of feeling.
Here are some examples of emotions:

- Anger/hate
- Love
- Sadness/sorrow
- Disgust
- Fear
- Happiness/joy

Emotions can be assets or barriers to communication. If the emotion obscures your ability to hear the other person clearly, it becomes a negative.

When emotion enhances understanding, it supports the communication process.

Gary was a very expressive child. When he was happy, you knew it. His eyes would beam, his smile would radiate, and his little arms would flail in the air as he barely could stand still. It was such a joy to observe the freedom in his movements as he excitedly told his story. Gary's emotions served him well. You knew what he felt and the message he sent was clear.

Emotions are such a large part of our interactions that they deserve a whole chapter of their own. If you can't wait, look ahead in chapter 18 and read about the impact emotions have on enlightened communication.

Projections

You expect that when you eat you will feel less hungry. You may project that if you don't get food when you are hungry you will start to feel irritated and lose your energy. Projections are many times correct, when they are predictions based upon previous experiences and the result thereof. As such, they can be supportive.

A projection may become a barrier when it is not an accurate reflection of the current reality, but the unconscious act or process of ascribing to others your own ideas, impulses or emotions that are undesirable or cause you anxiety. A part of projecting is when you are predicting and anticipating what and how the other person will respond based upon your previous experiences and preconceived ideas that may or may not be applicable to your current situation.

Wendy's experience was that if she was loud and excited in her home as a child her mother would get angry and hit her. Wendy learned quickly that the pattern of her own behaviors became trigger points for her mother's actions.

Wendy started to project (expect) that her mother would get angry and then hit her, so she would try to make sure that she wasn't too loud or too excited. Wendy's projections in this context served her well, by being able to know what to expect, Wendy could use her projections to protect herself from her mother's abusive behavior.

However, at times, she couldn't gauge accurately how loud she was, or maybe her mother's tolerance level changed. Wendy's mother would get angry even when Wendy thought she had been "perfectly good."

To avoid being at the mercy of her mother's anger, Wendy started to suppress emotions that propelled her to be loud and excited. This created sadness for Wendy. She did not experience any conscious anger since it would provoke too much anxiety.

Based upon Wendy's experiences, later in life, she unconsciously projected that her excited and loud behavior would trigger the same responses in all other people that she had experienced with her mother. Wendy continued to suppress her loud and excited part as often as she could. However, at times, her excitement "got the best of her" and she became loud.

When Wendy became animated during an interaction with Bob, it didn't take her long before she realized her excitement. She immediately became scared that he would get angry with her. Wendy unconsciously projected the anger she had seen in her mother, and the anger she had not been aware of in herself on Bob. To Wendy, Bob was angry. In reality, he was not. Wendy instantaneously adopted her familiar behaviors of retreating and withdrawing. She became silent and still as her gestures and facial expressions ceased. Bob didn't know what just happened. He thought he had done something wrong.

Wendy told herself she better disengage. Bob is just another angry, unpleasant person who she doesn't want to be around. Bob didn't want to ask Wendy what was wrong, since he was afraid she wouldn't answer him. She suddenly seemed so cold and distant. So they ended the interaction and left feeling uneasy and confused.

Wendy's projections were not appropriate reflections of her current interaction. Hence, they became barriers. Wendy's unconscious projections prevented her from experiencing and getting to know Bob and didn't permit her to take the risk of reality-testing her experience by asking Bob some questions.

Since unconscious projections are unknown in the present, it becomes difficult to deal effectively with this barrier. However, at times, if you can heighten your awareness you have a better chance of being able to evaluate whether projections are present, depending on the context of the interaction. Refer to logic when you feel confused. Take a moment and use the following tools:

- Be aware of strong negative emotions that seem out of proportion to the event. It may indicate a faulty projection
- Explore your earlier experiences and determine how they may affect you today
- Don't personalize when your instinctual response is—*This doesn't have to do with me*
- When you don't feel seen or heard, explore the possibility that it may have something to do with your own or the other person's projections

- When you get emotionally charged, step back and take a deep breath
- Ask questions, many questions, and *listen* to the answers
- Become curious and watch your judgments, since your ability to judge wisely is impaired when you are projecting

If you suspect that you are projecting, it is helpful to ask yourself if the current interaction reminds you of a similar past experience. If you suspect that the other person is projecting, you can ask her the same question. Unconscious projections are barriers that are extremely difficult to deal with. It will take a lot of time and practice to become aware when these forms of barriers are present.

Experiences and Preconceived Ideas

Though relatively easy to understand on the surface, past experiences may become complicated and challenging barriers to communication. Based upon your experiences, you may have fairly predictable reactions to various situations. When these situations have the desired outcome, it reinforces those experiences as accurate. You then conclude that your experiences are serving you well as a guide to how you should respond.

Out of your experiences, you often develop preconceived ideas. These ideas are fixed and predetermined. Independent of the nuances that may be presented in the future, if there are enough similarities to your earlier experiences, you are apt to fall into the trap of allowing your preconceived ideas to inappropriately influence your responses. When you are engaging in an interaction where your preconceived ideas are in the forefront, you often project on the situation or the person you are interacting with. You are assuming that you know the answer, or the point the person is trying to make without openly listening to all the facts and information. You are setting yourself up for misunderstandings. A no-win situation is being formed since it generally precludes you from being curious and open-minded to the person in the moment. Since you already *know* what is going to happen it will significantly color what you *hear*, whether it is actually said or not. Unconsciously, you adopt a rigid position.

Stacy had worked for a company for ten years. She was allowed to make autonomous job-related decisions as long as she delivered an excellent product at the end of the day. Stacy perceived herself as competent and highly effective.

Stacy's experience was

- *she was allowed to make independent decisions in her job*

Stacy's preconceived idea was

- *that her competence and efficiency should allow her to make autonomous decisions independent of what else was going on in the company*

The company changed ownership and the new employer made many changes. One change involved Stacy's relationship and reporting procedures to her new supervisor. The new changes reduced some of Stacy's freedom as far as making autonomous decisions. Stacy didn't like the changes. However, she did not approach her new supervisor to discuss them. She "was sure" he didn't think she was competent or efficient and the new changes had been an indirect way of pointing that out to her.

Stacy's preconceived idea is based upon conclusions that she had made from her earlier experiences. This predetermination prohibited her from asking her supervisor how he perceived her, and from the opportunity to verify whether her preconceived idea was, in fact, true and accurate. As a result, Stacy felt hurt, unseen, devalued, and less motivated in her job.

To summarize, experiences can be excellent guides to learn from, as long as you don't use your previous experiences as a means to justify holding a rigid and close-minded position. Preconceived ideas are just that, preconceived notions based upon information from the past. To be present in the now and available for the future, preconceived ideas need to be put in the background as you allow your curiosity and desire to learn and understand to be in the foreground.

Judge, Judgment, Faulty Judgment, and Judgmental

You are judging when you form an idea, opinion, or estimation about a matter. You are also judging when you think, suppose or criticize. Judgment is the act of judging, the ability to form opinions about things, the power of comparing and deciding as well as the capacity to understand and have good sense. It can be a conclusion or an assessment.

Being judgmental has to do with the exercise of judgment, to make judgments as to value or importance. A person who is being judgmental is often considered to be lacking tolerance, compassion, and objectivity.

In everyday communication, judgment is often perceived as something "bad," the reason may be that a judgment may be confused with being judgmental. Have you ever been asked in a hostile and accusatory voice, *"Are you judging me?"* Or heard someone say, *"You are so judgmental"*?

Judgments can interfere and act as barriers in communication when they are made carelessly, irresponsibly, without sufficient information or knowledge, in fear or used to compensate for fears, and unaccepted or unrecognized needs. As such, they can be referred to as faulty judgments. Another reason that a judgment can be a barrier is if it is delivered in a judgmental way lacking compassion, tolerance, and objectivity. To be able to make a wise decision, draw an accurate conclusion and form a useful opinion, it is important to have all the facts and be able to be as objective as possible.

When experiences and preconceived ideas are clouding the ability to make a wise decision, and the judgment instead is based on biased and distorted information, the judgment has become an obstruction instead of an asset in the communication process.

The key is to become aware of how you make judgments.

- Are you conscious of how you form a judgment?
- What are some of your judgments?
- What are some of your fears of being judged?
- Are you generally surprised when someone asks you if you are judging him or her?
- Are you generally responding with a no when asked if you are judging the person?
- If your answer is yes, do you generally feel neutral about your position?
- If your answer is no, do you feel defensive, or do you deny having made a judgment?

The first step in overcoming a judgment barrier is to become as objective as possible. Objectivity can be accomplished by separating emotions from logic and reasons and disengaging from a reactive communication style.

For example, Chris, a forty-five-year-old unmarried man has strong negative feelings about the use of alcohol. His father was an alcoholic and it caused Chris and his family tremendous pain and suffering while he was growing up.

Chris is involved in the business world where he spends a substantial amount of time entertaining. He is single and meets women for dinner frequently.

Chris's experience is *His father was an alcoholic and it caused Chris a lot of pain.*

Chris's preconceived idea, therefore, is *Anyone who drinks is an alcoholic and will cause Chris a lot of pain.*

Chris's faulty judgment is *Anyone who drinks alcohol will eventually become an alcoholic and can't be trusted or respected.*

Chris's unprejudiced and objective judgment is *Some people who drink alcohol may become alcoholics. Alcoholism or other forms of addiction is often hurtful and harmful for those afflicted by the disease. Chris has the opinion that when it concerns his friends and business acquaintances, it is their choice to drink alcohol or not. If a time comes when their alcohol use interferes with the quality of the relationship Chris will make appropriate choices and set suitable boundaries.*

If Chris were asked if he had a judgment about alcohol, the answer would be yes.

The question is whether his judgment is based on an integration of the following:

- Previous experiences
- Objective evaluation of problems that may arise out of an addiction
- Unemotional analysis of the effect that his father's alcoholism had on him and the other family members
- Understanding of how other members of the family system contributed and enabled the dysfunction to continue
- Acknowledgement and acceptance of the pain that he did experience
- Awareness of his own needs in the past and present
- Recognition of limitations and boundaries
- Responsibility for making choices that work for Chris

Or if Chris's judgment is prejudiced by the following:

- Preconceived ideas based upon limited knowledge or information
- Emotional reactions from his past projected on people in the present

- Inability to separate the now from the past
- A generalization of the issue as a whole
- Blame and unresolved anger
- Unrecognized needs
- Uncontained fears

Because we are human beings, it is impossible to arrive at a completely objective judgment. However, it is possible to weed out one's past from one's present, separate emotions, fears, and needs from logic and reason; and that is what is required when arriving at a beneficial judgment that can support enlightened communication.

Often when the question is asked, *"Are you judging me?"* or a statement is made, *"You are so judgmental!"* the person who asks the question or makes the statement is scared; he will be looked upon unfavorably, or someone will wrongfully judge his whole character as flawed. Sometimes the person asking the questions has a faulty judgment about his own action or choices. His own faulty judgment, therefore, colors his receptivity to hear accurately what the other person is saying.

Many faulty judgments are based on limited knowledge, feelings, or fears. These are taken out of context and, if voiced, could sound like this:

- You are bad!
- You are worthless!
- You can't do it!
- You are stupid!
- You are nothing!
- You are inferior!
- You are pathetic!
- You will never make it!
- Who do you think you are?
- How could you have been so crazy to believe that you could make it!

Other faulty judgments come from unrealized fears and are used to defend against experiencing the fear:

- If I can't do this right maybe there is something wrong with me?
- If I can't do this then I will be rejected!
- If I make a mistake I will be seen as a loser!
- If I fail I will die!

- If I am found out, I will be humiliated!
- If I am less than perfect I don't deserve to be respected!
- I am inadequate and this is the proof!
- If I lose control it will be clear that I can't do the job!

Pam is a highly accomplished woman in her thirties. She is managing a staff of twenty-two. She has been a manager at her current job for one year. Several of her subordinates are men who are older than she is.

The major complaint Pam receives from her subordinates is that she doesn't seem interested in listening to what they have to say. She often dismisses them and their input in a judgmental tone of voice. The morale has gone down significantly lately, and as the situation worsens, Pam's demeanor has become increasingly rigid and unavailable.

Pam may be aware on a conscious level or not aware consciously of her fears, such as the following:

1. *She is going to lose control.*
2. *She may fail.*
3. *She won't be respected.*

Since Pam is either not recognizing these fears or willing to deal with her fears responsibly, she uses a common response: she tries to discard them by projecting *those fears. She does not look at herself. Instead, she sees the fears she has in herself in her subordinates. "The subordinates are out of control, failing, don't deserve to be respected." Pam's fears about herself are changed into faulty judgments about her subordinates. This is often an example of reactive unconscious behavior.*

In essence, Pam's fears are likely to come true as the situation becomes unattainable.

Another example: Peter feels unsure how to approach women. He thinks if a woman turns him down, it is because he is not smart enough and he doesn't make enough money.

The fears consist of the following:

- *That he is not smart enough*
- *That he doesn't make enough money*

The faulty judgment based on those fears is this:

- *That there is something wrong with him*

Instead of exploring the fears and faulty judgment, he ignores them, and projects his faulty judgment and fears on the woman. If she doesn't talk to him, in Peter's mind she confirms his faulty judgment that there is something wrong with him, which is unacceptable to Peter. So he projects his own faulty judgment and sees the woman as judgmental, not realizing that it is his own faulty judgment that he is experiencing.

If she talks to him, he may project his fears and faulty judgment about himself on her, thinking that she is probably not smart enough and there is probably something wrong with her. Peter is setting the scenarios so that he doesn't have to confront or explore the fears and faulty judgment that he has about himself. Unfortunately, by doing that he is indirectly validating his fears and faulty judgment. He does not realize he is projecting.

Faulty judgments are often tied to needs that are sometimes not recognized or accepted. Together the faulty judgment and the unresolved need create flawed thought patterns.

- If I need to be reassured, I am weak.
- If I need attention, I am selfish.
- If I need to be validated, I am egotistical.
- If I need support, I am incapable.
- If I need you to explain it to me again, I must be an idiot.
- If I need to ask you to satisfy my needs, I must not be important enough.
- I should be able to resolve all my problems without talking to anyone if I don't want to.
- I should be able to find a solution on my own.
- I shouldn't have to remind you to listen to me; you should know what I need.

An excellent tool to use to challenge inappropriate and faulty judgments is curiosity. As you start feeling the judgment coming use your curiosity and ask yourself:

- What is the person's intent?
- What is it about your previous experiences that may be affecting you now?
- Why are you getting so angry?
- What is the person trying to convey?
- How can you find out what she may need from you now?

- Is the person angry with you?
- Does the person want to hurt you, if so why?
- Are you being too sensitive?
- Are you overreacting?
- How can you better understand this person?
- What are your immediate needs?
- What is your understanding of the nonverbal communication?
- What is not being communicated?

To summarize, judgments are appropriate when they are consciously made and based on information, knowledge, objectivity, and logical analysis. However, when judgments are derivatives of fears, unrecognized and unaccepted needs, unawareness, lack of information and knowledge, they can be called faulty judgments; and they are barriers that can be extremely disruptive and destructive in communication. Curiosity is one of the most effective antidotes to faulty judgments.

4

Intimidated No More

What does intimidate mean?

In this chapter, intimidation *is referred to as a behavior that is intended to make someone timid or fearful. Intimidation is used to frighten, discourage, or suppress by threats or violence.*

Blatant examples of intimidation may sound like this:

- If you don't stop what you're doing right now, you are grounded!
- You are not smart enough. You'll make a fool out of yourself if you move forward with that project.
- Stop crying. You have nothing to cry about. *I'll* give you something to cry about!
- If you are lying to me, I don't know what I'll do to you.
- If you don't listen to what I am saying, I'll walk right out of here, and I won't come back!
- I have a really bad temper! You don't want to get on my bad side, if you know what I mean!

In the long run, obvious intimidation is unpleasant and unproductive. Then again, it can be very effective in the moment to promote instantaneous behavioral changes.

When intimidated, the *intimidatee*[27] may withdraw, get quiet, and placate the *intimidator*[28] by altering his or her behavior. However, since the overriding

---

[27] An intimidatee is a person who is being intimidated.
[28] An intimidator is a person who is intimidating.

experience is that of fear, the changes are often more temporary, and as the imminent threat subsides the behavior reverts. An imbalance has been set up where the *intimidatee* feels forced and responds as a victim without choices. If intimidation is used habitually, resentment will develop as time progresses. The *intimidator* often experiences power in the moment and perceives behavioral changes as direct expressions of the success of the intimidation. Therefore, the cycle of intimidation is reinforced.

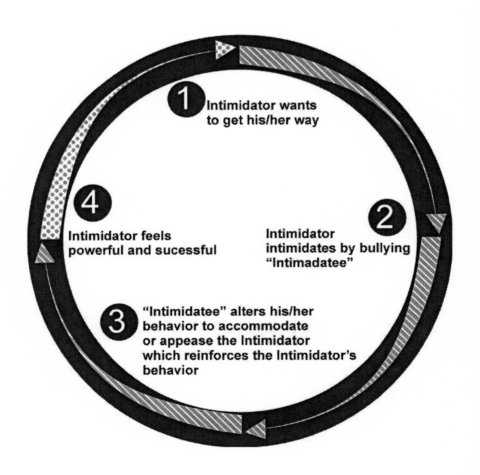

Intimidation Circle

1. Intimidator wants to get his/her way
2. Intimidator intimidates by bullying "Intimadatee"
3. "Intimidatee" alters his/her behavior to accommodate or appease the Intimidator which reinforces the Intimidator's behavior
4. Intimidator feels powerful and sucessful

Intimidation can be overt and easily recognizable. It can also be covert and more difficult to identify. Both forms of intimidation can be challenging to deal with. However, intimidation that is concealed or covert can throw you off without you having any awareness that you are being intimidated.

Nonverbal signs accompany both overt and covert intimidation. Some typical facial expressions and eye movements can be a clenched-tight jaw and teeth and intense staring with a slight contraction of the eyes. Some gestures and postures may be displayed in the form of a rigid upright position, slightly leaning forward with the shoulders and chest, and tilting the head somewhat upward and back. When this form of intimidation is apparent, body movements that follow are many times exaggerated and volatile in nature. It often includes large gestures specifically using the arms and fists. The *intimidator* often places her body above, or in a higher position than the *intimidatee's*.

It becomes more difficult to realize that it is intimidation when the movements are understated by being slow and still. A feeling of the potential threat will then influence the interaction when you experience uneasiness from not yet knowing, but you can still sense that "something awful may happen." There are other subtle cues, such as pausing, that can be observed during covert intimidation. Depending on where the pause is placed, for how long the pause lasts, and the tone that is used, it can drastically impact the experience.

Contrary verbal and nonverbal messages are often deliberately used to throw the other person off guard. By creating insecurity, it reduces the *intimidatee's* ability to recognize intimidation and make conscious choices of how to best deal with it.

Here are some examples of conflicting messages:

Verbal Message	Nonverbal Behavior
1. I wouldn't do that if I were you	A patronizing smile
2. Go ahead, why don't you try it?	Cold stare

Effects of Intimidation

Intimidation Exploits Your Fears and Creates Faulty Judgments

The intensity behind intimidation comes from a pending threat. It is sometimes verbalized but more often conveyed indirectly through behavior, unspoken feelings, a forceful self-serving intent, and words that are implicit. The threats, fears, feelings, and subsequent faulty judgments that get developed, and behaviors that follow are formed in early childhood. Since they are internalized at a very young age, they are often blown out of proportion to the event, since a young child doesn't have the same capacity to discriminate, use logic, or have perspective as an adult. The behaviors that develop become instinctual and habitual to defend against the perceived threat. They are largely unconscious and will remain that way unless you, as an adult, become aware of your learned behaviors and *retrain* your reactions to your feelings, fears and faulty judgments accompanying intimidation.

What could some of the *threats* sound like, if they were verbalized?

- If you challenge me, I will feel uncomfortable and I will stop loving you.
- If you resist me, I will abandon you.
- If you question my authority, I will reject you.
- If you insist, I will withdraw my affection.
- If you persist, I will disengage.
- If you push me, I will punish you.
- If you object, I will leave you.
- If you don't give in, I will ignore you.

The *fears* that are directly derived from the above threats may sound like this:

- If you stop loving me, *I'll die.*
- If you abandon me, *I will not survive.*
- If you reject me, *no one will love me.*
- If you withdraw your affection, *I'll starve.*

- If you disengage from me, *I will suffer severe pain.*
- If you punish me, *I'll be hurting.*
- If you leave me, *I'll have no one.*
- If you ignore me, *I'll be lost.*

The *feelings* that get generated may be these:

- Sadness
- Depression
- Hurt
- Anger directed at self
- Hopelessness
- Pain
- Anger toward others
- Self-hate

The *faulty judgments* that then get formed may be these:

- If you stop loving me, *I am not lovable.*
- If you abandon me, *I am nothing.*
- If you reject me, *I am worthless.*
- If you withdraw your affection, *there is something wrong with me.*
- If you disengage from me, *I am bad.*
- If you punish me, *it is because I am a horrible person.*
- If you leave me, *I don't deserve to be with anyone.*
- If you ignore me, *I should expect others will also ignore me.*

The *behaviors* that follow the faulty judgments may be these:

- Complying
- Agreeing
- Obeying
- Withdrawing
- Attacking
- Defending
- Leaving
- Acquiescing

The degree of leftovers from your childhood experiences will color today's experiences. Despite your adult resources to use logic, analyze, categorize, discriminate, intellectualize your value, and know you will not die if someone leaves, they take a backseat to the emotions that get activated during intimidation. Your conscious knowledge that you have survived rejection and disappointment before sometimes does not override the unconscious, instinctual reactions that were ingrained early in your life. The solution to freedom from intimidation and the exploitation of your fears is to integrate your early experiences with your current intellectual abilities.

Intimidator and Intimidatee

Children are vulnerable and dependent on adults for survival. Therefore, to a small child any adult, independent of their behavior, can be intimidating. Since the power rests with the adult, the starting point of the adult-child relationship is one that is out of balance. In simplified terms, it is most helpful for the adult if the child is compliant, listens, and follows directions. When the child is intimidated, obedience is more readily achievable which makes parenting "easier."

An adult may use a stern or sharp tone in her voice to ensure she'll be taken seriously to prevent a child from endangering himself. Often the adult doesn't recognize that she is, in fact, using intimidation as the tool to achieve her intent: to discourage the child from engaging in the activity. If the intent of intimidation is to prevent an accident, the use of intimidation can be justified. However, since the use of intimidation is by and large unconscious, neither the adult nor the child is aware of their choices and subsequent behavior. Instead of being proactive, they respond to each other and the situation reactively, setting off a chain reaction. It is from your childhood interactions that you learn about intimidation.

The power and influence of intimidation is not an area widely recognized or understood, thus, its dynamics often remains automatic and instinctual. Intimidation will continue to be an unconscious influence unless you raise your awareness level, create conscious choices and establish the kind of relationship you want to have with it.

Intimidation works two ways: the child is not the only one in the adult-child relationship that gets intimidated. Very quickly the child intuitively gains knowledge by observing the adult's verbal cues, nonverbal cues, and subtle nuances in tone, and demeanor. The child then integrates what he has learned by duplicating the adult's behavior.

The following happens when the adult feels intimidated:

1. Feelings will automatically trigger.
2. Depending on the feelings, a variety of reactions take place.
3. This happens if the adult feels angry when intimidated; the behavioral reaction may be to verbally attack and retaliate.

This sends a number of unconscious messages to the child:

1. The adult is scared.
2. The adult doesn't know how to handle me.
3. The adult is out of control.
4. I am a threat to the adult.
5. The adult doesn't love me.

The child will then react to the adult's behavior depending on what unconscious message he received. The child may react this way:

1. May become frightened and intimidated by the adult's reaction and back off
2. May challenge the adult further by matching or exceeding the adult's emotional reaction
3. May lose some trust and safety and withdraw

Sandra was six years old and a very smart little lady for her age. Her mother, Diana was very proud of her daughter. Sandra had always been "an easy" child. She listened to Diana and went along with her suggestions or explanations. As time progressed, Diana found that she had more difficulties getting Sandra to obey her. Sandra would no longer just agree with Diana, she would ask more questions. When Diana didn't have the answers she would feel very uncomfortable. She had a faulty judgment about not knowing the answers to these questions. To Diana, it meant that she didn't deserve to be given respect if she didn't possess the answers to all of Sandra's questions.

When Diana felt uncomfortable, she would often give short and abrupt answers, turn away, and change the subject. It didn't take Sandra long before

*she intuitively felt Diana's discomfort, and she started to test Diana further.
"Mom, why can't you explain to me, I only want to know?" Diana would reply
in a sharper voice, "Sandra, I told you no, I mean it, end of discussion." (Diana
would use intimidation as a means to avoid dealing with her own discomfort
of not knowing.) But Sandra would not give up, saying, "I want to know and
don't understand why you can't tell me." (Sandra would raise her voice to match
her mother's; she would move forward toward Diana and stare her in the eyes.)
Diana would respond, "Enough, Sandra, I will have no more of this nonsense; go
to your room." (Diana would remain still in her position and then deliberately
remove herself physically by increasing the distance between the two, pick up a
magazine, and avoid any further contact, clearly indicating that she had ended
the conversation.)*

In the interaction described above, both Diana and Sandra used
intimidation for the following purposes:

1. To avoid dealing with feelings and faulty judgments. In Diana's case,
    she avoided dealing with her discomfort and the faulty judgment of
    not deserving respect if she doesn't have all the answers.
2. As a means to achieve a goal and to learn by testing her mother. In
    Sandra's case, she tried to get a satisfactory explanation from her
    mother.

The roles of the *intimidator* and the *intimidatee* shifted throughout the
conversation. In the end, Diana's use of intimidation was more forceful
and effective, so she managed to avoid dealing with her discomfort and
Sandra retreated. Unfortunately, Diana didn't realize that by using force, she
continued the cycle of unconscious intimidation and deprived Sandra of the
experience of learning appropriate tools to deal with intimidation. If Diana
would have been more aware of her own dynamics in relation to intimidation,
she might have realized that *there was a moment* where she had a choice to
do either of the following:

1. *Let Sandra's curiosity, persistence, and her (Diana's) own faulty judgment
    intimidate Diana,* thereby indirectly role modeling insecurity, the
    need to be all-knowing, rigidity, and pressure.
2. *To accept that she didn't know the answer.* Diana could be curious
    and appreciative of Sandra's quest for knowledge, thereby role
    modeling trust and security in herself and the process. In addition,

she would be creating a safe and open atmosphere for Sandra to learn and grow from.

Many times the child will unintentionally intimidate the adult, by being insistent, overly demanding, or challenging in other ways. Depending on the awareness and relationship the adult has with her own judgments, needs, experiences, preconceived ideas, and fears, she may feel intimidated. The adult will inaccurately draw the conclusion that it is the child's behavior that intimidates her. For example, *"the child wouldn't stop or the child continued to try to challenge me."* Instead of recognizing that it is her underlying unresolved relationship and lack of awareness that is the source of the intimidation.

> *The child's behavior is simply the messenger triggering*
> *the events, not the source.*

This is a key point to understanding the dynamics of intimidation, since it changes where the power lies. The less the adult tries to control the child's inquisitive behavior, often using intimidation, the less reactive the adult becomes to the child's actions. If Diana didn't have a faulty judgment attached to not knowing, she could have provided a simple answer for Sandra, *"I don't know but I will see if I can find out and get back to you when I have the information."* Hence, Diana would not have felt intimidated by Sandra's insistence, which in fact was the trigger for Diana's faulty judgment to become activated. It was Diana's own faulty judgment that was the actual source of the intimidation. In essence, Diana intimidated herself without knowing it.

In order to change your experience with intimidation it is essential that you integrate your experiences by evaluating thought processes, faulty judgments, needs, feelings, fears, and preconceived ideas. You need to make choices and create a strategy for how to better deal with intimidation. Yes, certain behaviors, demeanors, experiences may provoke intimidation more easily than others; *that doesn't change the fact that you are the one with the ultimate power* to choose *whether to be intimidated or not.*

As long as you remain unaware of your inner relationship, you will find yourself in situations where you will be intimidated. You will experience the unpleasant feelings that accompany intimidation and engage in self-protective behaviors defending against the intimidation and the perceived intimidator; consequently, spending a lot of unnecessary and unproductive energy in the chain reaction of intimidation.

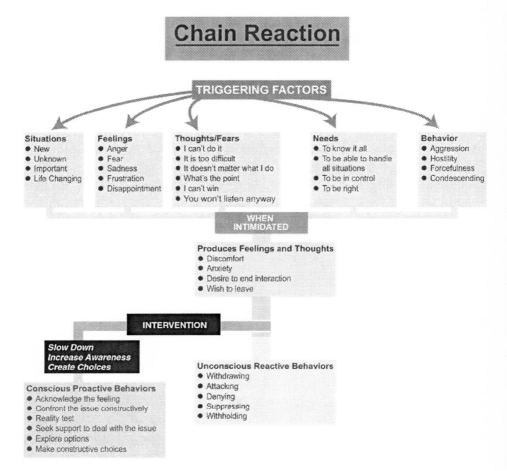

If you remain unconscious about the issues associated with intimidation, you are a victim. You give your power away when you react, and act out, instead of proactively choosing how to deal with the issue, feeling, situation, need, faulty judgment, behavior, and person in the moment. The long-term effect is that the more you engage in unconscious intimidation processes the more it erodes your self-esteem and self-respect. It undermines your trust in yourself and in others. As a result, you develop faulty judgments to compensate for the lack of self-foundation that is lost over time. You will continue to project your past on your present and create confusion and disruptions in your life.

There are seven specific steps that are helpful in the process of raising your awareness about intimidation:

1. Identify what situations, feelings, needs, behaviors and people in your life that have intimidated you.

    -   Do you get intimidated if you need to speak in front of an audience?
    -   Do you feel intimidated when you are in a room with new people?
    -   Do you feel intimidated when you are in a one-to-one interaction?
    -   Does it intimidate and frighten you when someone yells and is angry with you?
    -   Does it create discomfort for you when someone is trying to discourage you?
    -   Does your own or someone else's need to control intimidate you?
    -   Do you feel intimidated when someone stares at you and pauses for a long time without smiles or head nods?
    -   Do you feel intimidated when someone moves toward you hastily and stands too close to you?
    -   Was it your mom who intimidated you?
    -   Was it your dad who intimidated you?
    -   Was it a teacher who intimidated you?
    -   Was it a neighbor who intimidated you?

2. Distinguish what it was specifically about each area that was intimidating to you.

    -   Was it the fact that you were scared that you would forget what you were going to say in front of all the people and be humiliated?
    -   Was it your fear that you would be rejected if you approached someone and others would be watching you make a fool out of yourself?
    -   Was it because you may be confronted about personal issues, and that kind of intimacy may create discomfort for you?

- Do you not know how to respond when someone is angry?
- Do you get anxious when you don't want to allow someone to discourage you?
- What was it about the other person's need to control that intimidated you? Was it the force behind the need or the urgency behind the need?
- Was it the intensity of the stare or the inappropriateness of the long pauses that intimidated you?
- Was it the surprise of the sudden move or the experience of disrespect that you perceived when your personal space was invaded?
- Was it the messages your mom told you about how the world was a dangerous place?
- Was it when your dad came home from work and wouldn't talk unless he was angry, and you felt like you and everybody else in the house were walking on eggshells?
- Was it the times your teacher had asked you to be quiet in class in front of the rest of the class, and then stood near you and stared at you every chance he got?
- Was it when your neighbor had gotten angry with you when you had made a mistake and scratched his car with your bike?

3. Identify the specific feelings that have been triggered for you when you have felt intimidated.

- Do you feel scared?
- Do you feel helpless?
- Do you feel angry?
- Do you feel frustrated?
- Do you feel disappointed in yourself or others?

4. Identify the behavior that you have typically reacted with when you have experienced the feelings you identified above.

- Do you withdraw when you feel scared?
- Do you get immobilized when you feel helpless?
- Do you retaliate when you are angry?
- Do you give up when you are frustrated?
- Do you become defiant when you or someone else is disappointed in you?

5. Assess what you may need to do to deal more effectively with your feelings that get triggered when you feel intimidated.

    - Do you need *reassurance* when you feel scared?
    - Do you need *contact* when you feel helpless?
    - Do you need time to *slow down* when you get angry?
    - Do you need to *take a deep breath* and count to ten when you are frustrated?
    - Do you need *perspective* when you or someone else is disappointed in you?

6. When and how do you intimidate other people?

    - Identify three situations where someone has told you, or given you the impression that you have intimidated him or her.
    - What was it about your verbal and nonverbal behavior that was intimidating?

7. Make a strategic plan based upon the information you have collected above.

    - When I start feeling strange I will ask myself, "Am I being intimidated?"
    - I will reassure myself that I can handle the situation. The worst that can happen is I will feel lousy for a while.
    - I will tell myself that I am an equal human being and deserve to be treated as such.
    - I will tell myself that I am choosing not to be a victim of the other person.
    - I will tell myself that I have choices. I will exercise my choices in this interaction to support a constructive interaction.
    - I will set appropriate limits and boundaries.
    - I will respect myself by not allowing the other person to scare or threaten me.
    - I will not use intimidation to get what I want even when I am tempted to do so.

The following questions are examples that you can use when you create your own steps to reach awareness about intimidation processes:

- How do you deal with intimidation?
- What intimidates you?
- When do you get intimidated?
- How do you respond to intimidation?
- Why do you get intimidated?
- How do you change your behavior in response to intimidation?
- How do you intimidate other people?
- When do you intimidate other people?
- What situations intimidate you?
- What feelings in yourself intimidate you?
- What feelings in others intimidate you?
- What feelings in you intimidate others?
- What needs intimidate you?
- Does conflict intimidate you?
- What reactions do you have to intimidation?
- What are some of your vulnerabilities to intimidation?

Intent Behind Intimidation

It is important to realize that there are numerous reasons why one chooses to use intimidation. It is, therefore, helpful to ask the question, *What is the intent behind the intimidation?*

Is it for the following purposes?

- Dominate
- Control
- Persuade
- Threaten
- Discourage
- Create fear
- Make timid
- Suppress an emotion, need, desire, or behavior
- Exert power over
- Challenge
- Humiliate
- Compensate for feeling inferior
- Shame
- Shut someone up

- Not be held accountable
- Avoid dealing with an issue, situation, person, need, or feeling
- Remain in authority
- Lead
- Achieve quick results
- Get help
- Feel powerful
- Prevent an accident from happening

Usually, the intent *is not* thought out in advance; and often, it is not conscious, since most of the behaviors involved with intimidation are learned unconsciously, and therefore, are reactive. By asking what the intent is, you slow down the process, you hold the other person accountable, you raise the overall awareness, and you take back some of the power in the interaction. Instead of allowing the intimidation to "throw you off," you take steps in becoming aware *and create choices* for yourself and the other person. You have the capability to change the *Chain Reaction-Intimidation* so that there are fewer incidents when you are intimidated but more times when you can feel good about yourself and your interactions.

Alternative Behaviors to Intimidation

- Become aware of your feelings, needs, and faulty judgments.
- Take responsibility for your choices.
- Expand your options.
- Empower yourself via constructive and equal interactions.
- Understand aggression—your own and others'.
- Confront your fears.
- Be curious about the process, the interaction, and the other person.

How to Deal Effectively with Intimidation

The more comfortable you become in dealing with intimidation the more balance you will be able to achieve in your relationships. By asking questions when you feel uneasy, you are proactively confronting the *intimidator*. Whether the intimidation is coming from the other person or from within you, you are being assertive.

Questions to Ask and
Boundaries to Set

Depending on how you formulate your questions you can set effective boundaries. By asking the questions you show that you are not allowing the intimidation to *shut you down*. You are setting a boundary that sends an unconscious message that you are not going to allow intimidation to *control you* in this conversation. By questioning the other person's intent, you convey that you are committed to keeping this interaction balanced and up-front. Some effective questions to be asked are the following:

- What is your intent?
- I don't quite understand what you want from me, can you please explain?
- For some reason, I have the impression that you are trying to persuade me, and that you won't take a no for an answer; is that correct?
- Are you trying to convey that I don't have a choice; am I understanding you right?
- Are you trying to scare me?
- How do you experience this interaction: positive and solution oriented, or frustrating and going nowhere?
- What would you like to achieve in this interaction?
- What are you willing to give me?
- How do you see this interaction creating a win-win scenario for the both of us?
- Is it more important to you that I do as you want now, to appease you, than that I actually understand what you are asking of me?
- Is it more essential to you that I agree with you than having a genuine, respectful relationship based on trust and appreciation?
- How would you like to resolve our differences in a constructive and respectful way?
- Do you realize that if you are pressuring me, and I am allowing your pressure to persuade me, the chances that I will follow through and stay committed to the change are slim?
- How would that benefit us?
- What kind of relationship do you want to have with me?
- When you are yelling, I don't hear what you are saying; so it is unproductive for the both of us. What would you like to do?

- I need some space between us so I can listen better to what you have to say. I can either move a couple of feet over here, or you can move over there. What would you like to do?
- Is this something you want to resolve now? If so, let's decide how we should continue this conversation.
- What do you suggest?
- How will you deal with your disappointment and possible anger if we can't reach an agreement?
- Do you realize that when you yell at me, my first instinct is to withdraw from our interaction?
- How would it serve you if I withdrew?

The trust and respect for the *intimidator* will, over time, diminish when intimidation is used habitually, whether the threat is actualized or not. By actively engaging instead of withdrawing, you are sending the message that you are not willing to be a victim in the interaction. Hence, over time, your responses will help increase the trust, respect, and balance in the relationship.

5

On the Defense

Defensiveness can be described as feeling under attack, thus being quick
to justify one's actions by being ready to resist the attack or danger.

There are a number of reasons why you feel defensive. You can feel
threatened, attacked, accused, misunderstood, unheard, or unseen. You may
feel guilty and not want to take responsibility. When someone is addressing
what you perceive as negative information about yourself, you may feel stupid,
or inadequate, and that may produce shame and humiliation. When you feel
attacked, low self-esteem issues such as feeling inferior can be activated. When
you experience danger from a situation or a person, you may feel out of control
and that can also activate defensiveness. It is understandable that the initial
reaction is to defend against the feelings and perceptions described above,
since they produce, among other things, uncertainty, and discomfort.

Defensive Behaviors

Here are many ways you may respond when you feel defensive:

- *Attack.* It is better to be on the offensive than the defensive so if you
  turn the conversation around, the original issue may be forgotten.
- *Retaliate.* If you say something that you know will hurt her, then
  she'll stop accusing you.
- *Withdraw.* If you don't say anything, and instead, simply let her rant
  then you are the one in control, and there is nothing she can do.
- *Disengage.* If you stop listening altogether and invest no energy, the
  other person will be left feeling frustrated and powerless.
- *Sulk.* If you feel sorry for yourself then maybe the other person will
  let you off the hook.

- *Justify.* If you explain what really happened and how there was nothing you could have done differently, then she must forgive you.
- *Provide numerous explanations for your behavior.* If she really understands that you did your absolute best, then what right does she have to question you?
- *Blame.* It wasn't your fault it was hers. If she would have handled the situation differently, then you wouldn't have to deal with this now.
- *Rationalize.* Even though you could have done it differently, you probably wouldn't because it really isn't a big deal.
- *Be close-minded.* Simply shut her out and not listen to anything she has to say.
- *Project.* She is exactly like your mother. Always attacking you and complaining about one thing or another.
- *Resist.* Of course you're opposing her; you're strongly against what she is saying.

When someone is defensive, it is easy to get irritated, frustrated, or angry. On one hand, there is the defensiveness; on the other hand, there are the emotions and reactions that defensiveness ignites. Before long, the interaction becomes unproductive, and there is more energy spent on attacking and defending than there is on actually finding a solution.

Behind Defensiveness: Unrealistic and Unaccepted Needs

Behind defensiveness lie the unrealistic and often unconscious needs to be perfect, to know it all, and to never make a mistake. On one hand, the needs are ridiculous since they cannot possibly be achieved. On the other hand, the needs are very real, deeply rooted by-products from your early childhood development.

Unaccepted needs for support are a second group of needs that cause defensiveness. For example, you demand that you should be able to handle a situation without help and it is unacceptable to need someone or something. There is a split between your logical, reasonable mind, and your emotional realm. Intellectually, you know the need to be perfect and to know it all is unrealistic. You also know that you cannot possibly do everything yourself without support or help. You may feel pain emotionally when someone points out to you that you are not perfect by questioning your actions or reasons.

You may become defensive when someone is showing dissatisfaction with you or something you have done.

It is easier to explore defensiveness when "you are not in it." You can then be more objective and clear. That is the time to reacquaint yourself with your unrealistic needs. Find out what kind of support you require to better deal with those needs, so that the frequency and duration of your defensiveness can be reduced.

Defensiveness is reduced from the inside out. The more comfortable and secure you feel within yourself, knowing and understanding the dynamics of your needs, the less necessity there is to be defensive when you have made a mistake.

Culprits: Fears and Faulty Judgments

Often the fears and faulty judgments that are derived from unrealistic and unaccepted needs are culprits that complicate the dynamics further. These are some fears derived from the need to be perfect:

- Fear of disappointing someone
- Fear of not being good enough
- Fear of being found out and exposed
- Fear of being rejected
- Fear of being abandoned

Here are also some faulty judgments derived from the need to be perfect:

- If I am attacking you and you give in, you are weak.
- If you agree with me, you become powerless.
- If you allow me to attack you without defending yourself, you are pathetic.
- If I challenge you and you do nothing about that, you will lose your pride.
- If you don't defend yourself, you will look like a coward.

It is a process where the unrealistic and unaccepted needs activate fears and faulty judgments that lead to defensive behaviors. If you focus on understanding your needs behind your defensiveness, you can avoid getting manipulated by your own faulty judgments and fears, thereby reducing the impulse to be defensive. Bringing to awareness your own defensive patterns will help you to better recognize defensiveness in others.

Deborah and Her Boss, Tim

Deborah was an excellent employee. She got her job done on time and delivered an excellent product. Deborah's boss, Tim, was very demanding. This didn't bother Deborah, since she could keep up with his demands. However, he had recently asked her to log all her incoming and outgoing calls, e-mails, and other correspondence on a daily basis. This meant that Deborah's workload would increase significantly. Deborah could understand the reasons behind her new assignment but was not convinced the value would be greater than the increased workload.

Instead of approaching Tim, Deborah started to resent the task and him. Deborah soon realized that she could not realistically keep her standards up in all areas while simultaneously performing the newly added task.

When Tim approached her after a couple of weeks and asked Deborah for the list, she responded as follows, "I just want you to know that it was impossible to log every single call and correspondence. I did my best but it is not going to be 100 percent accurate."

Tim responded, "Deborah if you had a problem with this, why didn't you approach me?"

This "made" Deborah feel even more defensive, she knew she was good at what she did, and he had no right "making her" feel this bad. He was unrealistic and too demanding.

What Deborah didn't realize was that she had an unrealistic need to be perfect, and that she had a faulty judgment associated with not being able to do it all on her own.

That combination prohibited Deborah from discussing the new task with Tim once she realized it was an unrealistic demand on his part and that she couldn't do it. Her unconscious fears were that if she couldn't do it, that must be because there was something wrong with her, or because she wasn't good enough. Deborah's fears and faulty judgments prevented her from realizing and accepting that she couldn't do it simply because of the logistics of the demand, and that the responsible thing would be to approach Tim and discuss the issue before it got out of hand. Deborah perceived Tim's comment as yet another attack and it triggered all the resentment that she had built up over the last two weeks. Instead of staying focused on Tim's legitimate question, "If you had a problem with this, why didn't you approach me," Deborah became increasingly defensive.

"I did my best, I am very hard working, and you know that I deliver an excellent work product." The conversation escalated from there, concluding with Deborah feeling invalidated and unappreciated by Tim.

How could this have been different?

Step 1

Deborah would have had to be aware of her tendency to take on too much and her expectation that she should be able to handle everything perfectly. By having an understanding of her unrealistic expectation to be perfect and unaccepted need to get help, she would have been able to separate those issues from the reality of the assignment. Deborah would have then been able to review the assignment objectively and, by doing so, realize that the assignment was unrealistic, and that fact did not in any way reflect badly on her. Those were separate issues. Once Deborah had been able to identify the problem with Tim's request, she could have moved to the next step.

Step 2

Deborah would have approached Tim and sit down to discuss the logistics of her new task in combination with her current workload. *"Tim, this is a list of my current daily tasks, including the actual time each task takes. As you can see, if I am to add the new task of logging all calls, e-mails, and correspondence I will have to deduct one or more of my current daily tasks in order to continue to deliver excellent work. How would you like to resolve this?"*

By communicating responsibly and assertively, Deborah would have shown that she had thought the problem through. By taking initiative, she would have supported Tim and herself in finding a solution. Deborah would have been respectful of reasonable limits and committed to providing the best possible work she could for Tim. Deborah would be removing reasons to feel defensive.

Step 3

Tim could then respond, *"Thank you for bringing that to my attention so promptly. I actually don't need you to log every single call, e-mail, or correspondence. If you can do that with info relating only to Project C, that will be fine. Do you think that is reasonable?"* Deborah would get a chance to respond, *"Yes, that is quite different from logging every single call in all areas. I can do that."*

As you can see, the defensiveness process starts much earlier than after the actual perceived attack. Even if Tim wouldn't have liked the reality of the limits and time constraints that Deborah presented, Deborah could still continue to stay centered provided that she has an awareness of her own issues and therefore is able to separate those from the reality of outside demands and pressures. Subsequently, Deborah will then be better equipped to deal with Tim's need for the impossible and not allow his needs to trigger her issues. This solution helps them both by preventing future disappointment, frustrations, resentment, and defensiveness to be acted out within their work and their relationship.

Logic and Proportions

Logically, there are no reasons to be defensive unless you are actually under physical attack and your life is being threatened, or if you are being accused of a heinous crime that you haven't committed and the right to your freedom is in jeopardy. Nevertheless, you may find that there are many occasions when neither of those scenarios is present and you still experience defensiveness, *because when defensiveness is activated, logic is in the background and emotions are in the foreground.* These emotions are the main reason why you may react by defending yourself when you feel that you are being accused, instead of using reason, logic, and curiosity to investigate the background behind the accusation.

A normal sequence of events is to revert back to behaviors that are based on early childhood experiences, where feelings, emotions, and faulty judgments were dominating and the cognitive mind was less evolved. Instinctual responses used to defend against physical danger and attack are activated and acted out inappropriately when no real danger is present. The danger is perceived on a psychological level but reacted to with the same intensity as would be appropriate if it was happening on a physical level. There can be an inordinate amount of force behind the defensiveness, often making it difficult to assess. It is almost as if the perceived danger was threatening a part of the individual's existence. It is important to appreciate this force since you otherwise may not realize what you are up against when confronted with defensiveness.

When the intensity behind the defensive reaction is out of proportion to the incident, then you need to slow down the process.

How to Deal Effectively with Defensiveness

Creating Strategies

Raising your awareness and understanding of the dynamics behind defensiveness is the first step in creating strategies to better deal with defensiveness. Your defensiveness escalates the more you are unaware of your fears, faulty judgments, unrealistic, and unaccepted needs.

You are not being defensive because of something the other person is saying or doing. You are being defensive because of *what gets triggered inside of you*. Granted, the other person may have been insensitive, hostile, aggressive, or inappropriate but that in itself does not warrant defensiveness. In that type of situation, the responsible response is to hold the other person accountable for her actions, not to react defensively. The person who you respond defensively to is a messenger. He is telling you to pay attention to what is going on inside of you. "Shooting the messenger" is displacing your feelings about the message to the messenger or the situation. Ask yourself some questions:

- Does the message have some value to me?
- Is the content of the message true?
- If I agree with the meaning of the message, does that mean that I also have to see myself as less, or stupid?

If the message doesn't have any value and you determine that it is *abusive*[29], then deal with that by setting a boundary against the abuse. When *defensiveness*

---

[29]   Abusive, in this context, means inappropriate, offensive, exploitative.

is activated, it is to be considered in relation to the type of relationships and awareness you have with the following:

- Your fears
- Your faulty judgments
- Your unrealistic needs
- Your unaccepted needs

When someone says something to you that you perceive as an attack, *"You messed up and the order didn't get processed in time,"* your immediate response may be to defend yourself and feel terrible instead of taking a look at the reality of what happened. Take responsibility if you made a mistake; apologize and learn from the experience, and move on without being held back by faulty judgments. If you learn from an error or poor choice, then you are doing the best you can and the experience can have value for you. If you get "stuck" in being defensive, you are no longer receptive to learning because you are too busy justifying your choice and explaining yourself.

Simplified Summary:

If you don't believe and react to faulty judgments, fears, unrealistic or unaccepted needs, you take away the reasons to be defensive.

Granted, sometimes when you are being defensive, it may be because your judgment or the other person's judgment about your behavior is not faulty but in fact appropriate. If you make promises and keep breaking them, or keep lying and a person is angry, you may feel awful. That would be appropriate. If you continuously engage in a behavior that isn't conducive to healthy relationships, you may feel defensive if you refuse to look truthfully at yourself. The same goes for other people in your life.

Here are some suggestions one should have to approach defensiveness:

- Curiosity
- Patience
- Focus
- Heightened awareness

Expanding Choices

The beauty of choices is that they are empowering. The following are choices you have if someone says something to you that you perceive as an accusation:

- Feel horrible and get defensive.
- Be really interested and curious in what the person is telling you.

The more unaware you are, the greater the possibility you will not experience having choices but instead will react and be a victim of the other person or the situation. Emotions, fears, and faulty judgments that you are not aware of interfere with your ability to explore choices. Hence, the more aware you are, the more you can expand your choices.

Being proactive not reactive
in introducing curiosity

Here are some ingredients that help you to be proactive:

- Heightened awareness
- Curiosity
- Commitment
- *Containment*[30] of emotions and fears
- Ability to identify faulty judgments

The natural instinct when you feel threatened is to defend, so the intervention needs to happen before you react with a defensive behavior. When you start feeling "bad" because you feel attacked, the tool of intercession is curiosity.

Your own curiosity will help you raise awareness of your needs, accepting them, and readjusting them to fit into your existing reality. It will help slow down the process so you can become increasingly curious about what you can learn from the other person and the interaction instead of worrying about what he is thinking about you.

---

[30]   Containment is the capacity for holding and being able to restrain yourself.

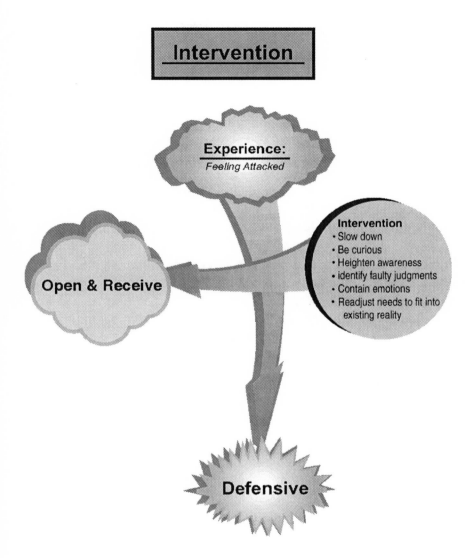

By staying committed to your curiosity, you will automatically contain your emotions and fears and help identify faulty judgments. As you practice using more curiosity, you will find that you don't experience the unpleasant emotions as they are replaced by your curiosity. The need to react is reduced and you can become more proactive in your interactions.

Instead of defending, you'll ask questions. Instead of waiting for the other person to move on, you'll ask about his intent; what he would like to achieve by bringing this information to you, how he sees this as an opportunity to improve your relationship. By not reacting, you are choosing not to be a victim of your emotions and faulty judgments that are generated by the messenger.

Criticism

Criticism can be described as the act of making judgments or finding faults and it is a part of life. Sometimes you may be criticized and sometimes you may criticize someone else. Criticism is an important factor to consider when defensiveness has been activated. It is difficult to deliver criticism in a productive manner since no one likes to have their faults pointed out to them. It is an area that is charged with many emotions. The first step when dealing with criticism, whether you are giving the criticism, or being on the receiving end, is to realize what it is and take responsibility for that. For example, when someone asks you in a defensive and accusatory voice, *"Are you criticizing me?"* the answer would be, *"Yes, I am."* It is common to be "thrown off" by the force of the defensiveness and accusation and instead answer defensively, *"No, I'm not."*

Since being critical is something many people perceive as negative and see as a quality they rather not be associated with, it is often difficult to accept. However, that is the first mistake, to not stand up for your behavior. Either make the choice not to criticize or accept the fact that it is exactly what you are doing. By taking this approach, you bring the criticism into the domain of objectivity and neutrality instead of remaining in the realm of feelings and emotions.

It helps when you clarify what your intent is. For example, you may point out a fault:

- What are you hoping to accomplish?
- How will this information benefit you, the other person, and your relationship with each other?
- Is this fault something that can be changed?

By discriminating when to criticize by means of qualifying the perimeters around criticism, you will be able to better evaluate when it is more likely to benefit the interaction in the long run. Furthermore, by understanding your own relationship with criticism, you can start to become sensitive to its dynamics in your life.

- Are you feeling threatened when you feel criticized?

- Who used to criticize you in your life?
- What areas are you most afraid of being criticized in?
- How do you deal with criticism?
- Do you perceive yourself as a critical person?
- Do you find that you feel criticized often?

If you find that you feel criticized often, you may realize that it may be your own inner critical voice that is being activated as well as the person being critical. At times, the other person may not even be criticizing you, but you still perceive any form of disappointment in you or questioning of your behavior as criticism.

By reality testing, you can differentiate between your own issues and experiences and the other person's intent, hence alleviating unnecessary conflict. Criticism is a loaded subject, and it takes time and patience to understand its impact on your relationships.

6

Power, Control
and Resentment (PCR)

Power *can be described as a person or thing having great influence, force, or authority. Power is the ability to do, act, or affect strongly. It means the right to rule, determine, make decisions, and enforce obedience.*

Control *can be described as exercising authority over, directing, commanding, holding back, curbing, or restraining.*

Resentment *can be described as a feeling of indignation or displeasure from a sense of being injured or offended.*

Power, Control, and Resentment
Go Hand in Hand

In many relationships, the forceful need for power and control encumber communication and significantly affect the enjoyment of the interaction. Resentment is a natural consequence when there is an inequity of power and control in an interaction *combined* with an undisclosed or direct objection to such inequity. The key is that the person who develops resentment is feeling and responding as a *victim*[31] often without realizing it.

The natural evolvement of power and control starts at the time you are born. During infancy and early childhood, the adult has the power and control. The child is dependent on the parent's goodwill. However, due to the infant's inability to cognitively understand that she and the adult are separate, the infant confuses the power the adult has as her own. As the infant is able

---

[31] A victim is somebody who is harmed by or; otherwise, suffering from an act, condition, or circumstance, and feels helpless to do anything about it.

to have her needs gratified, often instantaneously, she perceives herself as being omnipotent[32]. It can be observed, throughout childhood development, how the issue of power and control often becomes a struggle between the child and the parent. Take the "terrible twos" when the child practices saying no to most everything and wants what he wants when he wants it. Move on to adolescence when the teenager "knows it all, what is best, how to do everything," and wants to "make all decisions" for himself. Large portions of these processes are natural attempts to separate and individuate.

You learn to respond depending on how your parents and authority figures acted in response to power and control during the different stages of your life. *Thus, you develop your own relationships with power, control, and resentment.* Many of these processes are unconscious, reactive responses to feelings that are triggered as a result of the use of power and control.

Feelings that may be triggered are the following:

- Anger
- Rage
- Hurt
- Disappointment
- Frustration
- Feeling powerless and vulnerable

Some *attitudes and core beliefs that may develop are the following:*

- I can only get what I want if I have all the power.
- If I control the situation, I will not get hurt.
- If I bully you, you'll respect me.
- The one who has all the power is the one who gets to make all the decisions.
- I have to have all the power; otherwise, someone else will take it from me.
- If I have power, I'll be happy.
- Without power, I'll be useless.

---

[32] Omnipotent means having unlimited power or authority. L. J. Kaplan, *Oneness and Separateness: From Infant to Individual* (New York: Simon & Schuster, 1978).

- If I don't have power, I'll be used by others.
- Power is annoying when someone else has it.
- When someone is trying to control me, I feel trapped.
- I will never allow anyone else to control me.
- I'm going to take all the control so you can't control me.
- You can make me feel stupid when you have all the power. I'd rather make you feel stupid, so I better become powerful.
- Anger gives me power.
- Power means that I am in charge and I won't be challenged.
- I'll do anything to maintain control.
- Being out of control is scary and unpredictable.
- When I have power, it makes me feel better.
- If I have the power, you'll listen to me.
- People use control to make themselves look and feel better.
- Sometimes, if the person is so out of control, he will be so close-minded that he will not even hear the views and opinions of others.
- I hate when you control me.
- I hate when you have power over me.

These are some resentments that come from feeling powerless and victimized:

- There is no point in arguing. I will never get what I want anyway.
- Why are you even asking me? I don't have any power anyway.
- It always has to be your way.
- You will push me until I give in.
- You will not listen to me. It is always your way or the highway.
- I am weak, so you'll just wear me out. I might as well give up.
- If I don't give in you'll punish me anyway.
- Trying to have a discussion will only make you angry.
- I hate when you tell me what to do, but if I tell you, you'll only hurt me more.
- You can control me now but I'll get even later.
- This is so unfair.

People rarely take the time to discuss or explore the attitudes and core beliefs that are formed unconsciously. Without the time, attention, and support to do so, behavioral responses become reactive and lack awareness. This reduces the opportunity of making strategic choices and becomes the breeding ground for resentment. One of the main characteristics of resentment is passivity. It is, therefore, essential to work diligently on assertiveness in the moment, since that supports empowerment and acts as a cure to resentment. With the above information in mind, it would be unrealistic to think that power and control issues would suddenly evaporate as you become an adult. On the contrary, leftovers from previous experiences shape how you respond later in life and influence your choices and behaviors.

Sometimes, the power is clearly defined as in employer-employee relationships. The expectations are that the employer is the person in charge and in control and that the final decisions and authority rest with him or her. In spite of the fact that this dynamics is understood and accepted by the nature of the contract when hired, some employees resent them and choose to undermine the employer. Similarities can be seen in a parent-child or parent-adolescent relationship. The unspoken (or at times loudly expressed) rules are that the parent is in charge. In spite of that, the child or adolescence often argues with the parent in the pursuit of power.

Behavior

There are a variety of behaviors that evolve when someone is objecting to the existing or proposed power structure. Some can be described as more indirect. Passive-aggressive behaviors will fall under this category and may involve the following:

- Withholding pertinent information
- Prolonging procedures to stall and reduce efficiency
- "Stonewalling"
- Making sarcastic remarks and claiming, "I was joking," if confronted
- Making agreements and lack in follow-through
- Gossiping behind the other person's back
- Being defiant
- Blaming others when confronted

Other more obvious behaviors can involve the following:

- Intimidating and bullying
- Threatening and scaring

- Yelling
- Becoming aggressive when challenged
- Lashing out inappropriately

Logically, there would be no reason for the employee to resent the employer if he takes responsibility for having chosen to accept a position as a subordinate unless, of course, the employer is abusing his power. Likewise, the child and adolescence would peacefully agree to the ordinance of power if they accepted it "as is." Yet it is not that simple. Developmental stages, experiences, learned behaviors, abuse, and unresolved issues significantly affect the power and control dynamics. It can be expected that children, as they grow, will engage in most behaviors described in this chapter at one time or another as a natural part of their development.

It is how the adult responds that will considerably
shape the child's behavior.

It is about *your* relationship with power, control, and resentment that ultimately will determine how you will act in response to other people and their needs to control and maintain power. You may want to explore this area further if you "hate" when someone is trying to control you, independent of the circumstances, whether it is appropriate or not, and you have an unwarranted strong emotional reaction to the situation or the person.

Some examples of situations when it is reasonable to be controlled may include the following:

- You are part of an organized group traveling together in Europe and are told to meet in one hour in front of the Mona Lisa painting.
- You are assisting a doctor performing an operation and are told to get an instrument.
- You are on a plane and are instructed to fasten your seat belt.

If you experience an intense reaction in relationships to one specific person in your life or one type of interaction, you may have some unresolved concerns with that particular person or that person may activate some feelings from your past that you may be projecting unto the person.

Some common responses when people feel controlled may include the following:

- Withdraw
- Pout
- Retaliate (e.g., I'll show you, I'll get even some way)
- Ignore or stop listening
- Agree while simultaneously having no intent to comply
- Resent the person in control
- Oppose
- Get very tired and feel exhausted
- Be impatient for the interaction to end
- Be aggressive and threaten the other
- Use drugs and alcohol to rebel

The following are some situations that may evoke resentment:

- You didn't think that your feelings were considered.
- You experienced the interaction as one-sided.
- You didn't feel heard.
- You felt overpowered.
- You gave in because you were too uncomfortable arguing.
- You were scared by the other person's anger and gave in to achieve peace.
- You were worn down by the other person's force and insistence.
- The other person didn't seem interested in what you wanted or needed.
- The other person treated you as if you didn't matter.
- You didn't care at the time, but realized later that you hadn't been treated right.
- You felt that you had been contributing more to the relationship than the other person.
- You thought that you are the one initiating conversations and making more of an effort to connect.
- You realized that the relationship is unequal.
- Any time you abandon yourself without being aware of it, you risk building up resentment.

The more assertive you are, the more empowered you become.
The more empowered you become, the less resentment you will
build up and the less you will act out.

Polarization

Sometimes you may find yourself in a power struggle and not quite know how you got there. *When you are in a power struggle with someone the process can be referred to as a polarization[34]. You and the other person tend to separate into diametrically opposed, often antagonistic viewpoints. This opposition reduces the flow of the interaction and often produces a gap between the people and a solution, since neither person is willing to give up their position.*

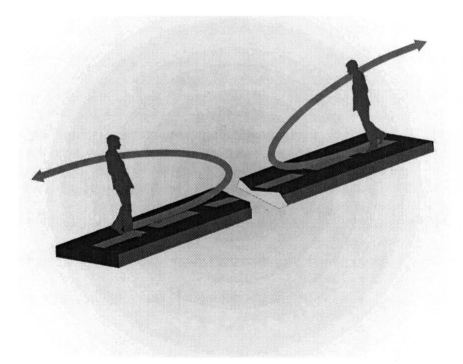

---

[34]   Polarization is a power struggle wherein you and the other person tend to separate into diametrically opposed, often antagonistic, viewpoints.

Recognizing when you or the other person is polarizing can have a significant impact on the interaction *as long as it is followed by a behavioral change.*

Mary and Ross

Mary didn't want Ross to continue having contact with his ex girlfriends. Ross saw no problem with his friendships, whether they were with men or women.

"You obviously have a need to be flattered or you wouldn't have to continue seeing your ex-girlfriends."

"That is not true, I enjoy their company. What's the big deal?"

"It bothers me."

"Well, that's your problem. You are obviously insecure and jealous."

"No, I'm not."

"Yes, you are. You have always been like this."

"That's not true. I'm not insecure. You're just insensitive."

"No, it is clearly your insecurity and your oversensitivity that's the problem."

"No, it isn't. You don't understand anything and you always think you are right."

The polarization continues to alienate Mary and Ross from each other. The point is not whether they are disagreeing or not. The point is that they are not (or willing to be) curious about the other person's experience, thought processes, and needs.

They are centered on who is right and who is wrong. The main intent is not to find a solution for the problem. Instead, it is about irresponsibly communicating feelings and often faulty conclusions. Mary's initial comment is made carelessly. She is making an accusation and using her conclusion as a matter of fact. The comment is intended to provoke Ross. He is provoked, and then he immediately rejects Mary's comment. The polarization has begun.

Ross *would not have* polarized if he, instead, had responded, *"I don't know that is the reason. I'm willing to discuss it with you. What is it that you want from me now?"*

By not taking the position that Mary is wrong, Ross is not being manipulated by the inflammatory nature of Mary's comment. He is disarming her while at the same time standing up for himself, since he is not committing himself to her conclusion. Ross role models an open-mindedness, which is a key component to successful interactions opposed to the close-minded position taken in polarization. By following up with a question, Ross is beginning to hold Mary accountable for what she wants in the interaction.

Practical Tools to Stop Polarization

✓ *Separate your logic from your emotions*

When you start to get angry or upset, ask yourself if it is logical and productive to respond with that emotion. *"Why am I getting so angry? If I choose to respond from this angry place, how likely is it that I will convey my message? Can I control my anger or am I going to be a victim of my anger and let it decide my response for me?"*

✓ *Contain your emotions*

Count to ten before you respond to give yourself an opportunity to slow down the process. *"One, two, three . . . "*

✓ *Maintain an open mind*

Use your curiosity about the other person's intent, wishes, thought processes, fears, and possible outcomes. *"I am curious about her intent. Is she trying to get closer? Is she acting out her frustration? Is she scared that we are going to break up? What is she thinking right now? How can we connect now?"*

✓ *Decode the message and respond to one point at a time*

Before you respond, be sure that you have separated emotional messages from any requests that may be imbedded in the message, and respond to them one at the time. *"I wonder if he is asking me or telling me. It seems like he is bringing up several points at one time. The first one seems to be whether I would like to go to the movies or not? The second part is a statement where he is telling me what movie we are going to see; does he not want to know what movie I would like to see? The third seems to be more of a question whether we should eat before or after the movie. "Are you asking if I want to go to a movie? Are you suggesting that we see XYZ? Would you be open to seeing another movie? If it doesn't matter either way for you, I prefer that we eat before the movie."*

✓ *Agree*

Most of the time, you will be able to agree with some part of the person's statement. Let's say you are suggesting using a specific method to achieve a goal and the other person's response is, *"That's so boring."* Your response can be, *"You are right, to many people that might be boring"*

✓ *Validate that you have heard what has been said*

When you validate the other person, you reduce the opportunity for the other person to polarize. *"I can see how that might be boring."*

✓ *Repeat back*

When you repeat back what you heard the other person say, you can help clear up misunderstandings. If you didn't hear the message correctly, the other person can let you know. You can also support the other person by allowing him to hear what he said. If his comment was hostile, he can realize this when he hears you repeat it out loud; and that can sometimes help to change the direction of the interaction. *"I hate when you ask me over and over again!"* You can respond with *"I can understand that you hate when I ask you over and over again."* And follow up with a second sentence to hold him accountable for moving forward constructively. *"I hate that too. So how would you like to resolve that issue?"*

✓ *Ask the question: What is your intent?*

This is a crucial question that will help you hold the other person accountable, and by doing so, help reduce destructive behavior from being acted out.

Lisa and Steven

Lisa is waiting for Steven to come home. They had a conversation earlier during the day when they talked about the evening plans, but nothing had been confirmed. During the prior conversation, Steven said that he might go and shoot some pool with a friend, and then go out to dinner afterward. Lisa had encouraged him to do so, saying that it had been a long time since he had done something like that and that he probably would enjoy it. Steven didn't know what he wanted to do but said he would go and shoot some pool and think about dinner. Lisa and Steven went about their business during the rest of the day and didn't talk again on the phone. Lisa did some errands and then went home. Steven went and met his friend around five in the evening. After they played some pool, they went out to dinner.

Around 8:30 PM when Steven entered his car, Lisa called him on his cell phone and said in an angry and sarcastic tone of voice, *"It would have been nice if you would have called!"* At first, Steven was taken aback, not quite relating to Lisa's outburst, but reactively and defensively responded, *"You could have called me!"*

The conversation then developed into Lisa maintaining her position and Steven maintaining his. They were polarizing. The conversation escalated into an argument where Steven got angry and Lisa got upset. Other issues were brought up and threats about the future of their relationship were thrown out. Both Lisa and Steven started to feel terrible about the conversation and about each other and the relationship. Doubt was brought into the picture—self-doubt, skepticism about the other person, and reservations about the relationship and its stability. The conversation had gotten out of hand. Problems that had nothing to do with the original interaction and only confused the matter further were brought up.

Neither Steven nor Lisa understood how something like this could become so out of proportion to the event itself. Lisa started to regret that she had made the call to Steven, and she certainly regretted having made the sarcastic remark; but it was too late. As much as she wanted to take back what she had said and start over, she couldn't. The angrier Steven got, the more justified Lisa felt in how she had approached him. They argued in circles until they were both too exhausted to continue. Steven came home and neither one of them felt like spending any time together. Later, they went to sleep without speaking.

The next morning, they didn't feel much better. They rushed off to start their day and felt disconnected and disappointed in each other, not quite knowing what to do or say. Lisa and Steven had not resolved what happened. They had not achieved closure or increased their understanding. They did not have the tools. Instead, they avoided each other, and later they avoided talking about what had happened. As a replacement for dealing with what had happened, they moved on. After some time, they "forgot" about the event and *rationalized*[35] that it wasn't really important, since it had "just" been a little spat anyway. If it hadn't been important, how come in the moment they had felt unresolved, distant, and ready to give up on their relationship?

- What really happened?
- What had in fact been said?
- What was Lisa's intent?
- Why did Steven respond so defensively?
- What was this argument truly about?
- Was Lisa angry at Steven for having gone out with his friend?
- Was Lisa trying to make Steven feel guilty for having had a fun evening?
- Was Lisa jealous?
- Was it simply a matter of Steven having been insensitive by not calling Lisa to let her know about his plans?

---

[35] To rationalize is to superficially formulate rational, plausible explanations or excuses for one's behaviors, beliefs, or desires usually without being aware that these are not the real motives behind the actions.

- Was it a simple misunderstanding?
- Had Steven tried to call?
- Was Lisa concerned and worried that Steven had been in an accident since she hadn't heard from him?
- Had Lisa been disingenuous earlier during the day, when she had encouraged Steven to spend time with his friend?
- How could their interaction have been handled more effectively?
- Does it make a difference what Lisa's intent was?
- Was there some other underlying issue that was causing Lisa to approach Steven the way she approached him?
- What could be gained by understanding possible underlying issues?

After the questions above were answered, it became clear that this was about resentment; and the real issue had to do with an agreement that had been made several months ago. The resentment was related to that agreement and how it had been made. Lisa had acted out her resentment without being aware of what she was doing. Lisa's intent (an unconscious intent) had been to "unleash" her resentment and punish Steven. She did so passive-aggressively by making a sarcastic remark. *So what was Lisa's resentment about?* Lisa didn't realize her resentment was based upon a different situation. After we spent some time exploring the connection between her previous night's reactions to Steven, we got a chance to answer the questions posed above. It then became clear that Lisa's reaction was related to the agreement between Steven and Lisa that had been made numerous months ago.

The topic of the previous agreement had centered on how Lisa and Steven are to keep in touch during the time they are apart, whether it is during regular business days, at night, or if one or the other is traveling. It was about how often and when they should call each other, how they should make themselves available to be reached, and how they should provide information to each other about their schedules and plans. They had talked about it and Steven told Lisa his solution. She listened and agreed without contemplating if the decision was reasonable and aligned with *her* needs as well as with Steven's needs. She never took responsibility for her own position. Lisa, without being aware, abdicated her power in the interaction, which she later came to resent.

When you don't think about what you want and simply go along with someone else's wishes because you don't take the time to think or explore your own needs, or because you feel pressure to do so, it often comes back as resentment acted out in your behavior. Especially if your behavior needs to be adjusted in order to comply with the request of the other. Behavioral changes are hard to do, even if we intellectually believe they are warranted. If our emotional half and our intellectual half are not synchronized and brought to a different level of consciousness, it becomes almost impossible to maintain the behavioral change on a long-term basis without resentment and subsequent acting out.

Steven and Lisa's first mistake was that they only "talked about" a serious subject without identifying it as an agreement process. In other words, they did not discuss the issue under the framework of an agreement. Lisa, at the time, listened and responded to Steven's suggestions, or as we later found out "his demands" as she perceived them, by going along with him without any discussion. Lisa's description of Steven's request as a demand is a clear sign of her responding as a victim in the interaction. She hadn't asserted herself and addressed her concerns with Steven. Because Lisa didn't take the time to explore what she wanted, or what she was looking for in their communication as far as plans and schedules were concerned, she indirectly gave her power away. After some time had passed, Lisa started to feel that Steven's demands were unreasonable, maybe on the controlling side. She didn't like it! But instead of admitting that his demands were complicating her life and making it more difficult or even questioning the issue, she went about her business and followed through as best she could; meanwhile, developing more and more resentment. It never occurred to Lisa that she could, at any time, bring up the subject again and renegotiate the original agreement.

When Steven didn't call her that night, it gave her a perfect opportunity to release some of the anger and resentment she felt toward him. *"See, he didn't follow his own demands, so why did she have to go out of her way to please him and do what he wanted."* This was Lisa's opportunity to regain some power. In Lisa's mind, Steven had to be perfect regarding this issue, since he was the one demanding it in the first place. Lisa would not allow him to make a mistake or deviate one moment from the demands that he had put on her. Lisa became rigid in her thought process.

Lisa is scared of conflict. Like many people, she doesn't have enough tools to deal with conflict effectively and productively. To Lisa, conflict is something negative, something she wants to avoid. Yet, interestingly enough, the comment she made to Steven inevitably produced precisely that—conflict!

Why?

On a logical level, it doesn't make sense. However, on an emotional level it makes perfect sense. Think of it as a pitcher of water. Once the pitcher gets full, the water spills over. It is the same with feelings that are unconscious, not contained, and not taken responsibility for.

Containment

The key is to bring awareness to the feelings and the power they have, so that you can make better choices and take better care of yourself by making appropriate behavioral changes. Lisa acted out her resentment because she wasn't aware of how much resentment she had developed. This is a common pattern among many people when they don't realize that it is tied to unresolved power and control issues. Lisa didn't have the tools to deal with her resentment any other way, and her "pitcher" simply spilled over and it presented itself as a sarcastic comment. It was her indirect, safer than being direct, way to let Steven know she was angry with him. It was an attempt to shift the power from Steven back to Lisa. Her anger was not only about the fact he did not call her. By not calling, Steven gave Lisa an opportunity to act out her resentment. Therefore, if we would have gotten sidetracked and only discussed whether Steven had called or not (we later found out that he had, in fact, called numerous times but the answering machine wasn't working correctly), we would have only resolved the superficial part of the problem. Lisa's resentment about the power and control dynamics during the agreement process would have remained unconscious. The resentment would have continued to grow until Lisa would have found future opportunities to act it out and it would have continued to cause problems in their relationship.

Hence, unidentified resentment stemming from an imbalance of power is often a hidden dynamics that causes unnecessary conflict. Often, a similar problem keeps repeating, which often is a cover-up for a more important and troublesome issue. The conflict doesn't get resolved, resentment continues to build, and intimacy and growth become, if not impossible, at least limited.

When Steven responded defensively to Lisa's inappropriate outburst, he was manipulated by his own and Lisa's emotions. This is the first place where a different choice on Steven's behalf would have changed the events that followed. There are many layers to communication, and often resentment connected to power and control dynamics is one of the underlying reasons for breakdowns and arguments that are unproductive.

Some good tools to deal with resentment are the following:

- Familiarize yourself with your own resentment.
- When do you resent someone?
- Identify ten times when you have resented someone in your past.
- Why did you resent that person?
- What had the person done that made you resent her?
- What do you do when you feel resentful?
- Are you generally able to identify when someone is resentful?
- What behaviors do you associate with resentment?
- How do you hold someone accountable when they are acting out their resentment?
- How do you hold yourself accountable?
- What behavioral changes can you make to better deal with your resentment?
- How does resentment get built up?
- Why does resentment grow?
- What kind of relationship do you have with resentment?
- What kind of relationship would you like to have with resentment?
- Raise your awareness about power and control by being curious.
- Pay attention to when you start feeling resentful and identify it early on by paying attention to your feelings and reactions.
- When you experience someone withdrawing from the interaction, ask questions; don't ignore the behavior because it is easier to do so.

- Ask yourself what kind of support you might need to learn how to better deal with your own and other people's resentment.
- Assert yourself in interactions and ask questions if you don't understand or agree.
- Become aware of how you negotiate and reach agreements.

Resentment is like a disease; as it keeps growing, it destroys the relationship. It chips away at your morale, wipes out values, and allures you to renege on your commitment to excellence.

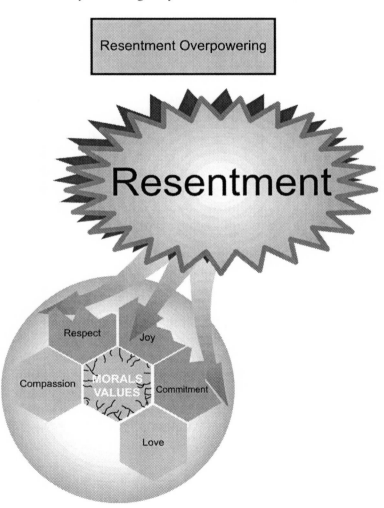

Have you ever found yourself making some sarcastic remark, or a comment halfway under your breath, humiliated the other person by exposing some secret told in confidence, said something mean or even vicious, laughed at the person not with him, gone behind someone's back, refused to make an effort that you would normally do, withheld your love or affection to punish, made a comment about something you had gone along with but *certainly never* agreed with? It cannot be stressed enough how important it is to learn about resentment and its direct connection to power, control, and *victimhood*[36], and find tools to deal with your own and other people's resentment.

Empowerment: the Answer

You are a victim when you are acting out your resentment. The intent behind your actions is to shift the structure of power and make the other person a victim. The dynamics of resentment is constant attempts to shift the power from one person to the other. Such behavior prevents you and the other from being empowered and locks you into power-struggles and polarized positions. When Lisa made her comment to Steven, *"It would have been nice if you would have called,"* Steven could have stated back *"I agree."* An answer like that acknowledges the truth about Lisa's comment and ignores her attempts to manipulate. Steven doesn't polarize, which is what Lisa is expecting. His nonreactive comment would most likely throw Lisa off balance. It may inflame her, since she is not getting away with her destructive behavior; it could force her to become more direct and less passive-aggressive or it may make her withdraw.

In either event, Steven has created a wall against the destructive behavior and has unconsciously offered Lisa some choices; she can remain a victim or become empowered. If Lisa chose to be empowered she could continue the interaction by stating the following: *"I am glad you agree with me. First off, let me apologize for my indirect comment. That was unproductive. What I should have said was that I have been getting angrier and angrier by the hour because you didn't call. Instead of getting lost in my anger while not having all the information, can you please explain to me why you haven't called?"* Lisa is still assuming that Steven hasn't called, but is showing some openness to hear

---

[36] Victimhood refers to somebody who experienced misfortune and feels helpless to do anything about it, or who was duped or taken advantage of, affected, or deceived by somebody or something.

what he has to say. Steven has a choice to react to Lisa's statement that she is angry or respond to her request for information. If Steven is able to decipher the various parts of Lisa's message, and only respond to one part at a time, he can avoid being manipulated by his own initial emotional responses to what Lisa is saying. If Steven chooses to react to her anger, he can get lost in the emotions that may prevent Lisa and him to understand the actual problem. If Steven, instead, is choosing to provide Lisa with information, he will support the process of getting clarity and resolution. *"Lisa, I called three times throughout the late afternoon, but the machine didn't pick up. Would you mind checking the machine?"* Now, there is a tangible action Lisa can take to resolve the problem. She checks the machine and it isn't working right. Lisa's anger may subside if the absence of a call from Steven is the real issue, since it now is clear that Steven had done his part and Lisa had reacted based on inaccurate or limited information. However, if this is about her resentment about the power and control dynamics that took place during the original agreement, then some anger will remain and Lisa will not feel resolved.

She may suppress her anger since she can't blame Steven anymore, or she may ask herself some questions to realize the underlying issue:

- Why did I react so strongly?
- How come I was being indirect when I was so angry?
- Why don't I feel better now that we have cleared up the misunderstanding?
- Is there anything else about phoning each other that bothers me?

> *The single most effective way to empower someone is to refuse to enable the person to be a victim, and to say no to becoming a victim yourself.*

7

It is About
Resistance and Receptivity (R and R)

Resistance *can be described as opposing, withstanding, and warding off. It hinders openness and receptivity. It can also be related to the psychological opposition of the bringing of unconscious material to consciousness.*

Receptivity *is the opposite of a barrier and can be described as being able and ready to take in suggestions, requests, and new ideas.*

Resistance can be difficult to identify unless it is transparent. Many times as you carry on a conversation, you may start feeling uneasy and irritated but not quite know why. The other person may be responding to you, yet you don't experience the interaction as open and productive.

Bob and Jeff

Bob decided he needed to have a conversation with Jeff about the project they were working on together. Bob was displeased with some of Jeff's contributions and wanted to make sure that some changes were implemented for the second half of the project. Bob approached Jeff in the hallway and asked if he could take a few minutes and come back to Bob's office, since there was something he wanted to discuss with Jeff.

Jeff said he was extremely busy right now. Bob replied that what he needed to discuss was very important. Jeff gave in and said he'll be there in a few minutes. Bob went back to his office and waited for Jeff. When Jeff came, he seemed rushed and anxious to get the conversation over with. Bob started to feel irritated but moved ahead anyway and said, *"Jeff, I have some concerns about you meeting your deadlines."* Jeff responded, *"I don't know what you're talking about, Bob. I have been on top of this project since day one."* Bob said, *"That is not my experience."* Jeff continued, *"I am really busy right now, Bob, so just tell me what you want, all right?"* Bob replied, *"I want this project to be done on time."* Jeff said, *"So do I. Can I get back to my work now, so I don't waste any more time?"* Bob felt angry and reacted. *"That's fine, Jeff. Make sure you don't disappoint me on this one."*

What Bob failed to recognize was that Jeff was resisting him. Jeff invalidated and devalued Bob during their interaction. During the latter part of the interaction, Jeff dismissed Bob by making the statement, "So do I," and followed it up with a sarcastic and underhanded question. With resistance often follows destructive behaviors, such as invalidation, devaluing, and dismissing. When those behaviors and intents are not identified, they are instead reacted to unconsciously.

Jeff did not contribute productive and useful input in his communication. Instead, he appeared hostile and close-minded. Yet Bob did not hold Jeff accountable for his choices but went along with Jeff's pressure to end the conversation as quickly as possible. Bob abandoned his goals and accommodated Jeff's resistance.

How could Bob have handled the interaction differently?

Step 1

Bob would have shown that this was a serious topic by choosing a more appropriate time. It may have sounded like this:

"Do you have a moment?"

This question is intended to aid in the process of creating a productive conversation by establishing if Jeff is available.

If Jeff answers, *"No, this is a really bad time."*

Bob can move to the next step and be curious if Jeff truly is swamped and doesn't have a moment or if he is resistant to communicating with Bob.

Step 2

"Since this isn't a good time, when will you be able to get back to me, Jeff?"

By asking that question Bob is showing that he is not going to be dismissed, while at the same time he is respectful of Jeff's time. The ball is back in Jeff's court and his answer will provide additional information for Bob.

"I'll call you later." By making that statement, Jeff is still attempting to dismiss Bob without giving Bob what he wants and needs. Jeff being

vague about a time, sets it up, so that Bob cannot later complain if Jeff doesn't call.

Jeff could then say, *"I said, I'll call you later."* What does later mean? Does it mean the same day, next day, later on in the week?

If Bob leaves at that time, allowing Jeff to dismiss him, he is being passive and victimized by Jeff's pressure to "get him off his back."

Step 3

The information Bob has gathered at this point is that Jeff is resistant to giving him a specific time. It is unclear why. Bob needs to support Jeff to agree on a specific time. By asking another question, Bob can qualify Jeff's answer:

"What does later mean?"

Jeff may show signs of irritation, which is common behavior when someone is being held accountable, and resistance is part of the dynamics.

"I don't know, Bob. Later this afternoon, I guess."

Jeff is trying to inflame Bob. Jeff's communication is indirectly letting Bob know that he is a "pain" and is being difficult. Jeff is again being unspecific and is taking no responsibility for his avoidance by not giving Bob a specific time.

Step 4

Commonly at this stage, Jeff's resistance would have worn on Bob. He would become victimized and give up or become manipulated and react with anger. Bob has a third choice: not react to Jeff's resistance, exemplified as vagueness, but instead be proactive and assertive.

"When you are being vague, it makes it difficult to plan for the rest of the day. I don't have a problem with you getting back to me later as long as you provide me with a specific time window of an hour. With that in mind, what time will you get back to me?"

Bob is gently and respectfully guiding Jeff to be specific.

"I'll call you between 5:00-6:00 PM. How's that, Bob?"

"That's great, speak to you then."

Bob and Jeff established a time that works for both of them. Jeff's attitude exhibited in his question "How's that, Bob?" indicates that he is resistant to having the conversation with Bob. Instead of being angry and reacting negatively to Jeff's question, Bob ignores it and, instead, responds to the first part that addressed his request. Bob recognizes that Jeff is trying to provoke him while Bob is trying to hold him accountable. Bob can use that knowledge to help him strategize on how to better deal with Jeff later.

When you are aware that someone is resistant, try not to react to that person's baiting. By anticipating their behavior, you can prepare for the interaction more effectively.

Step 5

Jeff calls.
"Bob, it's Jeff, what is it that you want?"
"I have some concerns about project A that I would like to spend thirty minutes discussing with you. When will you be available?"
"I don't know, Bob, it's really crazy here right now."

Jeff is again trying to avoid having further conversations with Bob. It is unclear what his motives are, but that is irrelevant at this time.

Bob's strategic move now is to validate Jeff, since that is in complete opposition to polarization. The intent is to reduce the resistance and at the same time respect the force behind it. By following up with a question that suggests that a positive result may stem from this conversation, Bob has an opportunity to better evaluate the degree of Jeff's resistance. Is it a 10 on a scale from 1-10, 10 being high and 1 being low?

"I understand that you are working really hard right now and that time is tight. Jeff, do you think that the results from our conversation may affect the structure of the workload so that it can become more reasonable and manageable if we have a conversation about project A?
"No, I don't."

Jeff's answer is very helpful, since it explains some of his resistance. Why would Jeff want to take any time out of his schedule to meet with Bob if he doesn't see any direct or potential benefit of doing so?

Step 6

Bob has reached an impasse and has some choices to make.

- Is he going to use pressure to have the meeting, let Jeff know what he wants, and ignore Jeff's resistance?
- Is he going to let Jeff "off the hook" and pass on the meeting?
- Is he going to ask Jeff some qualifying questions to establish how he is going to move forward?

It is helpful to understand some of the underlying dynamics of resistance so you can take it less personally. As with many of the hidden dynamics that have been discussed so far, as long as they remain unconscious you will be more susceptible to manipulations both by the other person and your own emotions that get activated.

Around & Around

Can you take a minute?

RESISTANCE
I'm busy right now!

This is important and I'll be quick!

RESISTANCE
No, I need to get this done!

PLEASE

RESISTANCE
I told you I don't have the time!

Busy Yet Receptive

Can you take a minute?

Receptive
I'm really busy right now.
However, I am interested in what you have to say.
Is it an emergency or can we talk in about an hour?

No, it's not an emergency.
An hour from now will be fine.

Receptive
GREAT!

How about I'll meet you back here in an hour?

Receptive
Sounds good, see you then.

Curiosity

Curiosity, to me, is what Windex ® Solution was to the father in the movie *My Big Fat Greek Wedding*—the cure for "all" ailments.

When curiosity enters into the picture, opportunities are created and faulty judgments and preconceived ideas evaporate. Learning can take place. Curiosity expands the space while rigidity restricts space. To be truly curious demands that you let go of knowing and embrace finding out. Curiosity requires patience. Some of the rewards from being curious are joy and excitement.

Resistance: When, How, and What About

What may be some underlying reasons behind the person's resistance?

- He doesn't perceive that the interaction, information, or person will have any value.
- He may fear that the interaction will be unpleasant, humiliating, or degrading.
- He may not be interested because he doesn't see the direct correlation to himself.
- He may be angry about how he was approached and this is his way of getting back.
- He may perceive any form of feedback as negative and unnecessary.
- He may experience the other person as negative and abusive.
- He may perceive the other person as self-centered and close-minded.

Using curiosity can be a very powerful tool in dealing with resistance. When you use curiosity, you can meet resistance with openness and creativity.

How to Approach Resistance

Here are other tools of approaching resistance:

1. Slow down the process.
2. Remain calm.
3. Identify the resistance, and don't take it personally.
4. Step back and be creative when you feel that you are hitting a wall.
5. Realize your limitations and the other person's limitations; don't insist.
6. Ask *qualifying* questions:

   a. Is this a good time?
   b. Are you interested in what I have to say?
   c. What value do you think this interaction may have for you?
   d. How important is it to you that we have this conversation, on a scale from 1-10, 10 being extremely important to you?
   e. What would you like to get out of this conversation?

f.   If we end this conversation now, do you think we have resolved the issue?

g.   Why do you think I want to have this conversation?

h.   How do you think this conversation will benefit you, our relationship, and me?

i.   What would you like to do now?

j.   If this is not a good time, when would be a good time to have this conversation?

1)   Depending on the answers you receive, it may be wise to remove yourself from the interaction and return at a different time.

2)   Be flexible.

3)   Gather information.

An additional, useful tool is to pay attention to the resistant person's body language and address it:

- When you look away when I am talking to you, you send a message that you are not interested. Are you not interested in what I have to say?
- When you roll your eyes, you send the message that what I have to say is meaningless, redundant, unimportant, and a waste of your time. Is that how you feel?
- When you yawn repeatedly, you send a message that this is boring to you. Are you bored?

The reason why it is important to address the various body language signs is so that you can help reduce the acting out by the person who is resisting.

As there are specific suggestions of what to do, there are suggestions of *what not to do*:

- Don't repeat yourself and your viewpoint over and over again.
- Don't invest more energy into the conversations than the other.
- Don't try to convince the other person about the benefits.
- Don't be rigid and polarize.

- Don't get manipulated by your own emotions or by the other person's emotions.

Resistance may take the following forms:

- Vagueness
- Dismissal
- Devaluing
- Invalidating
- Lack of interest and engagement
- Short answers
- Changing of the subject

When someone is resisting, there is no point to polarize with him. However, it is very important to recognize resistance in the form of vagueness and dismissal, so you don't fall victim to its force, develop resentment, and subsequently act it out. When you feel that the conversation is more important to you, and you are trying very hard to move the conversation along, or you feel that there is a clear imbalance in the conversation, then you might want to ask yourself the question: *"Am I being met with resistance?"*

Awareness of resistance starts with you:

- When are you resistant?
- What do you resist the most?
- Why do you resist that?
- How do you respond when you are resistant?
- What kind of support do you find most helpful when you are resistant?
- Who holds you accountable when you are resistant?
- Identify four different behaviors that you engage in when you are resistant.
- Where in your body do you feel the resistance?

There are a number of situations where it is reasonable to expect resistance to be present.

The following situations are some examples typical of resistance:

- You are negotiating.
- You are compromising.

- Sensitive or difficult subjects are being discussed.
- Someone is uncomfortable.
- Someone doesn't understand.
- Family matters are discussed.
- Behavioral changes are suggested or required.
- Authority is given or taken.
- Feedback is given.
- Advice is given without being solicited.
- Someone is scared.
- You're planning events.
- You want to change an existing structure of power and responsibility.
- Someone is separating.
- There are physical limitations that require changes.
- Someone is letting go.
- Someone is finding it difficult to accept limitations.

Receptivity

What a beautiful word! Receptivity is the opposite of resistance. Instead of a barrier it is an *enhancer*[37] in the communication. When someone is receptive, you feel heard, seen, validated, and respected; all the things missing when met with resistance. Receptivity can be an invigorating, supportive, and positive experience. It is important that you become clear about the behavioral responses that can be seen when someone is receptive, since that can help you raise your awareness about resistance.

What are some signs of receptivity?

The receptive person may do the following:

- He may have good eye contact with you.
- He may use head nods and other body language signs to acknowledge what you are saying.
- He may smile.
- He may verbally let you know that you are heard and understood.
- He may validate your points.
- He may agree at times.

---

[37] An enhancer is something added that improves an interaction.

- He may interject with complimenting suggestions.
- He may ask questions.
- He may mirror back what you have said at times.

If you want to make sure you are providing appropriate signs of receptivity, then it is a good idea to start paying attention to your own behavior, as it will also heighten your sensitivity to other people's behaviors. If you truly know what receptivity feels like, you will have a better chance at recognizing resistance, its polar opposite.

8

Fear and Anxiety: Fear Me Not

Fear can be described as a feeling of anxiety and agitation caused by the presence or nearness of danger, evil, pain, timidity, dread, terror, or fight. It can be a feeling of uneasiness or apprehension.

On one hand, fear can occur on a biological level when you feel physically threatened. It can then trigger instinctual reflexes such as the autonomic responses of your central nervous system[38], endocrine glands, and various other bodily functions. On another hand, there is the psychological fear that gets triggered when you feel emotionally threatened. This kind of fear may be self-imposed like the fear of speaking in front of an audience. Or, it may be resulting from an actual, or perceived external source, such as when you experience that someone else has the control, which can be a threat to your self-esteem.

Internal and external fears can cause a lot of trouble in your interactions and communication with others unless you understand, recognize, and learn to deal with the fears effectively. It is often difficult to identify fear unless it occurs in a situation where danger is blatant. There are specifically four words that *do not* go along with fear:

- Clarity
- Logic
- Patience
- Reasonableness

---

[38] Kathleen D. Ryan and Daniel K. Oestreich, *Driving Fear Out of the Workplace: How to Overcome the Invisible Barriers to Quality, Productivity, and Innovation* (San Francisco: Jossey-Bass Publishers, 1991).

Fears are often irrational, sometimes imagined, over exaggerated, and taken out of context. They are often slippery and disguised behind faulty judgments and irrational, reactive behaviors. That doesn't mean that fears are less important to understand or that they need any less attention. On the contrary, getting to know your fears, the how and when they show up, and what kind of behaviors you engage in when you are scared are imperative in removing them from the hidden-barriers list.

What kind of relationship do you have with your own fear?
What kind of relationship do you have with other people's fears?

Common ways of evading fear:

- Deny that the fear exists
- Avoid dealing with the fear
- Pretend it isn't there

By doing any of the above, you give the fear more power to undermine and sabotage your relationships. As long as fears remain unconscious, you are precluded from having choices to proactively deal with them and are instead prone to react.

The list of what the fear might be is long and involved. Is the fear about?

- Failing
- Making a mistake
- Upsetting the other person
- Conflict
- Other person's anger
- Your own anger
- Retribution and punishment
- Rejection
- Not being liked
- Being wrong
- Not being perfect
- Being humiliated
- Being shamed
- Being tied down
- Being out of control

- Having to feel some unpleasant feeling
- Success
- Betrayal
- Dying
- Being stuck
- Hurting people's feelings
- Being abandoned
- Losing
- Not measuring up
- Not being recognized
- Not being appreciated
- Not being special
- Being stupid
- Being unlovable
- Being crazy
- Being vulnerable
- Intimacy
- Losing power
- The truth
- Losing control
- Being exposed
- Not being believed
- Not being trusted

When fears aren't recognized or identified, there is a greater likelihood that you will lose perspective and that the situation will be taken out of context, thereby escalating the intensity of your experience.

If your fear has a dialogue with you, the fear *may make the following statements to you:*

- I am powerful because I know everything.
- I get my strength from keeping you scared.
- My purpose in life is to dominate and control your every move.
- When I am around, you surrender your power to me.
- I can control you because you let me.
- If I wasn't so strong, you would not keep me around.
- If you weren't so afraid of me, I wouldn't be so powerful and you would have the freedom to choose.

The more scared you are, the more power the fear has over your life, your choices, and your behavior. *If you are run by your fear, you are dominated and controlled, which is connected to the core of the issue, being controlled by someone or something else.* When you are scared, you are disempowered and reactive. The fear can control you as long as you remain unconscious of its force. The fear has to be strong or you would question its purpose and contribution to your life. The more afraid you are, the more power you give away and the fewer the available choices you have.

Turning Symptoms Into Signals

It is easy to become overwhelmed by the power of the fear and develop faulty judgments about the symptoms that are only expressions of the fear. If you do so, you become a victim of the fear and are at the mercy of reactive behaviors.

What may some symptoms of fear be?

- Headache
- Sleep problems
- Depression
- Anxiety
- Tension
- Procrastination
- Avoidance
- Stress
- Faulty judgments
- Inappropriate tone of voice
- Anger
- Changing of the subject
- Extreme tiredness
- Feeling overwhelmed and agitated
- Feeling hopeless and helpless
- Giving up and withdrawing
- Rejecting needs and perceiving the need as a nuisance and unnecessary

Commonly, your fear can be activated by another person's fear without you being aware. This typically happens if the message is perceived unconsciously as a potential threat to your well-being or self-esteem.

Megan and David

David's fear: *You are never going to marry me because you don't really want me. It is only a matter of time before you will take our relationship away from me, and I will be left with nothing.*

Megan and David have been in a relationship for three years. They have been discussing marriage, but Megan has some reservations. David has been growing increasingly agitated during their discussions.

"Megan, why do you keep avoiding the subject of marriage?"

(David is trying to hold Megan accountable for avoiding the subject.)

"I do not."

(Megan is either not aware that she is avoiding the subject or she is trying to get out of taking responsibility for doing so.)

"Yes, you do. When did you last bring it up?"

(David is yet again trying to hold Megan accountable by asking her a specific question.)

"I don't know, I have a lot of things on my mind and I have been very busy lately."

(Megan is making excuses and using her excuses as attempts to "get David off her back.")

"Yeah, you're always busy and always have an excuse."

(David is expressing his resentment and frustration. His fear is activated.)

"That's not true, David."

(Megan is resisting David's input and invalidating his comments.)

"Megan, can we be real for just a minute. I'm getting really sick and tired of being the one bringing this up."

(David is being manipulated by Megan's invalidation and resistance and reacting by making a sarcastic comment to inflame Megan. David is being a victim.)

"Then don't bring it up."

(Megan takes the opportunity to use David's comment against him, challenging his passive position to take some action.)

"That's great, Megan. Maybe we should just break up instead!"

(David is exposed, he wanted Megan to show some compassion and understand that he is tired of being the one bringing this topic up. Instead, she exposed him. He gets angry and reacts by escalating the antagonism between them using a statement instead of a question, which would have been more vulnerable and risky for David.)

"No, David, you know I don't want to break up."

(Megan is reacting to the escalation of the interaction and realizes that she has taken it too far; she is attempting to calm David down by giving him some reassurance.)

"Maybe you don't . . . "

(Instead of taking in Megan's reassurance, David is seizing the opportunity to take as much power back as he can by making a comment that is intended to make Megan unsure.)

"Don't threaten me, David. I thought we were past this."

(David's veiled threat angers Megan as she realizes he was taking advantage of her being vulnerable and reassuring. She can sense that he is attempting to shift the power away from her. Megan is not about to relinquish her power to David. She makes a strong direct comment setting a boundary and follows up with an indirect comment intended to make David insecure. What is Megan referring to? She seems annoyed with David. The uncertainty activates feelings of loss of control that will activate David's original fear that Megan doesn't want him or the relationship.)

"Past what? Past me bugging you?"

(David is receiving the indirect jab from Megan and is pushing her to state it directly so he can hear her say that he is bothering her, and by doing so, verify his fear that he is unwanted.)

"Yeah, past you bugging me! Just let me be! Why can't you just be patient?"

(Megan falls into David's "fear trap" and validates his fear, and then adds a request in an accusatory and disappointed way.)

"Because I have been patient for three years?"

(David's resentment is evident by his comment when he adds the length of three years, without continuing with some form of constructive suggestion to move toward resolution. David is again "throwing" powerless statements out that will further *disempower*[39] him in the interaction.)

"That's ridiculous! You didn't know you wanted to marry me the day we met."

(Megan is invalidating David's comment again. She adds a judgment about his comment as she is changing the subject, instead, to discussing whether he knew or not three years ago.)

"Maybe I did? Who are you to say I didn't know?"

(David didn't catch the change of subject. Instead, he is taken off course and they are now discussing what happened three years ago, instead of what David is wanting in the here and the now.)

---

[39] To disempower is to take or give power away.

"I'm only saying that it's not realistic to know if you want to marry someone the same day you meet. It's ludicrous."

(Megan is more comfortable now since she is discussing something hypothetical and she is temporarily off the hook. She is using inflammatory descriptions that are intended to manipulate David to react. By doing so, she maintains control and power.)

As you can see, Megan and David are going around in circles, not accomplishing anything. Instead, they are alienating each other. The dynamics of power, control, polarization, and acting out of resentment and fears are dominating the interaction. Thus far, David's problem is not being resolved. Eventually, they are both worn out and want to have nothing to do with each other. The issue is left unresolved and depending on where they both are on the "giving-up scale," they may suppress their emotions, drop the subject, and pretend everything is back to where it was before David approached Megan. However, if they do that, it is inevitable that this conversation will be repeated in one way or another; and each time that happens and the issue is left unresolved, Megan and David will have created deeper and more serious scars in their relationship. The more resentment that builds up, the more the trust and closeness between them will erode.

The communication could have sounded quite differently if David had been aware of his fear, taken responsibility for it, and approached Megan from an empowered position.

"Megan, I have something important that I would like to discuss with you. Do you have some time to sit down with me now?"

(David is taking his topic and fear seriously and realizes the importance of setting some time aside, and to achieve an agreement with Megan to participate. By doing so up front, David is showing Megan that he respects himself and his needs as well as Megan and her needs.)

"I am really busy, David. Can it wait?"

(Megan says she is busy. Whether that is true or not is irrelevant. What is important is to gather information to evaluate how interested Megan is and how resistant she may be.)

"Yes, Megan, it can wait. If this isn't a good time, then when will you have the time during the next five days?"

(The topic isn't urgent and since David is not operating out of his fear, he doesn't need to respond as if this is an emergency. This gives David balance in the interaction. However, David is not allowing Megan to dismiss him. He asks her a question that will hold her accountable for giving him a time that will work. By setting up the time frame of within five days, David is showing that he is reasonable, yet demands respect and reason.)

"How about tomorrow after work?"

(Megan is giving David a clear and appropriate answer.)

"That's fine, let's sit down around 7:00 PM. Will that work for you?"

(David is agreeing. He is suggesting a time, so there will be no reason for misunderstandings or confusion the next day. David's clarity and effective communication is attractive and builds trust and respect.)

"Yes, that's good. You're on."

(Megan verifies that they have reached an amicable agreement. The frame and container is set in motion for tomorrow's sensitive conversation.)

When David recognizes that he is scared of something, he creates an opportunity to explore numerous choices:

1. David can *deny* his fear, ignore its force, and become a victim. He can act out his fear and subsequent resentment that will inevitably build up over time, causing fights with Megan.

2. David can *pretend* that he does not have the fear and avoid discussing the topic of marriage with Megan. He will grow increasingly frustrated and angry with her over time when she does not initiate conversations about their future. David may, instead, start to complain about other aspects of Megan's character, behavior, communication, and interaction as a way of releasing some of his accumulated frustration and anger; shifting the topic away from the marriage issue to a less-threatening issue. One example would be to complain that Megan doesn't spend enough time with David.

3. David can *avoid* his fear and, instead, start to convert his fear into bodily symptoms in the form of increased anxiety, headaches, or stomach pain.

4. David can *suppress* his fear and when it threatens to break through from his unconscious to his conscious mind, David can use alcohol or drugs to numb him from experiencing the discomfort and anxiety caused by the fear.

5. David can *confront* his fear and *become curious* by reality testing. He can initiate a conversation with Megan about the topic of marriage and their future together. Thus, his fears can be validated that Megan does not want that type of future with him or that she does want to marry but the timing is not right. In either event, the "truth" can

provide David and Megan with options. One option may be for David to break up with Megan if their goals and aspirations aren't compatible. Another option may be to address the timing issues that were raised during the conversation and work as a team in finding a solution to that issue.

Remember that un*confronted fears often become* un*contained fears and as such remain* un*conscious and ready to interfere in your life at any given time.*

Healthy Strategies to Break Down Fear

- Identify and assess the fear.
- Accept and admit that the fear exists.
- Recognize and own resistance that often comes along with fears.
- Identify and separate faulty judgments from needs connected to fear.
- Evaluate your need for support to deal effectively with your fear or other people's fear.
- Explore what you need in the form of the following:

  o   Contact
  o   Encouragement
  o   Reassurance

- Learn to practice asking for what you need.
- Slow down the process.

The goal is to *reframe*[40] the symptoms of fear into signals, to recognize the fear, and learn how to deal with it constructively, without allowing the fear to interfere with your own or other people's well-being and productivity. When you do that, you can see the symptom as a signal to pay attention to the fear without developing faulty judgment. The symptom is the signal alerting you that you have an opportunity to act consciously instead of reacting.

First, you identify that fear is present before it interferes with the interaction. Once it has been identified, you need to establish what it is about:

---

[40]   Reframing is taking an already existing viewpoint or belief system and challenging it by adding new and different information and proposing a new outlook.

Are you scared that the other person is going to be angry with you? Are you anxious that you are wrong? If you have difficulties handling conflict, you may need to spend some time exploring your thoughts, fears, and past experiences that were involved in conflict.

Containment

Containing *can be described as the capacity for holding, enclosing, and restraining something, someone, or oneself in the moment. It does not refer to power and authority.*

The key to dealing effectively with fear is to learn how to contain yours and other people's fears. That means you do not allow your own feelings that get generated in reaction to fear, to determine your actions. In order to contain fear, you have to understand what the need is behind the fear.

Uncontained fear occurs when the fear is dominating the interaction, resulting in irrational and impulsive behavior. Communication is often exaggerated and contains "for sure" statements. It is close-minded and absolute. Contained fear occurs when the force of the fear is being respected and the fear is given appropriate attention. The fear is not being dismissed. Yet, it doesn't dominate or control the interaction. Rational and logical thoughts and actions are present.

The need behind the fear will determine the following:

- Intensity of the fear
- Power of the fear in the interaction
- The remedies that you will use to "get rid of your fear"
- How successful you will be in dealing with your fear effectively

Behind the fear may be these needs:

- To belong
- To be held
- To be loved
- To know
- To control
- To be right
- To understand
- To accept

- To be validated
- To be reassured
- To be supported
- To be taken care of
- To be nurtured
- To feel committed
- To be sure
- To give up
- To surrender
- To be understood
- To be known
- To be seen
- To be attended to
- To get attention
- To give
- To be received
- To feel connected
- To feel special
- To feel good
- To dominate
- To maintain power
- To be intimate

Once you are connected to and have explored the need behind the fear, you can choose suitable tools to contain the fear. *Until you have reached that knowledge, how can you possibly resolve the situation?* If you are tired and dehydrated but don't know it, and you start feeling dizzy and physically weak, you may simply go to bed and rest. The fear may be that you will otherwise faint. If you go to bed and rest, you are not resolving the problem of the dehydration but in fact exacerbating the situation further, since the need that requires attention is the need for water, not the need for rest. The same holds true when you are dealing with fear. If the need behind the fear is to receive reassurance but instead you harshly judge yourself as inadequate, the fear may instead increase and worsen the situation. One tool to use is curiosity. When you get scared you can become curious about what you are scared of, why you are scared, when you get scared, how you get scared, and what you need when you get scared, instead of immediately condemning yourself and seeing yourself as weak and pathetic.

- *Do you need reassurance?*
- *Is it okay to be scared sometimes or does that mean you are a weak person?*
- *Do you need to be able to separate yourself from the fear?*
- *Do you need to set a boundary that can better protect you when you get scared?*
- *Do you need to take some time to yourself and get perspective?*
- *Do you need some contact from another person that can identify with your situation?*

The easiest path to choose is to ignore the fear and act out the need behind the fear in a destructive manner. However, if you increase awareness and contain your fears you will be afraid less of the time, and when you *are* afraid you will feel more comfortable dealing with them. Subsequently, you become more sensitive to fears; they pass in less time and have less effect on your life. With this increase of awareness, you are less affected by the impact of other people's fears, which increases the trust you experience in yourself and the trust others have in you.

Anxiety, Fear's Closest Relative

Anxiety can be described as a state of being uneasy, apprehensive, or worried about what may happen. It is similar to being concerned about a possible future event. Anxiety can also be described as a state characterized by a feeling of being powerless and being unable to cope with threatening events.

Anxiety is often felt in the pit of your stomach. Sometimes it moves around throughout your body and makes you have a difficult time sitting still. You may want to tap your fingers or feet, rock some part of your body, and eventually you become increasingly agitated. Sometimes your anxiety may make it difficult to sleep. Other times, sleep may be all you want to avoid experiencing the effects of your anxiety. Taking some form of calming or relaxing substance to ease the effect temporarily, is many times a seductive solution when afflicted with high levels of anxiety.

Identifying Anxiety

Sometimes it is difficult to establish whether it is fear or anxiety that you are experiencing. In either event, you need to respect the force and power that fear and anxiety can have on your life. Learn to recognize it and use appropriate tools to deal with it. Anxiety sometimes shows up as irritability, shortness, and sharp responses. Behaviorally, it can also exhibit itself as withdrawal and isolation.

Questions to ask yourself when you see some symptoms that may alert you that you are anxious:

- What is going on in my body right now?
- Why am I feeling so tense?
- What is the irritability about?
- Why am I getting a headache?
- Do I need to reach out right now since my inclination is the opposite—to isolate?
- Could I be feeling anxious?
- What may I be anxious about?
- What has happened in the last day that may have triggered anxiety for me?
- What was said that I may be anxious about?
- Are there any demands or pressures that are different today than yesterday?

- How has my anxiety affected my desire to reach out?
- When did I start feeling irritable?
- What can I do right now to feel better?
- What do I need right now?
- Who do I need that from?

The same suggestions that hold true for dealing with fears apply when you are dealing with anxiety. Tools that can be applied overlap since they are so closely related.

9

Trust, A Must!

Trust *can be described as a firm belief or confidence in the honesty, integrity, reliability, and justice of a person or thing; it can be referred to as faith and reliance.*

Trust is an imperative part of a relationship, whether it is in the relationship you have with yourself or that which you have with others. Without trust, your internal life can become quite chaotic. The extreme opposite of trust can be described as paranoia. Imagine if you went around mistrusting and suspecting people of having malicious intent or being "out to get you," how would that change your interactions?

To better understand trust and the immense effect it has on your life, it may be helpful to start by asking some questions.

Where does trust come from?

Are there different degrees of trust?

Can you trust somebody if you don't ask questions?

Self-Awareness

Have you ever done an inventory about the levels of trust you have had in the five most important relationships in your life?

- Who has trusted you the most in your life?
- What did you do to earn that trust?
- What have you done to sustain that trust?
- What is the current level of trust in that relationship?
- Who betrayed your trust the most?
- How have you repaired the trust since then?

- Did your trust in yourself suffer from that experience?
- What resources in yourself do you trust the most?
- What are three major steps you take to build trust in relationships?
- What do you trust the least in other people?
- What did your father teach you about trust?
- What did your mother teach you about trust?
- Has your experience of grief affected your trust?
- Do you trust your ability to set boundaries?
- Do you trust that you can hold others accountable?
- Do you trust your impulse control?
- Do you trust your ability to deal with changes of subject?
- What book has taught you the most about trust?
- Have you ever wondered why trust is important to you?
- Do you trust your unconscious to provide comfort and trust?
- Do you trust that you can handle anger, your own, and others?
- What do you trust least about yourself?
- What do you trust the most about yourself?

Depending on what your answers are to the above questions, you can assess what kind of support you need and what actions you need to take to work on the trust-building process. There are several factors that are fundamental and easy to identify when you develop trust for someone. Some may be, you don't lie, you tell the truth. You keep your commitments and follow-through on agreements. You do what you say and you say what you do. You are up-front and forthcoming with information. You give the person appropriate amount of eye contact. You are interested in what the other person has to say and show that in behaviors congruent with your verbal responses.

Here are some of the hidden dynamics that may not be recognized as necessary in trust-building processes:

- Initiating conversation when you are unsure or questioning your experience
- Sharing vulnerable and intimate information in an appropriate fashion
- Being able to contain your own emotions and the other person's emotions

- Able to handle conflict without being intimidated or intimidating
- Noticing manipulations and knowing how to handle them effectively
- Holding someone accountable when he or she is acting out
- Being patient, while simultaneously encouraging growth
- Giving respect and requiring the same in return
- Not letting the other person get away with lies and excuses
- Addressing resentment
- Identifying withdrawal and asking questions about the behavior
- Being genuinely curious about where the other person is coming from
- Acknowledging judgments and dealing with them nondefensively
- Able to change tone of voice or volume if that is negatively impacting the interaction
- Being able to slow down the process
- Recognizing when the subject is being changed
- Able to maintain focus in the conversation
- Capable of tracking the other person's attempt to inflame you to react
- Taking yourself and the other person seriously
- Respecting boundaries and role model boundary-setting behaviors
- Knowing when it is time to stop the conversation because it is no longer productive and get agreement to continue at a later specified time
- Recognizing when the other person is not receptive to your input and know how to handle those situations
- Recognizing when you are no longer receptive and make conscious choices instead of reacting and acting out
- Making proactive choices that will enhance the chances of maintaining a constructive interaction
- Allowing feelings to be present and not take them personally
- Be aware when emotions and communication are escalating and be confident that you can stay centered in spite of that
- Reaching a reasonable and amicable resolution
- Knowing how to distinguish between gut instinct and fear
- Recognizing anxiety and feeling comfortable dealing with it
- Being willing to deal with discomfort, your own as well as the other person's

- Being clear about your intent
- Asking the other person what his or her intent is when unsure
- Allowing for each person to have a different experience
- Validating that you have heard what has been said
- Mirroring back information accurately and sensitively
- Treating yourself and the other person with respect and integrity

Have you ever wondered why there are some people that you seem to trust quicker than others? Or have you experienced that a large number of people seem to trust you or someone else very quickly, and are able to open up and share even the most intimate details about their personal life in a very short time frame? What makes one person seem more trustworthy than another?

In a new relationship, it is easy to get lost in the excitement of the moment, and then as the relationship progresses and disappointments occur, you may feel awkward and scared discussing them. Many times, you may think that you can *"let it go."* You may be irritated about the other person's behavior, but due to your discomfort and fear, you rationalize, using the following thought: *"Approaching the other person may be harmful for the relationship."*

In essence, you create an excuse so you can avoid dealing with the following:

- The behavior that bothers you
- Your own discomfort and fear of potential conflict
- The other person's discomfort, difficult feelings, and other unknown responses
- The possibility that you misread the behavior and may look "silly" for bringing it up

The fear of losing the relationship or offending the person are in the forefront and is used to rationalize your decision to avoid dealing with the person and the situation.

Avoidance of uncomfortable situations and unpleasant feelings are missed opportunities to build trust.

Each time you give in to your fear or discomfort, you prioritize protecting yourself from taking reasonable risks instead of prioritizing your trust in the relationship, the trust you place in yourself, and your abilities to handle difficult situations and emotions. When building trust, it is a good idea to keep priorities in the forefront and use realistic tools to deal with your own fear and discomfort. Long-term goals are effective tools compared to short-term goals since naturally, on a superficial level, it is much easier to let your irritation go in the moment than it is to bring a sensitive subject to someone's attention and especially since sharing your interpretation means that you would put yourself at risk of being vulnerable to getting criticized and corrected if you are mistaken. That is a risk many are not willing to take. When you tell yourself, *"It is not a big deal, I'll let it go,"* and you don't take the time to get in touch with and respect your experience, you don't slow down and evaluate if it was a big deal or not. You may not really be willing to commit to letting it go. If you are not, the chances of you letting it go and moving on *without* resentment are unlikely. It is unrealistic to believe that when you have a strong emotional reaction to something, or someone, you won't need to take some time to explore your reaction before you make a major decision, such as letting it go. *If your emotions were strong enough, in the first place, to demand acknowledgment, then logically, does it make sense that they will disappear because they are inconvenient or uncomfortable for you to deal with?*

Typically, you may let it go *then*, but when the behavior that irritated you is repeated in a future interaction, you'll go right back to your previous experience and the irritation doubles. The more times you let it go without care and attention given to that decision and then continue to subject yourself to experiencing a similar situation, the more you are allowing your resentment to build up.

How can someone trust you, if you don't take responsibility for managing your resentment constructively?

Unconsciously and over time, this hidden dynamics impacts the trust level. If you do not apprise the person of his or her irritating behavior and he or she keeps repeating the behavior, you will eventually act out your resentment. You will reach a point where your resentment is overflowing.

Behaviors That Support Long-Term Goals

Rewards and Costs I

**Behaviors that Support the Long Term Goal:
To Develop Enriching Relationships**

Address the issue
Don't shy away from the conflict
State your position
Keep an open-mind
Spend the time up front to resolve the problem
Invest your energy by being fully committed
Listen, even when you don't want to
Don't take comments personally
Don't get discouraged when met with resistance
Be creative
Don't polarize

Rewards and Costs in the Moment

Rewards
- Diminished occasions of being reactive
- Less frustrating
- Not as much chance of being disappointed
- Reduced risk of being manipulated
- Opportunities to learn

Costs
- Takes more time up front
- Is uncomfortable at times
- Challenges your patience

Rewards and Costs in the Long Run

Rewards
- Saves time in the long run
- Increases opportunities for integrated growth and learning
- Helps build self esteem
- Increases self respect
- Promotes integrity
- Supports balance and empowerment
- Expands choices and reduces victimhood
- Lesser chance of the same problem occurring over and over again
- Reduces build up and acting out of resentment

Costs
- Some people in your life may be too uncomfortable to continue a relationship with you

How unsafe is it to be around someone who may all of a sudden attack you for some behavior you engaged in, when you had no awareness that it had been perceived as annoying in the first place?

Resentment is an extremely important factor to manage responsibly since it critically affects the trust-building process. The behaviors that support long-term goals such as having a relationship based on integrity, trust, openness, safety, respect, and love are many times more demanding and difficult in the moment compared to behaviors that support short-term goals. Using a lot of energy in the beginning, toward your long-term investment is well worth the rewards, since there is a greater chance that you'll be experiencing less conflict long term, and the conflicts that will occur will be less time consuming. The occurrence of frustration and irritation will usually take place less frequently. You'll get an opportunity to experience more joy, peace, and balance in your life and relationships. Uncomfortable and stressful interactions will be reduced. When resentment is positively managed it will free up creativity, and you will feel better about and within yourself than you have before.

Behaviors That Support Short-Term Goals

Rewards and Costs II

**Behaviors that Support the Short Term Goal:
To Avoid Dealing with Discomfort in the Moment**

Avoid dealing with the issue
Shy away from conflict
Be rigid
Suppress your feelings or act them out
Intimidate and bully to get your way
Don't commit to the interaction
Be preoccupied, don't listen
Take comments personally
Be manipulated by resistance
Polarize
Give in if you are intimidated
Withdraw
Withhold

Rewards and Costs in the Moment

Rewards
- You may temporarily feel powerful
- You don't have to deal with conflict
- You don't have to make choices since you don't experience having any
- You can change the subject on a whim
- You can feel sorry for yourself when you feel victimized
- You may fool the other
- You may manipulate the other

Costs
- You can remain unconscious
- Wastes your time
- Uncomfortable and leads to a lack of choices

Rewards and Costs in the Long Run

Rewards
- The relationships that you are involved in require you to take less risks

Costs
- Creates dysfunctional relationships
- Reduces intimacy
- Promotes imbalance
- Supports victimhood
- Builds up resentment
- Encourages acting out of resentment
- Reduces safety in the relationship
- Damages trust
- Increases disrespect
- Provides room for self loathing and depression

The behaviors that support short-term goals, such as experiencing less conflict in the moment, decreasing the immediate time spent being uncomfortable, avoiding taking risks, having to deal with unpleasant and challenging feelings, reducing the opportunities to vulnerability and therefore potentially getting hurt by the other, will give you more of an immediate relief and provide the *illusion* that you have to deal with less grief.

It is an illusion, since the reality is that with those immediate rewards come the price, and it is high. In the long run, your short-term goal behaviors will erode your self-esteem and negatively affect your sense of well-being, since there is a place inside of you that knows that you chose the "easy way out" those times. When you do that consistently, you lose trust in yourself and your ability to make healthy choices, since you know that you gave in to fears and discomfort at the expense of your self-respect.

Trust-Building Questions for New Relationships

- Have you thought about the level of trust you would like to have in our relationship?
- What three behaviors do you need from me to help build trust between us?
- How long does it usually take for you to build trust in another person?
- What will you bring to this relationship that will help me trust you?
- How would you assess the levels of trust you have in other relationships?
- What are some of your difficulties with regard to trust?
- When we first met, what were your impressions of me with regard to trusting me?
- How important is it to you that we trust each other at a high level?
- Who is your role model for trust-building?
- What do you think of when you think about building trust with me?

Broken Trust

When trust in a relationship has been broken, there is often an expectation that the relationship will revert to its original functions and qualities without much work. This is a fallacy; broken trust comes at a price. Sometimes the price is paid immediately with ending the relationship. Other times, the price is paid in installments over a longer period of time. In either event, the pain and suffering that come along are frequently detrimental to the parties affected. What actions may break trust?

These are some obvious actions as mentioned previously:

- Lying
- Cheating
- Stealing
- Not following through on agreements

But how does it feel when you sense that you have done something that bothers the other person, yet he or she doesn't tell you directly? How do you respond when someone has a smile on his face, but the voice is harsh and the body speaks loud and clear to you that there is something wrong? What about when you ask for feedback and you get the feeling that the other person is withholding some information from you? How about when you ask the person directly if what you said offended her and she tells you no, and you later find out from another source that she was indeed offended and is holding a grudge?

When someone doesn't take responsibility for having caused the breaking of the trust, further resentment will develop in the person whose trust was betrayed. Because trust is a delicate aspect of a relationship, it needs to be handled with care and respect. That does not mean that you should rationalize or avoid dealing with uncomfortable situations.

Handling trust with care *does not mean* the following:

- Avoiding it
- Pretending that problems don't occur or need to be dealt with
- Using excuses about not wanting to hurt him so you can avoid confronting him

Handle with care and respect means that you take trust seriously, and that you give the trust-building process the necessary time and attention that it needs, that it be nurtured and challenged. If I get away with lying to you, how can I trust that you will be able to support the healthy part of me that realizes that lying is coming from an unhealthy part of me and used as an escape from taking responsibility? Even if I get away with lying to you, and you tolerate my behavior without any negative consequences, other people may not respond as favorably. It comes back to short-term versus long-term gain. In the short term, it is rewarding, since I don't have to deal with whatever it is that I am trying to avoid. In the long run, my behavior may alienate me from establishing productive and intimate relationships with other people. It is not possible to evolve constructively in a relationship when trust has been jeopardized unless some time, attention, thoughts, and actual behavioral changes are implemented to repair the trust.

One step to use is asking questions and being committed to listening carefully and respectfully to the answers. The second step is to take responsibility for having broken the trust. One way to demonstrate that is to apologize sincerely.

Trust-Repairing, Trust-Building Questions
Repair Existing Relationships

The following are examples of trust-repairing and trust-building questions:

- Do you remember the last time you needed to rebuild trust in a relationship?
- Were you the perpetrator or the injured party?
- Do you want to rebuild the trust between us?
- If yes, why?
- What will you commit to in order to rebuild the trust in this relationship? (Identify specific action steps to take.)
- Do you have any resentment toward me that you need to share with me?
- Who will be supporting you to help repair and rebuild trust in this relationship?
- What are your concerns/fears about rebuilding the trust between us?
- How do you plan to deal with those fears/concerns so that they won't interfere with, or sabotage our trust-building process?
- What was your best experience in rebuilding trust in the past?
- What was your worst experience in rebuilding trust in the past?
- What would you like the next step to be as we rebuild the trust?
- What do you need from me to support this trust-building process?

As you answer the questions above, you and the other person will begin to negotiate new rules for the relationship. When both of you are ready to commit to a game plan of specific actions to rebuild the trust, you can move to the next phase of implementing your new behaviors. It is wise to pay attention to what you are agreeing to, and not agree simply to feel better in the moment, since follow-through is an extremely important step when rebuilding trust.

10

Trusting Deeper: Jackie and Ned!

The factors in the circle that impact trust-repairing processes are presented in a random order, not in accordance with importance.

Circle of Trust

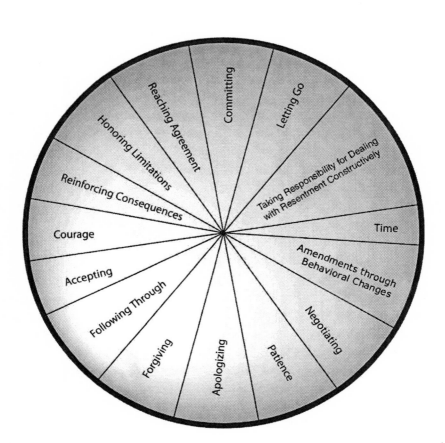

Negotiating

When you have broken the trust and want to repair the relationship, you first have to establish if the wish is mutual. Once that has been done, you can start to negotiate an agreement. Realize that you have lost some of your negotiating power in the relationship if you are the one who has faulted. When you chose to break the trust, you created an imbalance of power in the relationship. It will be helpful if you are humble and reach an acceptance of the consequences that are inevitable after the trust has been breached. That doesn't mean that you shouldn't negotiate, it simply means that you do not have as much leverage as the other person. You will have to bend more, give more, and have less say until the trust is rebuilt. Keep in mind that it was your trust-breaking behavior that created this unequal dynamics. Now, it is important to deal with the consequences in a responsible and patient way by accepting the current reality.

Reaching Agreement

Establishing an agreement represents a commitment to working to rebuild the trust. Without an agreement, how can you or the other person gauge how far along you have come in the trust-building process? An agreement can clarify expectations, detailing what is agreed upon, and what will be expected from each of you. It is a good idea to make sure you both have a clear understanding of the agreement. One way of doing that may be to repeat back to each other how you understand what has been said and what has been agreed upon. Getting closure and clear parameters are essential since that will enhance the likelihood of follow-through and reduce misunderstandings later. What actions do you think may be part of an agreement to repair trust? Based on what has taken place, what is reasonable?

Committing

Unless you are 100 percent committed to repairing the trust, the chances of other factors interfering are greater. Some factors may be anger, resentment, avoidance of responsibility, the need to forget the shame, and disagreeable feelings associated with the breaking of the trust. Likewise, if the other person is not committed to wholeheartedly partaking in this process you will both be wasting your time and creating additional aggravation. Some examples of commitment being exhibited in behavior may be accepting the unpleasant consequences such as being subjected to answering a number of repetitive questions patiently, continuing to give reassurance when you think that is "all" you have been doing, allowing the other person to express and share his or her feelings of disappointment in you without being defensive, or minimizing your responsibility by making up excuses for your behavior. In order to fully commit to this process, it is essential that you both have established boundaries around the needs and behaviors described above. Setting clear time lines and discussing expectations are part of that process.

Forgiving

How important is forgiveness to you in the context of the trust repair-building process?

If *you* broke the trust, the forgiving that needs to take place is with the other person. It is helpful if you are realistic and understand that forgiving may take time. If the other person forgives you too easily and too quickly, the forgiveness may not have been fully integrated. The risk is that the anger from the betrayal may later resurface in the form of destructive and punitive remarks, prolonging or undermining the repair process. Ask a number of questions about the other person's thoughts, experiences, and feelings that relate to forgiveness, so that you can learn about the other person. Find out what kind of support she may need from you, and from outside sources to best achieve the goal of forgiveness. Remember that if you broke the trust, it is appropriate that the other person's feelings and processes take priority in your interactions. That does not mean that you do not exist. It simply means that you are there to support the other person to reach forgiveness. During that process, it may require that you generously allow an inequity of time and attention to exist between your needs and the other person's needs in the interaction. Your feelings and needs are best supporting the process if they are placed in the background during the initial repair-building process. Forgiveness may not take place until a significant amount of time has passed during which time, the agreed upon behavioral changes have been integrated and recognized.

Letting Go

What does it mean to you to let go?

Letting go may mean different things to different people. Therefore, it is wise to first establish what it means to you and to the other person. Retrace how each of you have let go of other difficult events in the past; that way, you can create a reference point for letting go. If the other person needs to let go of her anger and disappointment in you, you may need to let go of the guilt, shame, and anger that you feel. Anger can often be misdirected. Pay attention to the anger you feel toward yourself and how it may be misdirected toward the other person when she takes longer to let go than you would like her to do. Patience is essential.

Accepting

Is there a difference between letting go and acceptance?

Acceptance is a key component since without it, you or the other person may ruminate "what if" questions and engage in behaviors that may set the trust back even further. Accepting can be to receive willingly. You cannot move on to the other steps of the repair process unless both parties agree to accept what has taken place. Furthermore, both parties need to accept that the repair work that happens next will take time and entail a lot of work. If the person who is betrayed cannot accept that the betrayal took place, and be willing to move forward, the repair process cannot be successful. Likewise, the person who broke the trust has to be willing to accept that repairing the trust will most likely be a hard and long process. During the repair process, it is reasonable to expect that the person who broke the trust will be placed in an imbalanced power position until the trust has been reestablished. If you are the one who broke the trust, it is essential that you accept and take responsibility for your behavior that created the current imbalance. When you do that, you are taking the first steps to heal and rebuild the trust. This is a difficult part of the process and cannot be taken lightly. *What kind of support do you need to accept something that can be hard to understand or painful to deal with?*

Following Through

Another key component is follow-through. Chances are that the person you betrayed will be watching "every move you make" for a significant amount of time. This is a natural response when trust has been replaced with mistrust. It is helpful if you are patient and accepting, knowing it is a necessary part of the repair work. After trust has been broken, there is a larger burden placed on you (if you broke the trust) to "make up" for what you did. That generally includes impeccable follow-through. Whereas before in your relationship, you may have been given the benefit of doubt when you occasionally slacked off and didn't follow-through on an agreement because, at that time, your behavior was trustworthy. Now that the trust has been broken, "all bets are off" and it is like starting from the beginning. However, it is even more difficult because when you start from the beginning, you do not need to add the baggage of betrayal into the equation. If you have any doubt that you are willing to accept this step, you might as well forget the rest, since without follow-through trust cannot be repaired.

Apologizing

Apologizing can be described as an acknowledgement of regret for a fault, wrong, injury, or insult.

There are two main parts in an apology: sincere and congruent verbal and nonverbal expressions of true remorse and showing a genuine interest and proactively finding ways to repent. If one or the other is missing, the apology very easily becomes ineffective and fairly useless in the process of rebuilding trust.

It is easy (at times) to say, "I am sorry." However, when you feel attacked, threatened, or defensive, it can be quite difficult to differentiate between your behavior that is being criticized and you as a person. It is often impossible to experience remorse and feel sorry when you are not able to separate those two aspects: your behavior that is under question and your character/identity. This is due to the fact that if you admit that you are sorry for your behavior, and at the same time take the position that your behavior defines who you are, then by saying you are sorry you indirectly say that you are sorry for who you are. When your understanding is *fused*[41], it is natural for you to have an urgent need to defend your behavior, since that is equal to you maintaining that you are not sorry for who you are. Being able to separate the two aspects of yourself is a critical step in forming a true apology. You can acknowledge that your behavior was negative and warrants an apology and possible behavioral change, which you are capable of, while at the same time, it doesn't define who you are. Unless, of course, the behavior that is being questioned is a

---

[41]   Fused means the inability to separate two parts from each other, whether it relates to experiences or parts of an identity.

common behavior and not out of the ordinary. An apology said during a time when you cannot experience the difference between your behavior in that moment and you in general is often forced and can sound both hostile and insincere, since you most likely don't believe it yourself at that time. Take some time and think about whether you are truly remorseful for what you did or if you are simply trying to placate the other person in the moment. Was your behavior—or *could it have been perceived* as—inappropriate, insensitive, hurtful, mean-spirited, selfish to the detriment of the relationship, or deceitful? If so, are you sorry for having engaged in that behavior? Do you think it *would benefit the relationship* if you apologized? How would it benefit the relationship? How will your apologizing affect your feelings and thoughts toward the other person? Are you able to take responsibility for having done something that is, or was perceived as "bad" while simultaneously be able to maintain an intact perception of your identity and self-picture, not as defective, but as someone who occasionally makes mistakes or poor choices? Do you see yourself as someone who can correct mistakes by apologizing, not repeat the same mistake over and over, and have choices and the ability to change behaviors that are destructive? Apologizing requires a certain amount of humility and letting go. An apology from the bottom of your heart can be one of the most freeing experiences that you can share with another human being.

Amendments through Behavioral Changes

Making Amendments by Implementing
Significant Behavioral Changes
in the Moment as well as over a
Longer Period of Time

You and the other person need to specify the behavioral changes that need to take place. For example, do you need to check in more often? Does she need to communicate more openly? Do you need to sit down weekly and discuss specific parts of the progress? Is there a time line that establishes when and how you will renegotiate, express feelings, and ask questions? How many times will you need to apologize? You may be required to allow more latitude for the other person to be inquisitive and suspicious. However, in order for this process to be successful, it is important that you (who in this case, broke the trust) together with the other person, set up some guidelines for how you will be receiving feedback on your progress. Otherwise, the other person may start to enjoy the imbalance and have no intent of moving forward, but instead use the situation to punish you and withhold from you. Such behaviors would be considered acting out and would clearly not support the goal to rebuild trust. On the contrary, such actions could start a circle of injurious behaviors that create resentment and more acting out from you as well. There is a fine line between allowing latitude and being abused. Therefore, it is important that you set appropriate boundaries.

Setting and Maintaining Boundaries

Creating clear boundaries is a must. Otherwise, with the imbalanced power structure the person who was betrayed can become abusive if she does not have appropriate tools to deal with her anger, hurt, and resentment. It is natural when one is angry to want to hurt someone back. To be realistic about that part of human behavior can prevent you from reacting and being surprised. If you are anticipating feelings of anger and revenge as part of the rebuilding process you can prepare ahead of time. You can better handle that part of the interaction by setting effective and supportive boundaries without developing a faulty judgment and becoming angry yourself.

Time

Repairing trust takes time. Healing takes time. It is wise to discuss the amount of time that each of you anticipate this process will take. If you think that it is reasonable to get over the betrayal in two months and the other person expects that it will take him one year, you need to have a dialogue to evaluate whether it is realistic or not that you both will be able to do the work to repair the trust. Exploring this aspect of the process can help you become more aware of your own needs as well as help you separate between what you wish, want, and can agree to live with.

Patience

Without patience, you and the other person have less of a chance to repair the trust successfully. You may have to be patient and answer a "million questions." The other person may not reach forgiveness as fast as you would like him to. You may, at times, have to use patience to overcome your anxiety and fear that keep telling you that it is pointless and will never work out. You may observe how the other person, at times, has to struggle with his patience either with himself or with you. This can be an opportunity to become more compassionate for life challenges.

Courage

Realizing that it takes courage to be willing to trust someone who betrayed you can be helpful for the person who broke the trust. When you realize that, you will automatically have more patience and empathy when she struggles to move forward. Taking responsibility for your mistakes and enduring the unpleasant parts of the repair process also takes courage. Drawing upon this courage can help you stick with the process even when you feel lousy about yourself and want to give up.

Honoring Limitations

Honoring yours and the other person's limitations is crucial. There is no benefit if you allow him to become abusive because, on some level, you feel that you deserve it. It is also important that you realize your own limitations. Maybe you are not willing to answer questions over and over again without getting angry or resentful. *How are you going to deal with your limitations? What are they?*

Reinforcing Consequences

You need guidelines. What happens if behaviors and agreements are not being upheld? Do you have planned consequences and strategies to reinforce them? Don't agree to a consequence in the moment that you doubt you'll be able to reinforce later. If you don't follow through you'll lose credibility and respect, which will undermine the trust.

Dealing with Resentment Constructively

Allow yourself and the other person to experience the various feelings that accompany betrayal and broken trust. Identify the feelings and spend time sharing them. Establish some clear parameters around the exploration of the feelings and create tools to deal with them and process them, so you can move forward. What kind of support do you and the other person need outside of your relationship to help you take responsibility for the feelings, so you don't act out the feelings and resentment later?

Trust

Your trust in yourself will be challenged. Your trust in your patience and in the process will be questioned at times. The worth of the work will be doubted. The more you trust in yourself, the more you can encourage the other person when she is ready to give up or be destructive. Being able to role model that you can hold the trust for the both of you can affect the repair process significantly. It can earn you a large number of points in the long run. *What do you trust the most about yourself? Do you trust that you will provide value to the other person while you are going through the trust repair-process? Do you trust that you will provide value in this relationship once the trust is built back up?*

Undermining the Trust: Jackie and Ned

Jackie and Ned, close friends for fifteen years, had discussed possible business ventures that they could do together. Jackie, an interior designer, was in the process of relocating her offices and she needed space immediately. Jackie asked Ned to come along and look at some office space to rent. As they discussed the space, they found out that the building was for sale. They started talking about the possibilities of buying the small office building instead of Jackie renting space. It could be fixed up nicely, leased out, and some money could be made. What a good idea to capitalize on Jackie's talents and interest in interior design and Ned's business sense. Ned, who was working for an accounting firm, was good with numbers and had a lot of contacts. Ned came up with possible suggestions for how the partnership could work. Jackie who had found the office space said she didn't quite understand the concept Ned presented. Ned suggested he'll explain it further and that she should give it some thought. Jackie said okay, and that she'd get back to Ned when she had spent some time thinking it over.

A week went by and when Ned called Jackie, she excitedly told him that she was on her way to open escrow. She had decided to buy the office building they had looked at last week. Ned was surprised, since Jackie had not called to discuss his proposed agreement from the week before. Jackie continued by telling Ned how excited she was about the space. Ned made a comment, *"So you decided to go ahead with the deal on your own then."* Jackie answered lightly with a smile, *"Yes, it didn't make sense to me that you would be involved. You know I could die tomorrow, and then you would be stuck with the whole thing."* Ned didn't know how to react, so he said nothing. Jackie continued, *"So can we meet after I leave my meeting?"* Ned said, *"Yes, sure"*

They made plans to meet later that day. Ned thought about how Jackie had handled the situation and he began to feel uneasy and anxious. As Ned's feelings of uneasiness and anxiety increased, he started to ask himself some questions about his experience. He came to the conclusion that he didn't like the fact that Jackie had chosen to ignore their agreement to discuss the business venture prior to moving forward.

For Ned it wasn't okay that Jackie had made a unilateral decision when the decision concerned him as well. Instead of giving Ned the courtesy of letting him know that she had given their idea some thought and concluded she didn't want to go into a partnership with Ned and planned to buy the property on her own, Jackie had ignored the whole discussion and communicated as if they never had the partnership conversation in the first place. Jackie had unconsciously or consciously chosen to ignore their agreement. She continued the betrayal with her reason why she was purchasing the building on her own. She had intimated that the driving force behind her decision had been to try to protect Ned, when in fact Ned, who was an intelligent man, had done the numbers himself and quickly realized that this idea could become quite lucrative. Ned's hunch was that Jackie's greed had gotten the best out of her.

For a number of years Ned and Jackie's relationship had been built on trust, respect, and integrity. In less than a week, Jackie had done substantial damage to the relationship by her actions that had followed what she perceived was an uncomfortable situation. Based upon his experience of what had taken place, Ned had some choices to make:

- He could pretend, like Jackie, that everything was fine. He could go along with her and allow her to ignore their agreement. He could accept her dismissing and lying to him, without her experiencing any consequences from her behavior.
- He could avoid dealing with the situation. He could stay away from Jackie and not have any form of real conversation with her.
- He could remain anxious, uneasy, and become angry. He could avoid taking responsibility for his feelings. Instead of being constructive, he could punish her indirectly by withholding or acting out his resentment in other ways.

- He could withdraw from the relationship or end it all together.
- *He could decide to be proactive and approach Jackie constructively by addressing her behavior and reality-test his experience with her with the intent to get clarity and closure on the experience.*

How Ned decided to handle his experience in relationship to Jackie would impact their future relationship. Jackie's behavior had affected the trust Ned had in her. To ignore that, he would not honor their relationship. To make a choice other than to take a risk by approaching Jackie face to face, he would compromise the closeness and intimacy of their relationship, which would harm the trust between them further.

When Jackie later saw Ned, she greeted him with the following comment:
"I have the paperwork with me. Maybe you can take a look at it?"

(Jackie continued to ignore the fact that she had not gotten back to Ned prior to making her decision)

Ned said,
"Maybe, but first I have something I need to talk to you about. Are you willing to listen to what I have to say?"

(Ned was not willing to help Jackie anymore until they had discussed her behavior and achieved some closure on the issue. He asked her the question if she was willing to listen with the intent to set up a framework of accountability, which would increase the likelihood of a constructive conversation.)

Jackie answered,
"I don't want to be "bummed out" . . . but okay, it's already out there, so just tell me."

(Jackie's response indicated some resistance, but she did commit to hearing what Ned had to say.) Ned had chosen to take responsibility for his experience by following his comment with a behavior that reflected that. He approached Jackie in a constructive way by sharing his experience with her and asking her for input. Ned was calm and constructive and genuinely interested in understanding Jackie's motive and response.

Jackie owned up to the fact that she had been uncomfortable about the situation so she had chosen to avoid dealing with it. She also confessed her greed played a part in her decision to do the deal by herself. She apologized for her behavior.

How did Jackie's behavior affect Ned and the trust between them?

When Jackie decided to break their agreement, she sent the message that she prioritized accommodating her own discomfort before the integrity and trust of the relationship. Indirectly, Jackie's behavior told Ned that she isn't trustworthy when it comes to managing her perceived unpleasant feelings and interactions.

By prioritizing discomfort and greed over the friendship, Ned realized that Jackie is likely to make unilateral decisions with any future business dealings. She can also be expected to avoid dealing with her discomfort without consideration to how that will affect the trust between the two of them. Jackie's behavior indicated that she was committed to short-term gratification instead of long-term trust. Jackie could get immediate gratification while avoiding any difficulties she might, otherwise, have had to encounter in a partnership when she chose to do the project on her own. Jackie would also not have to split the profit when the time would come to do so. What Jackie might not have given consideration to was the fact that this could have been an excellent opportunity to explore a partnership between the two. If this partnership worked out well, it could have set the stage for future work between Jackie and Ned. If it did not work out well, they could put "partnership talks" behind them. That way, Jackie and Ned would know that any projects in the future, whether big or small, would not be a good fit between the two of them. Maybe Jackie thought that she could make a unilateral decision, avoid an uncomfortable interaction with Ned now, and still continue to work together in the future when Jackie might want to do so. It is evident that the short-term goal that was supported by the short-term behaviors was in the foreground when Jackie made her choices.

For Ned, the information he gathered from this interaction would support a choice of not being involved with Jackie in future business ventures. Jackie's acknowledgment and apology of her destructive behavior wasn't followed by a direct behavioral change that would repair the trust. Jackie had acknowledged that her discomfort and greed had led her to her decision, yet she continued the purchase on her own. After Ned's discussion, it didn't seem to occur to Jackie that she could further explore the basis for her decision, maybe discuss her thoughts on the short-term versus the long-term goal with Ned, and include him in the conversation she had previously made the decision to avoid. Jackie did not suggest that she was interested in having a discussion about pros and cons of doing this deal on her own, versus as a partnership with Ned. Jackie seemed to lack an awareness of how her continued passivity in relation to having a dialogue with Ned now, in contrast to her proactive actions to finalize the deal on her own before, continued to affect their relationship. Jackie kept operating as if in a vacuum, which may indicate that she was uncomfortable again, and didn't possess the tools to continue a conversation with Ned.

How did that affect the trust?

Jackie's reaction diminished the trust further. Her previous choices and subsequent actions had been done unconsciously and therefore were more understandable. Now, Jackie had reached a different awareness but her choices remained the same. That could indicate that the discomfort and greed were still the determining forces in Jackie's decision-making process and subsequent behavior. Which leads to another question: *"How can Ned trust that in the future Jackie will exercise good judgment when making important decisions if discomfort is a part of the equation?*

What could Jackie have done to repair the trust?

Apologizing is a first step, which Jackie had done, but unless she takes the apology to the next step, the trust in not being repaired. Lack of actions *can many times affect the trust as much or more significantly than actions.*

The next step could have been for Jackie to initiate a dialogue with Ned about how she had made her unilateral decision. She could have acknowledged that her behavior was not conducive to a partnership. Jackie could have recognized that her behaviors were breaking the trust between her and Ned. She could then have done what she should have done the previous week, honored her agreement, and gotten back to Ned and discussed the actual topic, their potential partnership, and the effect her decision now might have on any future partnership between them. When Jackie again refused to approach the partnership agreement, she once more exhibited an avoidance of what she may have perceived as an uncomfortable topic.

The message Jackie sent is that it doesn't make a difference whether she has the awareness or not. She is not able to make the behavioral adjustments necessary to repair the trust. If Jackie had an interest in the two of them working together in the future or not, it would have been beneficial as part of the trust-building process if she would have shared her thoughts on how that would work out or why it would not work out, by giving specific examples. Jackie could have continued by giving some explicit illustrations of how she would be prepared to deal with discomfort, disappointment, and greed when it may come up in the future. She could have explained how it would be different from how she handled this situation. If Jackie intended to stay firm on her decision to move ahead on her own, she could have stated so directly to Ned. Jackie could also have acknowledged that she understood that her choice might jeopardize them working together in the future and that she was willing to take that risk. She could have asked Ned if her maintaining her original decision would in fact preclude her from being involved with Ned in a business venture in the future. Jackie could have asked Ned if he saw any other solutions to the situation with the additional information she had provided.

By bringing up the sensitive and somewhat awkward points described above, Jackie would be repairing the trust by showing that she was willing to take full responsibility for her actions and choices. She would also demonstrate that she could and would deal with discomfort constructively without giving into her fears.

If Jackie would have been exhibiting the trust-building behaviors described, Ned could be fairly confident that he could trust that Jackie would be up-front with him from this point on. Ned may not have liked Jackie's choices and actions, but it would leave him feeling safe that he could make his own choices having full, up-front disclosure from Jackie.

In either event, Ned and Jackie's interactions would most likely alter the course of the relationship in one way or another. The benefit is that they had had an opportunity to learn about themselves and each other from the experience. Jackie left the interaction without sharing her thoughts on future partnership ventures, as if they never had discussed that in the past. Ned decided that he had been as proactive as he was willing to be in the interaction without taking care of her when she didn't, wouldn't, or couldn't show an interest in going any further. Ned acknowledged that he had learned that Jackie has certain limitations in the area of trust and trust-repairing processes. He also came to understand that she either wasn't willing to, or couldn't, for whatever reasons move beyond those limitations. Ned made a conscious decision to accept Jackie's limitations and adjust his own behavior in accordance. Ned trusted that he could maintain a close friendship with Jackie under the new conditions of their relationship without sacrificing his own integrity and self-respect or carry resentment with him.

At a different time, this situation may have prompted Ned to end the relationship instead of making adjustments to it. Ned was able to put this experience and the outcome in the context of other aspects of importance in their relationship. Ned determined that this area was not as important as other areas in their relationship where he did have faith that Jackie was trustworthy. As a conclusion, Ned made the decision that he would not place himself in a situation where this aspect of their relationship would be repeated.

Trust Cup

Trust is like a cup. If you drop it once, you may be able to glue it together without too much trouble depending on the placement of the damage. The cup may function as well as before it broke, even though you know and can see that it is different. If you break the same cup again, this time in two places, you may have more trouble gluing it together without suffering more serious consequences. After this incident, it might not hold liquid without leaking, so you may have to use it for another purpose. Realizing the cup is more fragile, after several repairs, you drop the cup again. This time it shatters in a thousand little pieces. The damage is irreparable. Depending on the cup, it may not be as easy to replace as you think!

The lesson is, think before you act and think long-term!

11

Boundary: One for You, One for Me

A boundary *can be explained as a line or thing marking a limit or a border.*

There are different sorts of boundaries. Some boundaries may be the parameters separating different countries from each other. Other boundaries may be a house that holds furniture or a glass that contains water. Such physical boundaries are easy to identify and relate to. Psychological boundaries can sometimes be more difficult to understand. They can't be seen, often are subjective and available for interpretation based upon each individual's frame of reference.

If you think about various forms of boundaries, you'll realize very quickly that the examples are endless:

- Laws
- Rules and regulations
- Agreements
- Various forms of containers: pitcher, cup, bowl, pot, to name a few
- Cars
- Clothes
- Time
- Space

In this chapter, your external boundaries will be compared to the tangible and visible parts of a house that you can easily see, such as walls and the roof. The internal boundaries will be likened to the foundation, beams and posts that you cannot necessarily see but know if the house is standing, must be there. Both kinds of boundaries are vital for your welfare. You are more likely to have an awareness of, and be able to identify what your external boundaries are. The internal boundaries, like the wooden studs in a house, are often hidden and operate more on an unconscious basis. With strong internal boundaries in place, there is a greater chance that you can better support yourself.

In either event, there is a certain amount of unknown territory that influences both forms of boundaries. That unknown territory can be referred to as the reactions and unconscious responses arising from various feelings, thoughts, communication, and behaviors that take place either directly in you, or as a by-product of an effect that happens in another person. The more in touch you are with your needs, feelings, responses, thoughts, the more likely it is that you will have better developed boundaries. However, it is fairly common that you may have well-developed external boundaries, but less effective internal boundaries.

External Boundaries

An external boundary can be described as having a clear line that enables you to do the following:

- Clearly communicate to others and set limits before someone gets an opportunity to violate your personal space.
- Advise someone to stop when he is communicating disrespectfully with you.
- Be aware of and effectively address what your needs are, and when those needs are being violated or ignored.
- Assert yourself in interactions. Recognize and set appropriate limits in regard to tone of voice, interruptions, interest, and availability.
- Be aware of and honor your own physical limitations and have others do the same.
- Communicate and follow-up with congruent behaviors setting an example for how to be treated with respect and integrity and receiving the same in return.
- Give in proportion to what you receive.

Some behaviors that indicate that you are consistent and respectful of boundaries may be the fact that you *don't* do the following:

- Allow others to mistreat you.
- Take yourself for granted.

- Treat yourself as less than in a relationship.
- Tolerate being abused, physically, verbally, sexually, or emotionally (applies to adults).

Instead, you can maintain a position of balance in your relationship to others.

Tony and Katherine

External boundaries generally become more powerful when they are communicated verbally, concurrently with clearly defined nonverbal actions and clues. For example, Tony and Katherine are discussing what they want in a relationship. She says that she wants to have a relationship that is built on trust, integrity, and respect. As far as she is concerned, she wants the both of them to communicate lovingly to each other and make sure neither one takes out his or her frustrations and anger on the other after a rough day. She wants to be able to be open and honest.

The nonverbal actions that she uses to reinforce and role model congruency may be these:

- She turns toward him when she speaks to him.
- She looks him in the eyes.
- She listens attentively by giving him her full attention.
- She provides appropriate head nods to acknowledge that she understands what he is saying.
- She patiently waits until he has finished what he had to say without interrupting.

In addition, she asks him questions when she is concerned about something he said or if he said something that was upsetting to her.

She pays attention to her own behavior in response to him, as well as being alert to the following:

- She observes how he responds to her when she speaks.
- She watches if he seems distracted and doesn't pay attention to her.
- Instead of ignoring his nonverbal cues, she observes them and responds appropriately. She does not continue to speak, if his nonverbal cues are indicating that he may not be interested. Being

ignored or not listened to, and continuing anyway, indirectly sends the message that it is okay for him to ignore her. It says she doesn't need to be respected or treated with integrity. Hence, it is okay for him to violate that boundary.

By responding to his communication whether verbal or nonverbal, Katherine role models that she is not afraid of dealing with her own discomfort or his. She also shows that she will not tolerate or support him treating her disrespectfully by violating fundamental boundaries. One way to deal effectively with Tony's behavior if he isn't looking at her when she speaks, he seems to be distracted, or disinterested, can be to stop what she is saying and look at him until he looks back at her. When Katherine has gotten Tony's full attention, she can inquire about his behavior. She can ask him if he is interested in what she has to say. If he says yes, she can continue. If Tony starts to repeat his behavior and seems distracted by the TV, computer, or anything else again, Katherine can calmly state that she is going to end the conversation at this time, since the interaction is not being productive as far as she is concerned. She can add that if he is interested in picking it up later, she will be glad to do so when he is ready and available. If Tony says he is interested and doesn't understand why she wants to stop the conversation, she can ask him if he wants her to tell him. The reason for that question is to support Tony to commit to either being interested or not. That way she can hold him accountable for his position in the event he ignores her later again. Let's say Tony wants Katherine to tell him. She is then given an opportunity to explain that when he looks away for longer periods of time, or seem more interested in what is on the TV or computer, the messages that he sends are that he is not really interested in what she has to say.

Her explanation serves two purposes:

1. She is giving him a chance to become aware of the message his behavior is sending. Hence, help create choices for him.
2. If he is aware of his behavior and knows the message it is sending, but he doesn't care, then she is indirectly putting him on notice that with her that kind of behavior is not acceptable.

Katherine is making it clear to Tony that she understands her own value and does not want to waste his or her time by communicating with him if he is not interested.

Tony has some choices:

- He can continue his current behavior and deal with the consequences.
- He can change it depending on what messages he wants to convey to Katherine.
- He can give Katherine his input and reactions to what she has said.

If Tony's response is that Katherine is too sensitive, then she can tell him that she will *mirror back*[42] his behavior to him when he is talking to her, and then he can experience if it would bother him or not. Tony may be committed to continue to be destructive. If he is, it is likely that when Katherine mirrors back his behavior to him that he'll respond by stating something like, *"It doesn't bother me one bit and it's obviously your problem."* If that is, in fact, how Tony feels and thinks, but is committed to being constructive in the interaction, his comment could instead have sounded something like, *"It doesn't bother me, maybe because I am less sensitive than you are. But I can see your point that my behavior could be interpreted as rude and disinterested. So I will stop it and pay closer attention when you are talking to me."* If Tony stops at the first response, it is important that Katherine respects her own boundary by realizing the limitations she is faced with in this relationship. Katherine's response to continued destructive behaviors is to end the interaction by taking responsibility for her boundary and maintaining it. She can do that by stating, *"There seem to be a vast difference between our goals and boundaries. While I can accept that, I also recognize that it doesn't work for me. At this time, I don't enjoy communicating with you under those conditions."* Katherine takes the position that the two of them are not compatible in this area and continues, *"It wouldn't support either one of us to continue the conversation at this time. I have some serious concerns about the future of our relationship."*

Obviously, if this is a one-time occurrence and Tony is generally attentive and respectful, Katherine will end the interaction in the moment and give him some time to think about his behavior. If Katherine is ending the relationship, she is either in the beginning of the relationship and these are early warning signs of what is to come, or it is a behavior that has increased over time and gotten to a point where it is no longer acceptable. The key to having boundaries respected is behaving consistently and following through.

---

42   To mirror back means to repeat back what was said as closely as possible to how it was said.

Flexibility is generally a good thing, but when it comes to boundaries, it is better to exercise some restraint, as long as one doesn't become rigid in the approach. There can sometimes be a fine line between upholding a boundary because it is serving us or upholding a boundary simply because we are rigidly attached to the principle of having that specific boundary.

As with most factors discussed in this book, putting the situations and interactions into the context in which they occur is imperative in order to make good choices that are followed by constructive behaviors.

Internal Boundaries

Internal boundaries can be described as having a clear line that enables you the following:

- Not take on someone else's discomfort, anxiety, anger, or fear.
- Clearly separate between the feelings that belong to us and those feelings that belong to someone else.
- Protect ourselves from unknowingly absorbing feelings in a room that aren't ours.
- Contain unpleasant and destructive feelings that are someone else's without starting to feel uncomfortable or reacting unconsciously.
- Experience unpleasant feelings, contain them, and make choices of how to deal with them constructively and consciously.

Sometimes the feelings that we experience can be so strong and create such a high level of discomfort that it is difficult to contain them.

Containing means (1) maintaining the feelings inside your body without it interfering with your well-being and (2) the ability to make logical and proactive choices without acting out unconsciously.

To contain other people's feelings is letting those feelings be, and then separating them from your own feelings without allowing them to pass through your internal boundaries and negatively affect your well-being and your ability to make conscious, logical and proactive choices.

When you cannot contain the feeling, it is common that the unconscious need in the moment is to discard the feeling as soon as possible. One way of doing so is to project the feeling unto someone else. The processes described are largely unconscious, happen very quickly, and make it almost impossible for you to have an opportunity to identify or even be aware of the feeling before you discard it. Feelings such as joy and love are generally not experienced as being threatening. They are often easily received and shared with others. The feelings that can cause anxiety or other unpleasant reactions when internal boundaries are not intact are more often anger, rage, disappointment, fear, shame, guilt, humiliation, discomfort, anxiety, or frustration.

It can be more challenging to conceptualize intangible, psychological factors that affect your interactions than it is to observe and understand tangible, physical factors. When you start to draw parallels to visible, more easily explainable reactions, you can more readily translate them to psychological hidden dynamics that affect your life and relationships.

The Vase

Visually, it can be helpful to picture yourself standing with a vase in your open hands. The vase looks fine. What can't be seen is a sharp piece of glass that is protruding out from the bottom of the vase. Your instinct (a spontaneous reaction) when you experience the pain of the glass in your hand, is to get rid of the vase as quickly as possible. Now picture a person standing in front of you watching you, not knowing that there is anything wrong with the vase. You throw the vase in the air, the other person instinctually reaches out to catch it before it hits the ground and breaks.

Both your reactions happen without thoughts, *happen fast*, and cause pain. *How could you have handled the situation in another way once you felt the sharp pain from the glass?*

- First, you slow down the process.
- You take one hand and grab the top of the vase, thereby removing the pressure from the piece of glass that is causing you the pain, instead of relieving the pain by throwing the vase away.
- This action gives you an opportunity to find out what is causing the pain, while simultaneously relieving the immediate pain you are experiencing.
- You are giving yourself a chance to make some choices of how to handle the vase without reacting.
- You evaluate the information. Is the protruding glass at the bottom of the vase detrimental to the function of the vase? Is there a way to remove the glass without it negatively affecting the function of the vase?
- You can help prevent potential unwanted and sometimes destructive chain reactions to take place. You may decide to dispose of the vase or you may choose to keep it.

- You create and experience choices. Another important aspect is that by heightening your awareness, you are not being a victim of the vase and the pain it is causing you. You are acting from an empowered position instead of throwing the vase away unconsciously without thinking.

The other person's actions will also change as you increase your awareness and subsequent behavior.

- The other person will not have a need to react and catch the vase if you don't impulsively throw it in the air.
- Not throwing the vase in the air limits his exposure to experiencing unnecessary pain.
- Not throwing the vase also alleviates a potential negative reaction that he may otherwise have toward you if he would have caught the vase and experienced pain from the protruding glass at the bottom of the vase.

When you deal irresponsibly with the consequences of your experience and allow yourself to be a victim of a situation, thing, or another person, without realizing it, you are encouraging another victim position to be created. In the above-described situation, the other person who caught the vase was made a victim. Granted, he was vulnerable to reacting unconsciously and becoming a victim because he didn't have the awareness or tools to deal effectively with this kind of dynamics.

If he had better developed internal boundaries, the response to the situation could have looked like this:

- The vase is in the air, the other person steps aside, and allows the vase to fall to the ground. (The other person is not responding in a codependent manner in response to your action—the consequences of your actions are yours to take responsibility for.)
- The other person becomes curious about your need to discard the vase.
- He or she asks you some questions about what happened to support you and the interaction.

As long as you continue to be unaware of the hidden dynamics in relation to internal boundaries, you are robbing yourself and the other person of a more wholesome and joyful interaction; void of the needs to protect, attack, and defend against painful and unpleasant feelings and experiences.

Value of Your Gut Instinct

Your gut instinct is only as good as the connection between your mind, physical body, and spiritual link.

It is helpful to realize and respect the deep force that instincts play in creating, maintaining, developing, and reinforcing internal boundaries. It is easy to be exploited by our own and other people's instincts in the heat of the moment. Instincts need to be listened to and sometimes a quick reaction is warranted. However, when it comes to supporting internal boundaries, the instincts need to be evaluated before action is taken.

In order to receive value from your instincts, it can be helpful to pay attention to the following five steps:

1. Instinct happens.
2. Instinct is recognized.
3. Instinct is listened to.
4. Instinct is evaluated.
5. Instinct is responded to.

The Intimate Link between Internal Boundaries and Feelings

Now let's translate the vase scenario into a feelings and internal boundary scenario. Unconsciously, when a feeling is causing you pain or discomfort, the natural instinct is to discard the feeling as quickly as possible in a similar fashion to what you would do with the vase. One way of doing so is to very forcefully reject the feeling and deny its existence. When a feeling is, for lack of a better description, "hanging in the air," it is easy for someone who does not have clearly defined internal boundaries in place to unknowingly absorb the feeling whether it is his or not.

The processes described in this chapter are primarily unconscious, waiting to be discovered. Not until you start to consciously ask yourself some questions about your internal boundaries and your past experiences with strong emotions can you raise your awareness level sufficiently. When that has been done, you can make choices and not be a victim of yours and other people's feelings.

- Have you ever started to feel terrible and not understood why when you have been around another person or a group?
- Do you find that you often become uncomfortable when someone else is experiencing anger?
- What reactions might you have had during, before, and after you bring up a sensitive or confrontational subject?
- When someone is discussing an uncomfortable topic, what reactions do you generally have?

Anger is a feeling that can often challenge boundaries. The more you understand anger and how it affects your life and interactions, the more equipped you will be at reinforcing your boundary when tested.

The first step is to familiarize yourself with anger by asking some questions:

- What is your relationship to your own and other people's anger?
- When you are feeling angry but are not acknowledging your anger because you are uncomfortable with the emotion of anger, what do you do?
- Does anger fit the image you have of yourself?
- Are you confident you can handle your anger?
- Does anger cause you anxiety because you lack trust that anger can be part of a relationship without destroying the relationship?
- Do you have any positive experiences to draw upon concerning anger?

The odds are that if you have an undeveloped relationship with anger, you will tend to project it outward, away from yourself.

When you do not see and acknowledge the anger in yourself and instead perceive the anger in the other person (i.e., project the anger), and when you perceive the anger in the other person even though it isn't there, the anger and its energy is not being contained within your boundaries. The anger is spilling out and needs a place to go. When the other person doesn't have sufficient internal boundaries to protect herself against *the spilled out anger that needs a place to go,* the anger easily moves through what can be described as holes in the internal boundary walls and is absorbed inside of the other person.

When you absorb the anger, it can cause many reactions, such as the following:

- Become angry and not know why.
- Feel very anxious, but not understand the reason for the anxiety.
- Unconsciously try to discard the foreign anger by acting out destructively, i.e., grab one too many drinks, overeat, have trouble sleeping, or take drugs.
- Become agitated and irritated.
- Exhibit hostility.
- Feel hopeless and helpless.
- Become enraged due to feeling powerless.

In essence, you have rendered yourself powerless and a victim of the anger when the internal boundaries aren't operating to support you and the other person. When your internal boundaries are effective, you will not allow yourself to be a victim of the other person and her feelings. Having solid internal boundaries supports you. It also supports people around you. You create win-win situations in your relationships when this area of your life is brought to a higher level of awareness, and the necessary behavioral changes have been implemented. Being able to differentiate and separate between what is yours and what is the other person's can create clarity and safety for both people involved. You have probably already realized how this aspect of your life affects responsibility and accountability on a deeper level.

When you discard unpleasant feelings and project them unto an innocent bystander, the messages sent could be these:

- You do not have to deal with things or feelings that you don't want to deal with.
- You are not able to handle your own discomfort.
- You shouldn't have to experience pain if you don't want to.
- You can do whatever you want with your feelings without encountering any form of consequences.
- Other people should take care of your feelings.
- You are not responsible.

What is a Healthy Boundary?

A healthy boundary is a limit that is being set with the intent to support the best part of others and yourself.

Why Can Boundaries Be So Difficult to Reinforce?

Difficulties in reinforcing boundaries may be due to the fact that we, human beings, often want to do the easy thing, take the short cut, receive immediate gratification, not respect limits, and remain in the fantasy that we have an unlimited amount of power to change and affect anybody, anything at any time. There is a direct connection between your ability to deal with discomfort, disappointment, and conflict to how well you are able to maintain your boundary in the face of pressure. If you have serious doubts about your ability to handle conflict, you'll most likely *give in to* the pressure when someone is trying her best to persuade you to give in.

Laura and Beth

Laura answered the phone. It was her friend Beth who asked if they could get together because there was something she wanted to talk to Laura about. Laura started to feel a little uneasy. She could hear in Beth's voice that she was upset about something. They decided to meet at the coffee shop the next day. As soon as Beth got there, Laura could see that this was not going to be easy. Beth started to tell Laura about an experience she had with a mutual friend. Laura realized early on that she was not ready to discuss this topic with Beth right then and there. This was a loaded subject; she had had no time to think about or prepare herself emotionally or intellectually for this discussion. But Beth insisted. So Laura told Beth that this was a difficult issue and that she didn't want to discuss it right then. Beth ignored Laura and insisted that Laura give her opinion about what had happened. Laura said once more that she'd rather not. Beth became even more agitated and again insisted, demanded that Laura give her some feedback. Laura started to feel pressured by Beth and soon she complied with Beth's request and told her what she thought about the whole thing. Laura had barely finished before Beth got angry and accused Laura of being insensitive and uncaring. They continued their discussion until Beth had to leave for a meeting. Laura felt horrible as she finished her coffee. She had known and tried to tell Beth that she wasn't in a great emotional state of mind to begin with, but Beth hadn't listened. Laura kept asking herself, "Why did

I give in when I knew better?" Laura told herself, "I didn't have to get into it with Beth." In her mind, she replayed their meeting over and over again. The more she thought about it, the angrier she got with Beth, and the more certain she became that Beth had pressured her, and Laura didn't like it.

Laura had been manipulated by Beth's pressure and demands, which made her angry at Beth. The hidden dynamics that Laura was not so quickly aware of was the fact that she was even angrier at herself for surrendering the boundary she had tried to set. When she did that, she had abandoned herself. Without Laura knowing it, she had made a choice, but first she had set her priorities.

These were the questions:

1. Should Laura maintain her boundary and not get into an in-depth discussion with Beth like her gut instinct had told her? (Laura didn't feel emotionally and intellectually balanced. She didn't think she could be her best. Thus, the probabilities of the conversation turning unproductive were quite high.)
2. Should Laura give Beth what she wanted, to avoid having to deal with her own discomfort, fear of conflict, and Beth's disappointment in her?

Laura's priority had been set many years ago. Her priority was to avoid conflict at all costs. That is the reason why Laura chose alternative number two, giving in to Beth's pressure and giving her feedback against her own gut instinct. The end result was the same, conflict between Laura and Beth, exactly what Laura had tried so desperately to avoid. Unless Laura gets comfortable dealing with conflict, discomfort, and disappointment, it will be almost impossible for her to maintain a boundary when she encounters someone who doesn't take no for an answer.

How, and what could Laura have done differently?

Laura could have responded to Beth like this: *Beth, you are an important person to me; our friendship is important to me. What you told me has an impact on me. You gave me a lot of information that I need to digest. I would love to give you feedback right now, however, this is significant. I am not willing to respond before I have had some time to give this some thought. So I'll tell you what I'm going to do. I'm going to go home and really think about this, and then there will be a better chance that my feedback will have some value to you. How about I will call you tomorrow around 5:00 PM, does that time work for you?*

Even with this response calmly presented, it would be naïve to think that Beth would go along with Laura and respect her boundary. Beth has her agenda and she is used to being successful at persuading people to give up their boundaries in order to avoid conflict. However, taking these new steps will slow the process down. It will let Beth know that Laura is willing to deal with Beth's and her own feelings, and that Laura is not going to give in without a fight. The conversation may go back and forth for a while. Laura will be tested a number of times by Beth. In the end, if Laura can maintain her boundary she will feel pleased and proud of herself that she *stood her ground.* Beth will respect Laura more for having done it, even if she doesn't like the boundary in the moment. Human beings have an uncanny ability to detect fear, and avoidance of fear, and intuitively know how to exploit those fears very early on. With years of practice, some people become masters when it comes to applying precisely the right amount of pressure and discomfort to break down boundaries. The end result is usually unproductive experiences that leave both parties uncomfortable. When we allow people to manipulate our boundaries, we are not supporting them to be their best selves. Not only are we not being our best selves, but we are also reducing the level of mutual respect and consideration that exists in the relationship. Do not abandon yourself; do not abandon the other by allowing her to *run you over.*

What to Do When Someone Violates a Boundary

Become aware, address the violation, adjust your behavior, and enforce consequences.

Identify Violation of a Boundary

First, get to know what your boundaries are, then you can find out if they are being violated.

How to Develop and Set Appropriate Boundaries

Patiently, diligently, and with a 100 percent commitment

Watch other people and their boundaries or lack thereof. Evaluate what kinds of boundaries seem to work and what kinds don't. Try a few on and see where they will get you. If a boundary is supporting the best parts of you, learn more about it, and use it.

Most importantly, start to practice setting, reinforcing, and mastering boundaries in relation to yourself!

12

Cynthia and Mark Challenge Boundaries

Cynthia was going through a rough time. She had been working for a small company during the last eight years. Her boss had been a personal friend as well as her employer. Cynthia thought they had a good relationship until the business started to falter four years into their working relationship. During that time, Cynthia voluntarily reduced her salary and supported her boss in his attempts to put some life into the business. At the same time, Cynthia came up with the idea of creating a separate division offering a new kind of service to their customers. Cynthia's idea and her hard work in building the new division was a success. In spite of Cynthia's achievement, the company was not doing as well as expected.

About two years ago, Cynthia's boss decided to take away some of her responsibilities and reduce her position from full-time to part-time. Cynthia was devastated by his decision. She had been there 100 percent for her boss over the years both as an employee and as a friend; now he decided to betray her loyalty. Without discussions or forewarning, he made his decision and informed her that if she didn't like it she could always find another job. As a result of the major change that took place, Cynthia and her boss's working and personal relationship was redefined.

Cynthia continued to do her best with the division she had created and was managing, but her trust had been betrayed and she no longer felt safe in her position. Her boss never did explain his motivation or treatment of Cynthia. The topic was never brought up again. Instead, Cynthia and her boss did everything they could to have as few interactions with each other as possible.

A couple of years went by during which time Cynthia and her boss didn't see each other much. When the lease renewal came up, Cynthia's boss decided that he needed the space Cynthia's division was in. Some decisions needed to be made.

When Cynthia was told about the upcoming changes, her wounds from two years ago surfaced and her feelings associated with the betrayal she experienced then, came up for her again. Once again, Cynthia was at the mercy of a boss with whom she thought she had a mutually respectful and supportive relationship during the first four years. The betrayal that Cynthia experienced was especially detrimental, since Cynthia had been such a part of her boss's family as well.

Cynthia was trying to figure out what her options were.

Cynthia and Mark Meet for Lunch

Over the years, Cynthia had numerous conversations with her good friend, Mark, about her work and her boss's behavior. She trusted Mark explicitly and felt he had supported her and their friendship for the past eight years. Cynthia and Mark met for lunch. Cynthia was venting about how devastated she felt, how her life was about to be turned upside down again. Mark listened and agreed with Cynthia; this was a very painful and difficult situation that she was facing. Cynthia continued by throwing out possible choices that she saw of how to deal with her boss. She said it wasn't fair and that her boss should do the right thing and should give her the division. It was *her baby.* She had built it from the ground up. Mark agreed with Cynthia and stated further that he thought that would probably not be the way her boss would view the situation based upon his past decisions.

Cynthia started to get upset. She said without her, the division would fall apart. No one else could run it the way she could. Cynthia insisted, once again, that the division for all intents and purposes was hers and should rightfully become hers. Mark agreed, and suggested that it may be helpful if Cynthia tried to look at how her boss might view the situation. That way she could get an understanding of where he might come from when she would approach him. He owned the company. He had given Cynthia the authority to create the division but it had been under his approval and ownership. The division was his whether he or someone else had built it. Cynthia looked at Mark as if he was against her. She said she had put in several years of her life to build this, and her boss had no idea of how to run it. Cynthia's response indicated to Mark that she was not feeling supported by his comment, but instead started to get annoyed with him.

Mark thought maybe if he would remove the example from Cynthia's situation and discuss something more neutral, he would be able to help Cynthia understand his point. Mark continued by giving an example of a similar situation and how it might be viewed.

Mark stated, *"It would be like a manager at a Big Five store who essentially worked his butt off and made that particular store successful. Then the manager would expect that the owner would appreciate that fact and give it to him when the owner didn't want to work with the manager anymore."* Cynthia dismissed Mark's comment and continued expressing her outrage about the unfairness of how she had been treated and betrayed.

Mark felt Cynthia's resistance. Instead of trying to provide more details of his example so that Cynthia could gather some tools of how to better approach her boss, Mark dropped the subject and sat back and listened to Cynthia. Cynthia made a few more comments about her situation, but the interaction was clearly starting to be more uncomfortable and strained. When the lunch was over, they went their separate ways. Mark could sense that Cynthia was agitated when they departed. She wasn't as warm and friendly as usual.

Later on that day, Mark was trying to understand what had happened during their lunch together. *Why had Cynthia seemed so agitated with him when they left?* Mark didn't have the answer yet.

Had he been rude or, otherwise, disrespectful? Mark didn't think so. He had certainly felt available and interested when she shared her experience.

Had he not been interested or supportive in the best way he could be? He thought he had. He definitely felt that he hadn't been received for reasons that were unclear to him at this point.

Had he not listened to Cynthia? He had listened. In fact, he could give a summary of most of their conversation. Mark had felt some unpleasant feelings during their time together. *Whose were they?*

Did he have a reason to be angry with Cynthia? No, Cynthia was being betrayed. She was in a difficult situation, not him. She had been on time and there was nothing behaviorally that she had done that would have made him angry.

Was there any possibility that there might be another reason for him to be angry with Cynthia? Mark couldn't come up with one. The previous week

Mark talked to Cynthia about something she had done that had irritated him and he was very up-front with her. Mark had felt good about how he had handled their conflict, so there was no resentment from his side, and no need to act out. However, Cynthia had not seemed comfortable. And she had not initiated to take any steps to resolve their problem at that time, or since then. Maybe that had left her feeling uneasy on some level. Maybe Cynthia felt unsettled about how she had handled their previous interaction. Maybe she was angry with Mark for having pushed her outside her comfort level by approaching her and confronted her about her behavior then?

Was Cynthia feeling angry? She didn't say so, but it seemed like it was logical that she might be. When someone is betrayed, she would likely feel anger and pain.

Did Cynthia seem frustrated with him when he was giving his examples? Possibly, she interrupted him several times. She looked away and around the room for longer periods of time when he was talking, which was unusual behavior for Cynthia who was typically very attentive and engaged when Mark was talking.

These behaviors are often unconsciously intended to manipulate the other person to take on anger or other unpleasant feelings by projecting the unwanted feelings outward. By engaging in rude, self-centered, dismissive, or devaluing behaviors, Cynthia would unconsciously attempt to manipulate Mark to get angry. Common reactions to those kinds of behaviors are anger, frustration, disappointment, or pain. If Mark felt dismissed and got angry, he might act out his anger and Cynthia can then sit back and experience Mark as being out of control instead of herself. As Mark gets angrier, chances are that Cynthia gets calmer since Mark is releasing the pressure Cynthia would, otherwise, have felt if her anger remained in her own body. Another unconscious motivation that Cynthia might engage in could be to create a fight/disagreement. In this scenario, Cynthia would only respond to Mark's anger, which would rationalize her own anger. If Cynthia is not comfortable with her own anger, or if she has a strong faulty judgment against anger and being out of control, she has "set up" Mark to act out her anger, creating a safer environment for her to release some anger as well. Cynthia may perceive that it is more acceptable to respond to someone else's anger, so as to defend herself, than to express her own anger without a real provocation. It very quickly can become a vicious circle of acting out unless one of the two people in the interaction has effective internal boundaries in place to support a healthy interaction. Mark who has strong internal boundaries had the ability to put Cynthia's behavior into the context of their long-term relationship. Their usual patterns did not include inconsiderate or otherwise disrespectful behaviors, so Mark did not take on those feelings or react to the message they were sending. Another sign that would lead Mark to believe that Cynthia might have been frustrated was the fact that she was repeating herself several times. That is an indication that she didn't feel heard or understood by Mark, which also could lead Cynthia to feel pain or anger.

Did Cynthia seem interested in Mark's comments? Maybe not, she didn't ask any questions. She didn't ask him to expand on what he was saying. In fact, her only response was that she didn't think it was the same thing at all, dismissing what he said as having any value.

If Cynthia was angry, in pain, frustrated, didn't feel heard or understood, and didn't express that, where might those feelings go? Out in the air between Mark and Cynthia, "hanging around," waiting to be "sponged up."

Cynthia's focus was exclusively on the betrayal, injustice, and pain. She discussed feelings associated with the betrayal. Cynthia did not express feeling any anger or fear. Mark thought it would be reasonable and logical if she would be scared. Potentially, her livelihood could be significantly affected by her boss's decision. Cynthia was once again left in a relatively powerless position with her boss due to the ownership factor.

Mark certainly sympathized with Cynthia, and he understood the injustice that Cynthia was feeling. He had been subjected to his share of betrayal in the past. However, as much as it made him angry for her sake, he didn't personalize the anger, which would have made it difficult to contain.

Mark's Message for Cynthia

Mark decided that he would call Cynthia later that day and leave a message on her home machine reassuring her that his intent during lunch had been to support her and that he felt compassion for her and the betrayal that she was experiencing. Since Mark did not experience any anger or hostility toward Cynthia, he was able to be reassuring and put his own needs for answers about Cynthia's behavior in the background. Mark left the message and then decided to let it go by trusting that Cynthia would respond when she was ready and more available to have a conversation with him.

Mark intentionally left a message that was reassuring, so that he would give Cynthia a chance to continue the communication instead of polarizing with him.

Cynthia Calls Mark

The next morning, Cynthia called Mark and started off by thanking him for having left the message on her machine the day before. She said it had meant a lot to her since she hadn't felt good about their meeting. Mark asked her what she thought that had been about. Cynthia said that, at times, she felt Mark could be mean-spirited, and yesterday's lunch was a perfect example.

Like most people, Mark knew that if he wanted to, he could be very mean. He also knew that he had choices, and that if he would act out and be mean, he would suffer the consequences of his behavior. It is likely that a need to be mean-spirited would come from resentment, followed by behavior acted out as an expression of the resentment. Mark knew how much trouble that behavior could cause and decided a long time ago that he would not be a victim of his own resentment. On a regular basis, Mark made sure he dealt with resentment, so there would be no need to act out meanness. He knew he did not feel resentment toward Cynthia.

Mark believed Cynthia when she said she had experienced him as mean-spirited; as much as that contradicted his intent and behavior, it also made him curious. Mark asked Cynthia to give him examples of when he had been mean-spirited in their relationship over the last eight years. Cynthia answered that last time it happened had been when her boss had put her through *the ringer* and reduced her position to part-time. At that time, she had felt that Mark had been mean-spirited during one of their lunch meetings when she had been absolutely devastated. She acknowledged that she never confronted Mark about her experience or dealt with it.

Mark also remembered the situation. He recalled that it had been very similar to yesterday's lunch with one major difference. At that time, Mark had responded by getting angry at Cynthia when she had looked away, seemed disinterested, dismissed him, and interrupted him several times. Those were the same behaviors that she had engaged in during yesterday's lunch. The difference this time had been that Mark stopped giving input and he did not address her behaviors. Instead, he simply ended the lunch calmly and unaffected. Another major difference was that after this lunch, Mark had made a reassuring call to Cynthia, which he had not done four years ago. When Cynthia's behavior had upset Mark at that time, he had confronted her. Looking back now, Mark had clearly been manipulated by Cynthia's emotions and his own reactions to them.

To be able to move the interaction along without getting polarized, Mark asked if there had been other times that Cynthia had experienced Mark as mean-spirited.

Cynthia said, *"No."* This question was intended to gather information as well as to support Cynthia to raise her awareness. Mark wanted her to become aware of her experience in the context of their long-term relationship. Mark hadn't felt mean-spirited four years ago, and hadn't felt that way yesterday either. Cynthia verified that she had only perceived him to be mean-spirited twice during their long-term relationship.

What was similar and different about the two incidents relating to Cynthia perceiving Mark as mean-spirited?

The differences were in Mark's responses to Cynthia. The similarities were that Cynthia had been experiencing severe betrayal in both situations. Cynthia perceived her boss as mean-spirited. Mark was the same sex as Cynthia's boss. Mark had most likely failed to respond in the moment to some of Cynthia's needs to vent. Cynthia's answers led him to believe that this issue might have to do with Cynthia's experience not in relationship to Mark, but in relationship to her boss. Mark still needed to gather more information before he could understand the situation. He thought it might be helpful if Cynthia would be willing to reality test her experience with him. In general, reality testing is more effective than to give another explanation, since that could increase the risk of polarization if Cynthia is still projecting, being defensive or resistant.

Mark asked Cynthia if she wanted to reality test and she said yes. Mark responded, *"Great, go ahead."*

There was a long silence.

After a while, Mark initiated the communication to move forward by once more encouraging Cynthia to go ahead and start reality testing her experience.

Cynthia said,

"I don't know . . . I thought you were going to say something else."

(It was clear that Cynthia didn't have the tools available to reality-test, so Mark realized it would be helpful if he provided some for her.) So he said,

"Cynthia, how about you ask me some questions about your experience with me yesterday, for example, was I being mean-spirited? What was my intent? How could the example I gave be helpful for you in your interactions and reaching your goal with your boss."

Cynthia asked Mark,
"Were you mean-spirited?"
Mark answered,
"No."
Cynthia continued,
"What was your intent?"
Mark stated,
"My intent was to support you to develop some tools by first understanding what your boss's position might be so that you could relate to him and his thought processes, since that often is helpful. It's like the saying "know your enemy."
Cynthia responded,
"Comparing a Big Five store that had nothing to with my situation wasn't helpful."
Mark said he understood. (Instead of polarizing with Cynthia and insisting that his example would be helpful if she understood it, Mark validated her by agreeing with her. It was clear to him that she was not available to receive any benefit from that particular example.)
Cynthia continued,
"I think maybe you were upset about the conversation we had last week and that was where your meanness was coming from yesterday. I have seen you be mean to others in the past. That's why I think maybe I'm more objective about this right now."
Cynthia brought up another topic, how Mark treats others. This is an unconscious attempt to shift the focus off the two of them. If Mark goes along with Cynthia's attempt to switch the subject, he could become enmeshed in trying to defend his behavior in relationship to others, instead of keeping the focus on their interaction. Keeping the focus on the two of them, using reality testing as the tool to get clarity makes Cynthia more vulnerable to find out about issues within herself. Instead of addressing Cynthia's comment about him being mean to others, Mark addressed her concern about him having left over feelings from their conversation last week.
Mark replied,
"I was done with our conversation when we finished it last week. If I hadn't been done, I would have approached you again. I don't have resentment toward you. I feel complete about that interaction."
By making the above comment, Mark indirectly gave Cynthia what she might have been looking for; reassurance about last week's interaction. So as not to get sidetracked, he did not attempt to further discuss last week's interaction. Maybe Cynthia had feelings leftover from that interaction that

she tried to act out now. In either event, that was not a topic to discuss now, maybe later. Mark then continued by asking Cynthia if she thought what he tried to convey at lunch yesterday might have some value for her. If so, did she want to hear him expand? (The intent was to hold Cynthia accountable for her position of being interested or not).

Cynthia responded,

"*Sure.*"

Mark continued,

"*Why do you think it may be helpful to understand how your boss thinks? How do you think that could be used to your advantage?*"

Cynthia said,

"*I don't know.*"

Mark added,

"*If you could offer him some incentives to give you the division, do you think that would make him more or less interested in exploring that with you?*

Cynthia said,

"*More, of course.*"

Mark said,

"*Great, so if you could figure something out, like if you take over the division, he still gets the benefits of its success without doing any of the work, it may increase your opportunities to reach your goal of getting the division, right?*"

Cynthia responded,

"*It might.*"

Mark said,

"*At the very least, it probably couldn't hurt?*"

Cynthia said,

"*Probably true.*"

Mark added:

"*Do you feel supported by me in general?*

Cynthia said,

"*Yes, I do.*"

Mark stated,

"*Do you feel supported by me now?*"

Cynthia answered,

"*Yes.*"

Mark asked,

"*Do you feel better now than when we first started the conversation?*"

Cynthia said,

"*Yes.*"

Mark continued,

"Based upon this additional information, do you think that I came from a mean-spirited place yesterday or from a supportive position?

Cynthia said,

"I'm not sure."

Mark could experience the resistance from Cynthia.

Mark then asked,

"Cynthia, could you see that maybe I was trying to accomplish the same goal as I have done in this conversation? Maybe you projected someone else's behavior or some of your disowned feelings to me and that colored how you experienced me yesterday?"

Cynthia said,

"I don't necessarily agree with that or know that to be true. That is your reality but not necessarily mine. Maybe you came from a mean-spirited place and you weren't aware of it."

Mark was curious about Cynthia's thought processes, since they didn't seem logical based on what they had discussed a moment ago. Mark's questions to Cynthia and her answers supported the fact that Cynthia had missed Mark's intent to support her. She had instead experienced him as mean-spirited, the complete opposite of supportive. In this interaction, Cynthia said that she felt supported by Mark, even though he had essentially delivered the same message that he had tried to do yesterday. Mark's intent yesterday had been the same as today, to support Cynthia.

Since Cynthia's experience was so far from the reality that Mark presented to her, it might indicate that either she had been projecting on Mark what wasn't there, and that had precluded her from receiving his support, or Mark was lying.

Mark continued by asking another question:

"Cynthia, would it cause you less pain if you didn't think I was mean-spirited?"

Cynthia's response was

"Of course, I don't want you to be mean-spirited."

Mark said,

"Yet at this time you're not sure whether I was or not, right?"

Cynthia responded,

"Right."

Mark said,

"So the information that you got in this conversation didn't really clarify that issue for you then?"

Cynthia evaded Mark's question and said,

"I feel better now. You may not have been mean-spirited. I may have been projecting, or maybe not. Maybe you aren't in touch with what you did?"

Clearly, Cynthia does not want to let go of her point that Mark was mean-spirited. If she would concede this point, it would alleviate some of the pain the belief caused her. In addition, she would no longer be a victim of Mark. Thus, logically, it makes sense for Cynthia to surrender the belief that Mark was mean-spirited. By retaining her belief, she remains a victim of Mark, since nothing would prevent him from exhibiting this behavior again in the future.

Why did Cynthia take a position that made her a victim of Mark's mood and behavior when the other position would have given her more choices?

What reasons might there have been for Cynthia to want to hold on to a victim position when she had an opportunity to relieve pain by changing her perception of her experience based upon new and additional information that had not been available to her yesterday?

Maybe, for Cynthia, it was less painful if Mark was mean-spirited once in a while, than it would be for her to admit that she wasn't perfect. Maybe Cynthia was more threatened by having been wrong about her experience. Perhaps in Cynthia's eyes, she would have had to admit she had been out of control. If she couldn't trust her own experience, she might think that she couldn't trust herself. Cynthia might have been trapped in a faulty thought process that led her to believe that if she wasn't aware *at all times*, there was something wrong with her, and that would make her inferior. It makes sense that Cynthia would resist giving up her position that Mark had been the source of her pain if those were her faulty beliefs.

Cynthia had projected that Mark would not listen or support her. She had projected that he would betray her by taking a position against her, like her boss had done. In the interaction with Mark, Cynthia was; therefore, not able to experience Mark's support.

Cynthia would have had an empowered position in her interpersonal relationship with Mark had she done the following:

- Recognized that Mark had been supportive
- Realized she misread the situation because of some of her past experiences
- Understood how uncomfortable she was with her anger, and how that prevented her from recognizing it in herself and expressing it constructively

By raising her awareness, Cynthia could learn to understand her projections. This understanding would give her more freedom, she would be less reactive and she would not be at the mercy of outside forces such as Mark.

Cynthia chose to take the position that her pain had been caused by Mark being mean. Thus, her pain had been inflicted by an external source. In spite of additional information, Cynthia resisted the possibility that her pain had been caused by her own projections; hence, the pain had been inflicted by her internal sources.

Mark and Cynthia ended the conversation with Cynthia feeling supported by Mark, while not committing to a clear position as far as yesterday's experience. Mark felt okay. He wasn't invested in Cynthia deciding one way or another. He was happy that she had taken in his support, better a day later than never.

This interaction had shown Cynthia and Mark that they could get through a difficult situation together. Cynthia made the promise to pay close attention to when she started to see similarities between her boss and Mark. Mark committed to trying to be more sensitive to Cynthia during stressful situations.

Mark had exhibited excellent internal boundaries in the interactions with Cynthia. His boundaries had supported him to stay on track and helped him from being manipulated by Cynthia or his own emotional reactions. Mark wasn't invested in being right, instead he respected the limits he encountered and became creative and inquisitive. Mark used his curiosity to support him from taking personally Cynthia's dismissal and devaluing of him; thus, he avoided polarizing with Cynthia.

13

Good-Bye, Victim

A victim *can be described as being harmed by or, otherwise, suffering from an act, condition, or circumstance. It can be somebody who experiences misfortune and feels helpless to do anything about it, or somebody who is duped or taken advantage of, affected, or deceived by somebody or something.*

Choice *can be described as selecting, having the right, power, option, or chance to choose, usually by the* free *exercise of one's judgment.*

Freedom *can be described as the exemption or liberation from the control of another person or some arbitrary power. Freedom implies the absence of hindrance, restraint, or repression.*

When one is a victim the experience of having choices is impaired, which means that one isn't free to exercise one's judgment to choose. During those times, one doesn't have the freedom but is instead controlled and repressed by the power of someone else, a circumstance, situation, feeling, or by one's own perception and experience. One is rendered powerless.

Nobody enjoys being a victim . . . or do they?

- How did you react to the previous sentence?
- Do you agree?
- Did it make you angry?
- Did it evoke any other specific thoughts or feelings?

When the term victim is used herein, it refers to a human being reacting to a situation, being at the mercy of the act, situation, other person, *or of oneself, without the experience of having choices.*

Examples are when your reaction is in relation to the following:

- Someone's emotional reaction to you or to a situation.
- Someone's attempts to manipulate you to react.
- Someone's unconscious projections that are directed to you.

The second part is in relation to being a victim of *yourself*:

- When you get manipulated by your own feelings, thoughts, faulty judgments, fears, or unwanted needs, and react
- When you are engaging in unconscious projections and acting them out

It does *not* refer to people in situations like the following:

—War
—Sexual or physical abuse of a child or adult
—Crime
—Physical violence

It is common to think of yourself as a victim when you are at the mercy of others. What one often fails to realize is that more often we are really victims of our own reactions and emotions. The true power to change the experience lies within each of us.

- Are you aware when you are acting, thinking, or feeling like a victim?
- Are you aware when others are acting, thinking, or feeling like victims?

Begin with Raised Awareness

When you begin to understand some of your unconscious, learned, habitual *victim stances*[43] and behaviors that you engage in, it can help raise your awareness. You can then move to the next step and discover *responsibility frames*[44] that will help you bring some of the unconscious thought patterns about victimhood into consciousness. After this step, change can start to take

---

[43]   Victim stances refers to somebody who is experiencing misfortune and is taking the position that he or she is powerless to do anything about it.

[44]   Responsibility frames is synonymous to dependable structures.

place. Some examples of how it may sound when one is thinking, feeling, or reacting like a victim:

- Someone spoke rudely to you for no reason at all, *and you left feeling horrible and powerless*
- Someone violated your boundaries and *you are sure that there was nothing you could have done to stop her*
- The deadline wasn't met, *but it wasn't your fault*
- Someone got disappointed in your performance, *but you couldn't help that you didn't have the right resources to do better*
- Someone accused you of being self-serving and not listening, *which made you angry so you withdrew*
- There was no point arguing. *You wouldn't have been heard anyway*
- You didn't get what you needed, *so why should you give him what he wanted*
- You tried to talk to her, *but she wouldn't listen, so why should you waste your time*
- No one else seems to care, *so why should you work so hard at this relationship*
- He never follows through, *and there is nothing you can do about it*
- She only makes you angry. *What's the point of arguing?*
- *It doesn't matter how hard you try, things won't change*

The thoughts and experiences described above have components of hopelessness and helplessness attached to them.

Feelings that often follow can be these:

- Depression
- Anger and frustration
- Disappointment
- Sadness and hurt

Actions/behaviors that are likely to follow when you experience the feelings associated with being a victim can be these:

- Withdrawing
- Giving in/up
- Reacting defensively

- Blaming
- Retaliating and punishing later
- Seeking out others to gossip with to receive misguided compassion

What you generally *do not* experience when you are being a victim:

- Choices
- Opportunities
- Freedom
- Growth and development
- Knowledge and expansion
- Curiosity
- Being proud of yourself
- Feeling self-respect and respect for the other person
- Dignity and integrity
- Joy and happiness

To better understand the victim dynamics, it is helpful to know why you sometimes may *choose* to be a victim. You may want to challenge that statement by saying that you don't *choose* to be a victim! I agree. Maybe at this time, when you react like a victim, you don't actually choose because when that is your reaction you are probably *not experiencing having choices.*

Change can happen when choice is experienced!

Therefore, part of the goal in this chapter is to discover tools that will help you increase the times, places, situations, and interactions when you experience having a number of choices. Then you can choose to be a victim or not.

There can be many unconscious reasons behind the choice to react like a victim:

- It may be a behavior that was role modeled to you as you grew up by a parent, a sibling, other caretaker, or friends at school, or in the neighborhood.
- Your need for attention and empathy may have been met when you acted like a victim. You may have confused the good feelings you received from having your needs met with being a victim. Therefore, the victim behavior became a tool to get those needs met.

- When you first practiced taking responsibility you may have received repeated negative feedback and unconsciously deduced that being a victim is easier and a quicker way to avoid feeling pain, shame, and humiliation. Have you ever heard a parent becoming angry when a child admitted doing wrong, and then punished the child, swiftly bypassing the opportunity to teach the child more about responsibility? The parent placed his need for instant gratification (releasing his/her anger and punish the child) over the opportunity to teach the child more about the responsibility process. The focus was on the child's behavior that evoked the anger, not on the part of the child's behavior that admitted having done something wrong and was the child's first move toward taking responsibility.

Generally, being a victim isn't a trait that anyone is teaching you directly, in contrast to having been taught how to bicycle, play a sport or an instrument; it is most likely learned indirectly and unconsciously. Through observations and unconscious deductions, you internalized the victim position. It is often difficult to undo something that you may have spent years practicing, especially when it was learned indirectly. Another reason why this may be a more difficult dynamics to retrain is because your victim position may not be very dominant in your character.

In most areas of your life, you may already be taking responsibility, so the area of victimhood feels even more foreign to you, and less necessary to spend time on. However, even if you rarely react as a victim, it is important to acknowledge these feelings.

It has been said that the only guarantee in life is death and taxes. It is time to add one more. If you are a human being you will, at times, respond as a victim. It doesn't matter how responsible you are or how much growth you have done, it is inevitable. The question becomes: *how can we increase our awareness enough, so that the frequency of victimhood can be reduced?*

How often would you say that you think, act, or feel like a victim?

There are many reasons why you may want to familiarize yourself with the victim dynamics. First, when you react as a victim you will miss out on being able to engage in a satisfying interaction. Second, awareness of victimhood will almost certainly increase your ability to be effective when you are on the receiving end of a victim interaction. This is especially profound when you are the victim of your own feelings and reactions. Third, it is less likely that a victim will be able to manipulate you to react emotionally when you understand the dynamics well. Subsequently, you will increase the respect you feel for yourself and the respect the victim will feel for you. *What kind of relationship do you have with your own victim?*

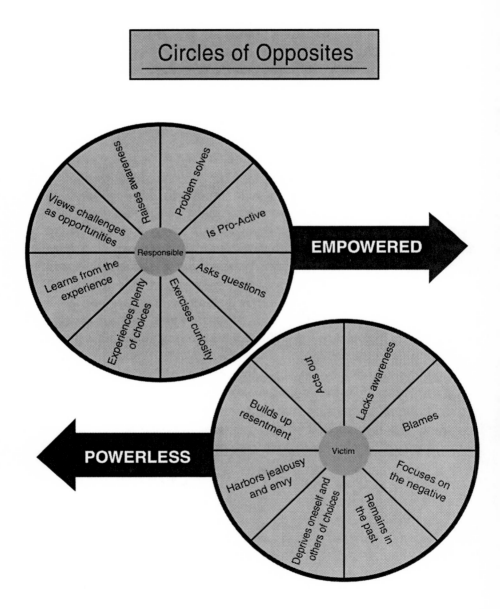

The experiences of having choices and behaviors that follow that are rooted in responsibility are the antidote for victimhood.

Some of the benefits that you can experience when you have integrated responsibility into your daily thoughts, communication, and actions are the following:

- Choices
- Opportunities
- Freedom
- Curiosity
- Growth and development
- Knowledge and expansion
- Being proud of yourself
- Feeling self-respect and respect for the other person
- Dignity and integrity
- Joy and happiness

If the list above seems repetitive, you are right. The same things that are listed as potential beneficial experiences when responsibility is involved are generally absent when you feel like a victim.

Victim and freedom are two words that are mutually exclusive, since as a victim you are a prisoner of others, or of your own reactions.

Roger and Eve

Roger and Eve were in their bedroom getting ready to go to bed. The TV was on and the news had just started. Eve went into the bathroom to brush her teeth while Roger was already in bed. As Eve went into the bathroom, Roger turned off the TV. Eve poked her head into the bedroom and asked Roger to leave the TV on while she was getting ready so she could listen to the news from the bathroom. Roger started getting very annoyed and responded in a hostile tone of voice, *"No, I want the TV off! I am really tired and want to go to sleep. I have to get up early because I have to work all day."* Eve who knew that Roger wouldn't go to sleep while she was still in the bathroom and the lights were on, walked into the bedroom and stood next to the bed where Roger still had the remote control in his hand and said, *"I only want it to be on for five minutes while I'm finishing up. Can you please turn it back on."* Instead of responding verbally to Eve, Roger gave out a big sigh, frowned, and with excessive force threw the remote control across the bed toward Eve. The remote slid off the bed, hit the floor, the back cover opened up, and the batteries tumbled to the floor. Eve got really angry and stated, *"It is all about you controlling the situation, what's the big deal keeping the TV on for five minutes? What difference is it going to make?"* Roger had lain down in the bed without saying a word. Eve waited a moment for Roger to respond, when he didn't, she stomped out of the bedroom and left the TV off. When she came back, she lay on her side of the bed with her back turned to Roger without saying a word. Roger had turned his back away from Eve and did not initiate any contact either. They both fell asleep without speaking to each other. Eve had become a victim of Roger's behavior and of her own reactions.

What happened?

The TV was turned on and they were both watching it. Eve got out of bed and walked into the bathroom. Roger turned the TV off. Eve responded to Roger's action by requesting that the TV be turned back on again while she was getting ready for bed. Roger said no. When Eve challenged the reasons behind his answer, Roger threw the remote control toward Eve. Instead of giving a verbal response indicating that he was granting Eve her wish, Roger's actions indicated he was going to give in by using excessive force and sighs of annoyance; his message became contradictory.

Roger's nonverbal communication spoke volumes. Eve reacted to Roger's behavior when she experienced a rush of anger. She accused him of being controlling, further inflaming the situation. When Roger reacted by withdrawing instead of responding, Eve left the room and left the TV turned off.

Why had Roger reacted so strongly against turning the TV back on for five minutes as Eve requested? Was Eve's request unreasonable? Did Roger's reaction seem out of proportion to her request?

Roger might have become *disappointed* when Eve asked him to turn the TV back on. Maybe he got upset that she didn't accommodate his needs in the moment. He might have felt *frustrated* or *gotten angry* that Eve didn't go along with his request. Roger's feelings could have been *hurt* because Eve didn't put his needs ahead of hers when he really wanted her to do so. Any one of the above scenarios is plausible, and perfectly acceptable to experience.

Having a feeling is never "bad." It is what you do with it that will determine whether you are taking responsibility for the feeling or being a victim of it.

It is the *behavior that follows* the feeling that can be thought of as productive or unproductive, constructive or destructive, supportive or unsupportive, and responsible or victimlike.

When you don't take responsibility for a feeling, it generally gets repressed, suppressed, denied, or acted out. Those reactions are mostly unconscious processes. Sometimes your experience of a feeling might be out of proportion to the event. When that happens, it often means there is something inside of you that gets triggered, which has very little to do with the external provocation.

In this case, Roger's reaction to Eve's request indicated that he did not take responsibility for his feelings; exemplified by his reaction and behavior that followed. Also, Roger's reaction seemed out of balance to the event. Roger's reaction might be stemming from leftover anger that he projected on Eve when she didn't respond in accordance with his wishes. In fact, we later uncovered that Roger had acted out anger from an earlier experience. At that time, Roger felt powerless in relation to this other person. Since Roger hadn't dealt with, expressed, or shared his anger, it was suppressed, and then stored somewhere in his body waiting to be released at a later time.

There are a number of reasons why we don't deal with our anger. Often the choice *not to* deal with our anger is unconscious. It is often a learned reaction that may stem from a variety of reasons. One reason may be that the anger is suppressed before you even get a chance to become aware that you are angry. That may happen if there is a faulty judgment or fear attached to the feeling of anger. Another reason may be due to discomfort or not having the tools to deal with anger safely.

A common result is to later, in a safer or more familiar setting, unconsciously set up a situation that would lead to a fight, so that the suppressed anger can be released. In this case, Roger created a fight with Eve. Roger in essence reenacted and set in motion a situation where he would feel powerless and angry, but this time it would be in relationship to Eve.

Why would Roger want to do that? It hadn't felt good the first time, so why put him in a position that would make him feel powerless and evoke anger again?

It is like a pressure cooker. Suppressed feelings need to have a place to go. In the moment, Roger wasn't aware of this setup. Roger was being a victim of his lack of awareness, suppressed feelings, and subsequent projection. Eve was a victim of Roger and herself. Eve allowed her reaction to Roger's feelings and projection, as well as her reaction to her own feelings to overshadow the experience of having different choices.

Victimhood

How can the cycle of victimhood be changed, if it is unconscious?

The cycle can be changed by becoming aware of the feelings, being able to identify, and deal with your own and other people's feelings. You also need to make appropriate behavioral changes. The responsibility process is a step to reach this goal of enlightenment.

On a positive note, the wish to repeat a behavior that is left unfinished might be the unconscious desire to *heal the wound,* i.e., be able to handle the situation differently next time. The problem that often occurs is that we tend to repeat behaviors with people that are not able to support us to reach a different solution or help us expand our choices and make behavioral changes. Unfortunately, that is what Roger did when he reenacted a powerless situation with Eve. She wasn't able to contain her own or Roger's emotions but instead reacted, consequently achieving no positive resolution.

When Roger objected to Eve's request, she challenged him since his reasons didn't make sense in light of the time limit of turning the TV on for five minutes. Eve reasoned with herself that if she requested to watch TV for thirty minutes or an hour, Roger's objections would have been reasonable. Eve knew that Roger didn't fall asleep until she was in bed and the lights were turned out. Eve approached Roger in a calm and logical fashion and Roger's reply was a disproportionate emotional reaction, which indicated that this was not about the TV being turned off, but about something else. If Eve slowed down the process at this point and responded instead of reacted, she might have been able to experience that fact.

Instead of either agreeing with Eve and amicably turning the TV on, or logically and reasonably explaining to her how the five minutes would make a difference, Roger gave Eve mixed messages. By withholding verbally from Eve, Roger created the illusion that he could maintain some power. There were two parts to Roger's nonverbal response. By throwing the remote control toward Eve, the message was that Roger granted Eve her wish to have the TV turned back on. While at the same time, he used excessive force to do so, which rendered the remote control temporarily useless, sending the message that Roger denied Eve her wish. Roger's contradictory behavior could have been his desire to indirectly show Eve how powerless he was feeling and the anger it evoked when he was giving in to her.

Roger was essentially giving Eve what she wanted (the remote could have been put together fairly easily), but it came at a price.

Eve got angry and without thinking or making a constructive choice, acted out the anger she felt in response to Roger's mixed messages. In that moment, Eve became a victim of her own emotions. She was no longer able to reason logically within herself or with Roger.

It can be noted that Eve was manipulated by Roger's indirect anger and by her reaction to it. If Roger had issues with his own anger, it would be safer for him to see it in Eve and acted out by Eve instead of seeing and feeling the majority of the anger in him. At the same time, when Eve got angry, it became justifiable for Roger to act out any suppressed anger that was still stored in his body.

Throughout the process described here, there were many opportunities for either person to stop acting out and to take responsibility for their feelings and make constructive choices. Neither Eve, nor Roger did so; instead they both became victims of the interaction.

If Roger had experienced an emotional reaction when Eve requested to keep the TV on, he could have responded to her in several different responsible ways starting with identifying his feeling to himself, and then sharing them constructively with Eve.

Here are some examples of how that could have sounded:

- Eve, it is *disappointing* to me that you want to have the TV turned back on when I turned it off.
- Eve, it makes me *angry* when you challenge my decisions.
- Eve, it *frustrates* me that you want the TV to be turned on again.
- It *hurts* me when you don't understand that I have a need for the TV to be off right now whether it makes sense or not. (Roger could be sharing his hurt and identified the irrational component of his reasons.)

If Roger would have chosen to take responsibility for his feelings, it is likely that he would have been open to a dialogue; he was not.

The strong emotional reaction indicated that Roger was projecting unto Eve. Feelings that may have been triggered for Roger may have been disappointment, frustration, anger, fury, hurt, humiliation, or feeling betrayed. (Other feelings that may at times be experienced or projected can be jealousy and envy.) Instead of taking responsibility for the experience and the feeling that the situation evoked, Roger acted it out. Some common forms of acting out can be to retaliate, punish, withdraw, or withhold.

Roger withheld, retaliated, and punished Eve. He withheld by not giving Eve a verbal response to her comment questioning his reasons. He retaliated and punished by using too much force so the remote control landed on the floor, and then would need to be put together before the TV could be turned on again. He continued to withhold by not responding to Eve's comment before she stomped out of the bedroom.

It is interesting to note that Roger's actions were more indirect than direct, which is another indication that he may neither have felt comfortable nor had the tools to deal with his anger and powerlessness directly.

Eve responded by giving in, the TV remained turned off, but she continued acting out, punishing Roger, and withholding by going to bed in silence, and turning her back away from him without speaking.

In order for this circle to be broken, one of the two people needs to take responsibility for his or her experience/feeling and make a constructive choice to deal with it and the other person.

The secret is being able to act rationally when the situation isn't necessarily rational.

When someone is projecting, the situation often has an irrational quality to it, and the feelings are often out of proportion to the event. A significant component in the heat of the moment is to be able to

have the ability to reason logically
with the absence of emotionalism!

This is a key point in avoiding victimhood. It is one of the most difficult things to do, since logic seems to fly out the window when emotions enter into the picture. It takes practice and an everlasting commitment to succeed.

When Eve reacted to Roger's emotional comeback, it indicated that she was being manipulated by Roger's emotions as well as by her own.

- *What kind of support do you need to avoid reacting and being manipulated by other's emotions?*
- *What kind of support do you need to avoid reacting and being manipulated by your own emotions?*

If Eve would have been able to reply rationally and logically to Roger's emotional response, she could have empowered them both instead of becoming a victim of their emotions. It doesn't matter *in the moment* of the interaction whether Roger was disappointed or angry with Eve, or whether he was projecting his anger unto her and it didn't have anything to do with her, the main point is his choice of behavior.

The vital point then became whether Eve would react or respond.

React = Emotions "run the show" and get acted out in the moment (we become victims and choices are absent).

Respond = Logic is used with the absence of emotionalism, followed by a constructive choice to act responsibly. (That doesn't mean that emotions are not there, it means that logic takes priority over the needs for the emotion/feeling to be acted out in the moment.)

The question is not who ought to be responsible. The question is who is willing to take responsibility for his or her actions *irrelevant* of whether the other person is acting responsibly.

We can find reasons and excuses to act out in almost any interaction. Therefore, set your own goals for your behavior, choices, and awareness level in each interaction *independent of* the other person's actions. That does not mean that you, or in this case Eve, should take full responsibility for "all interactions *at all times.*" However, it does mean that, in the situation described, if Eve would have taken on the responsibility to stay constructive, it could have benefited both Roger and herself. It could have empowered them, and created an opportunity for intimacy and closeness instead of isolation and withdrawal.

The choice was in Eve's hands *after* she experienced the rush of anger. A window of opportunity can be accessed when there is some time, space, sensitivity, and awareness allowed to surface *right after* the feeling is experienced. When that step is overlooked, we tend to become victims and react instead of respond. That is why slowing down makes a difference.

It is important to note that either person can at any time choose to break the acting-out circle or feed it further. That is, of course, if the person has become aware that he or she has some choices. That is why raising awareness makes all the difference in the world of interpersonal relationships. Without awareness, we are victims of our emotions, lack available choices, and follow with unconscious behaviors. One way to raise awareness is to understand the hidden dynamics that exist within us and between people.

During later discussions with Roger and Eve, Roger shared an experience he had earlier that same week with his supervisor. He had been denied additional support that he needed to complete one of his projects in order to meet a deadline. Roger had left the meeting feeling furious, but had dismissed his feelings and instead focused on his deadline.

The pros of being a victim such as getting attention, feeling sorry for yourself, and receiving compassion from someone, all have a price. Justifying hostile and angry feelings by taking the victim position is also costly. Pretending to be a victim, so others won't experience you as a threat means giving up vital parts of a relationship such as equality, balance, freedom, and empowerment.

Can you receive the pros of victimhood without having to pay the price? If not, maybe it is time to evaluate your relationship with your victim part and make different choices?

14

Hello, Responsibility

Being responsible *can be described as expected or obliged to account for something to someone. It means being answerable, and able to distinguish between right and wrong. It includes having the capacity to think and act rationally, hence, being accountable for one's behavior, by being dependable, and reliable.*

Responsibility *can be described as a condition, quality, fact, or instance of being responsible.*

The Responsibility Process

The responsibility process can be broken down into four specific areas:

- Raising awareness
- Taking a responsibility inventory
- Untangling the feelings, fears, thoughts, and faulty judgments
- Making changes and doing it now

Raising the Awareness

A step in the process of becoming more aware is to answer the following questions:

- Is it reasonable that you are responsible for your conscious actions?
- Is it natural that you perceive yourself as being responsible if, in general, you

  o   make good choices when it comes to life decisions;
  o   are a good student;

- o   are successful at your job;
- o   make good money;
- o   function well in society;
- o   possess appropriate social skills;
- o   are perceived by others as honest and reliable;
- o   take care of yourself;
- o   are independent;
- o   care for others;
- o   contribute to society?

- When you engage in an action that contradicts your self-image as a responsible person, do you know how to deal with the conflict that may arise?
- Does it automatically mean that you are not going to feel miserable, or that you are not going to have to deal with other unpleasant feelings if you act out and are disrespectful, then later take responsibility and admit that it was hurtful and wrong?

- o   Why would you react and act out if you are a responsible person?
- o   Is it acceptable that you sometimes react to a feeling without making a responsible choice to respond logically?
- o   How often is it acceptable for you to do so?
- o   Do you think it would be worth your while to become aware of your own unconscious behaviors?
- o   Do you think that to more completely integrate the responsibility process, it may be helpful if you investigate the underlying dynamics that determine some of your unconscious behaviors?

Now that you have started to raise your awareness it may be helpful to continue your exploration.

Taking a Responsibility Inventory

Actions that produce positive results are generally not something that we are asked to take responsibility for, or questioned about later.

On the other hand, actions that produce negative outcomes are more often questioned. As a result, the following often happen to them:

- Blamed on someone else or something else
- Denied that they ever happened
- Taken responsibility for and explained

How often do you think responsibility is questioned for one of the following actions:

- Having cleared the table without being asked?
- Made the bed and cleaned up the room without being told to do so?
- Delivered a great speech?
- Done a superb job?
- Been kind and considerate in a relationship?
- Patiently explained a difficult task without getting frustrated?
- Spoken to someone in a polite and respectful way?
- Given a gift to someone for no reason?
- Shared happiness and joy?

In contrast, how often do you think responsibility is questioned when a person has done the following:

- Lied?
- Cheated?
- Broken an agreement?
- Not followed through on a commitment?
- Changed his mind and made a unilateral decision?
- Broken a valuable possession?
- Gotten into an accident and been the one at fault?
- Acted carelessly?
- Gotten into a fight at work?
- Spoken rudely or disrespectfully?
- Yelled?
- Not listened?
- Been angry and inappropriate?
- Disappointed someone?
- Made poor choices?
- Not paid attention?
- Left an argument in a foul mood and taken it out on someone later?

- Gossiped behind someone's back?
- Missed an appointment?
- Not shown up for a meeting?
- Missed a deadline?
- Delivered mediocre work?
- Failed on a test?
- Forgotten someone's birthday?
- Messed up an order?
- Misunderstood directions?
- Behaved irresponsibly?
- Acted out anger or frustrations?
- Reacted with hostility?
- Been unreasonable?
- Not accepted a limit?
- Broken a rule or regulation?
- Not known?
- Been lazy?
- Misread a situation?
- Avoided dealing with discomfort and withdrawn?
- Given into the fear of conflict and withdrawn?
- Not maintained a healthy boundary?
- Blamed someone else?
- Been self consumed?
- Given in, resented it, and punished later?

It can be helpful to identify different areas of responsibility and divide them into categories:

1. Thoughts
2. Feelings
3. Communication
4. Impulses
5. Behaviors

1. Thoughts

There is a difference between taking and not taking responsibility for a thought. Let's say that the thought is, *"It will make no difference whether I try my best or not."* That thought can *lead to* a feeling or it may *stem from* a feeling.

The feeling might be despair. Whether despair was the reason for the thought to occur or whether the despair came after the thought doesn't matter.

Once the thought occurs, we can go along with the thought and become victims of it, i.e., the first thought may lead to a second thought. *"Since it won't make a difference if I try my best, I'm just going to give up trying altogether."* That thought may then be followed by an unhelpful behavior such as withdrawal, isolation, or abandonment of one's goals and aspirations.

As victims of our thoughts, we are no longer using logic or reason to make choices. We need logic so we can take responsibility for the thought:

- Slow down.
- Acknowledge the thought.
- Identify the feeling behind it.
- Examine the value of the thought by asking some questions:

  o How does this thought support your goals?
  o How can it benefit you to trust a thought that tell you that it won't make a difference to try?
  o How does this thought help you be a better person?
  o In what ways does this thought make you feel better about yourself and the world?
  o How does this thought promote choices and options?

- Explore what choices are available:

  o You can choose to trust that the thought is accurate. You can go along with whatever feelings and impulses may follow. Then you can let those feelings and impulses make choices for you.
  o You can choose to believe the thought and feel really lousy about yourself. That will give you a reason to be punished. You can do that by giving up on yourself.
  o You can choose to ignore the thought and suppress the feeling that comes along with it. Then you can take your discomfort out on someone else later.
  o You can choose to stop doing your best. What a relief, you don't have to work so hard anymore.
  o You can choose to use your previous knowledge about yourself of how you sometimes get into a place of despair and hopelessness

to support yourself to make a better choice now. You can choose to have perspective and realize that feeling good and feeling bad goes in cycles and is part of life. Therefore, you can choose to not allow the thought to bring you down or give you an excuse to act out your frustrations.

o You can choose to be curious and wonder why that thought came up for you now. You can choose to leave your faulty judgments behind and reach out for some support.

o You can choose to write in your journal, then run five miles. After that, you can choose to check in with yourself to see if your thought is still the same.

o You can choose to take some time to find out if there might be some needs of yours that demand some attention from you right now. If that is the case, you can choose to give those needs some attention and see if that has an impact on your thought.

- Follow up the choice by taking the appropriate behavioral action.

If we take responsibility for the thought, we can acknowledge it and also recognize that our thought may be inaccurate. If the thought is not a true reflection of reality, then we can choose to restrategize. *How can we create more support for ourselves and explore what other options may be available instead of giving up and abandoning our high standards?* If we choose to act out destructively, we may have the illusion that we don't have to take responsibility. It is an illusion because even if we are not held accountable by ourselves or someone else, we will still suffer the consequences of our acting out over time. Alienating ourselves from someone we care about is a common consequence. We may feel increasingly miserable and keep escalating our acting out, engaging in behaviors such as drinking excessively, using drugs to try to numb the feelings, or overeating to try to make the thoughts stop.

All those actions we are responsible for because we do them.

2. Feelings

To take responsibility for a feeling, we first need to be aware what the feeling is. If it is a pleasant feeling such as joy or happiness, it may not cause much trouble. Unless, of course, we are expressing it inappropriately, e.g., we start to laugh hysterically when someone is giving a serious speech or expressing grief.

If we are feeling anxious, frustrated, angry, or disappointed we may want to quickly dismiss or ignore the feeling. Ignoring feelings may not be such a good idea, unless we believe that suppressed feelings will have no effect on our choices and behaviors. Let's say that the feeling is anger; the trigger point may have been someone else's behavior. Once we experience the feeling, we may have an impulse to react. Since this is where choices come in, we can do the following:

- We can take responsibility for the feeling.
- We can become victims of it by following it up with a destructive behavior such as lashing out emotionally, withdrawing, or retaliating.

Out goes the logic and in comes the acting out when we don't take responsibility for the feeling.

The same strategy we used when we addressed taking responsibility for a thought applies to taking responsibility for a feeling:

- Slow down.
- Acknowledge the feeling.
- Identify the trigger point and what it is about the trigger point that made you angry.
- Examine possibilities about the other person's intent:

  o Did the person try to manipulate you to react by using inflammatory language?
  o Is this your anger or are you taking on someone else's anger?
  o Can you support the interaction by responding back angrily?

- Explore what choices are available:

  o You can choose to ignore the answers you received from examining the other's possible intent, and choose to yell at her because that is what you feel like doing right now.
  o You can choose to withdraw because your anger makes you uncomfortable.
  o You can choose to express your anger constructively, choose to set boundaries in your interaction, and then choose to ask if and how, at this point, you can resolve this issue.

○ You can choose to ignore the anger you are feeling and choose to suppress it as quickly as possible. Then you can choose to take your discomfort out on someone else later.

○ You can choose to be curious and wonder why the feeling was so strong. You can choose to leave your faulty judgments behind and see how you can reach out for some support.

○ You can choose to end the interaction right now and make an agreement to continue once you have had some time to sort out the intensity of your experience. You can choose to write in your journal then run five miles. After that, you can choose to check in with yourself to see if your feeling is still the same.

○ You can choose to take some time to find out if there might be some needs of yours that demand some attention from you right now. If that is the case, you can give those needs some attention and see if that has an impact on your feeling.

- Follow up the choice by taking the appropriate behavioral action.

You can see that there are a number of choices and there are almost as many choices as there are people.

3. Communication

How we take, or do not take responsibility for our communication tells a lot about how we think, behave, and what kind of relationships we have.

It is easy to use words to hurt someone in the moment. Unfortunately, those moments often become everlasting memories.

This is a good reason to choose to take responsibility for how we communicate before we utter the first word that may be with us for the rest of our lives.

If we are angry, there are a number of ways to communicate our anger:

- "I hate you and I will never forgive you!"
- "You are a liar and that's all you ever will be!"
- "I'm out of here!"
- "I'll never speak to you again!"
- "I'll throw you out next time!"

Then there are some other more constructive and less inflammatory ways:

- "I am really angry with you and it will be difficult for me to forgive you."
- "I don't have the words to describe how angry I am with you right now."
- "When you lie, you undermine the trust between us; and in the long run, it will destroy our relationship."
- "I am furious! *Right now* it feels like I will never get over it."
- "I am so angry that *in this moment* I can't see how I will ever want to speak with you again."
- "Simply stating that I am angry doesn't give my anger justice *right now*. I suggest that, as soon as possible, we start to redefine some of the boundaries in our relationship so we can avoid having this occur again."

"Right now" and *"in this moment"* are phrases that are qualifying the moment from the rest of the time. They are used as tools to maintain perspective during a difficult and emotional time.

Words are not the only aspect of taking responsibility for the way we communicate: the tone of voice, volume, pitch, rate, and articulation of speech must be included. Without thinking, we can communicate in absolutes, use certainties, and choose words that are intended to hurt, sabotage, undermine, belittle, intimidate, antagonize, or provoke.

The question is what we prioritize:

- To satisfy our need in the moment; to act out whatever we may be thinking, feeling, or having the impulse to do?
- To create a relationship that we can be proud of that will give us satisfaction, support, and peace of mind?

As with taking responsibility for a thought or a feeling, the process when you take responsibility for your communication follows the same steps:

- Slow down.
- Explore what choices are available:

o   You can choose to say anything that comes to your mind. You can choose to not care how cruel it may be or how it may affect your relationship long-term.

o   You can choose to yell at the top of your lungs and use as many profanities as you can come up with. You can choose to not care if you destroy the relationship.

o   You can choose to express your anger as constructively as you can by stating how you feel and choose to not make any threats.

o   You can choose to ignore the anger you are feeling and suppress it as quickly as possible. Then you can choose to take your discomfort out on someone else later by finding some fault or inadequacy that you can point out.

o   You can choose to be calm and collected and deliver your words with ice, and make sure that you find words that you know will hurt him.

o   You can choose to end the interaction right now, since you recognize that you don't want to say anything you know you will regret later. Then, you can set another time when you can continue the interaction.

▪   Follow up the choice in your communication with some form of constructive behavior.

Questions are great! When you are heightening your awareness, the more questions you ask yourself, the more insight and understanding you'll get about yourself.

▪   *How do you think your communication style is impacting your current relationships?*
▪   *What kind of situations do you find to be the most difficult for you to control your emotions or impulses to act out in your communication?*
▪   *What kind of support do you receive on a regular basis to raise your awareness of the tone of voice you are using when you are frustrated, angry, or disappointed?*

4. Impulses

An impulse is a sudden forceful inclination to act. Until it has been given some time and attention, it is almost impossible to contain. However, an impulse is not beyond consciousness. *With training and attention, we can learn to recognize the impulse after it is happening and* before *we have acted it out.*

We can also become aware of subtle signals that often precede our impulses.

- When I feel anxious, my impulse is to grab another cookie.
- When I feel threatened, my impulse is to attack.
- When I get disappointed, my impulse is to give up.
- When I am scared, my impulse is to make someone else feel scared by threatening him.

The more familiar we become with ourselves and how we operate, the less victimized we will be by our impulses. As with thoughts, feelings, and communication, taking responsibility for an impulse follows these steps:

- *Slow down.*
- Acknowledge the impulse.
- Identify the trigger point and what it is about the trigger point that sets off the impulse.
- Examine the other person's possible intent:

  o   Did the person try to manipulate me to react by using provocative language?

- Explore what choices are available:

  o   You can choose to act on your impulse without giving any thought to potential consequences.
  o   You can choose to give in to your impulse and let it take priority over your relationship.
  o   You can choose to acknowledge your impulse, be curious about where it is coming from, and not act out, but instead, find another way that you can satisfy the need behind the impulse.

- Follow up the impulse by taking the appropriate behavioral action.

5. Behavior

Actions speak louder than words! Keep that in mind as you are making your next move. It is as important to take responsibility for a behavior as it is to take responsibility for a thought, feeling, communication, and impulse. You can do that:

- *Before.* After the thought, feeling, impulse has been experienced and before action is taken.
- *During the time it is happening.* As we are retaliating by withdrawing, we can stop ourselves in the middle of the withdrawal and change our course of action by making the choice to be proactive.
- *Immediately after it has taken place.* When the other person is crying due to the hurt we have inflicted, we can apologize and express remorse in the moment.
- *Sometime after it has taken place.* We might realize our behavior was hurtful or someone might complain to us about our behavior, and we can then apologize and make amends.
- *Never.* We can never take responsibility if we believe that is the way to achieve fulfillment and joy in our lives.

Untangling the Feelings, Fears, Thoughts, and Faulty Judgments

It can be concluded that we as human beings, at one time or another, will do something that we are not proud of. Later, we will feel terrible and regret what we did. The easiest thing to do is deny that we ever did it, explain away what we did as something that was out of our control, or blame someone else so we won't be held accountable. Thus, try to avoid unpleasant feelings and potential conflicts.

The responsibility process requires that we take a completely opposite direction. The process requires that we go back and investigate what we did: our thoughts, feelings, choices, actions, and reactions that may have led up to the behavior that produced a negative outcome. Instead of avoiding unpleasant feelings or potential conflicts, we deal with them head on. That is often a scary proposition, since we will have to subject ourselves to having to deal with the other person's feelings and judgments toward us, on top of whatever feelings, thoughts, or judgments we may discover that we have about our own behavior. This is the first juncture at which we may be derailed by our fears of not knowing how, what to do, or what might happen.

The fears may evoke all kinds of negative feelings, thoughts, and faulty judgments such as the following:

- Feeling stupid
- Less than
- Inadequate
- Out of control

When these fears surface, the easiest way out is to avoid responsibility, blame another person, or make up an excuse for our behavior. One of the reasons for doing so may be the fear that if we instead take responsibility, we might realize how hurtful, "stupid," inconsiderate, or selfish our behavior was. The fear often leads to a faulty conclusion. *As long as I deny what I did and pretend that it didn't happen or wasn't my fault, I don't have to feel awful. I can also* prevent *the other person from arriving at the same realization; that I was hurtful, "stupid," inconsiderate, or selfish. If she doesn't realize that, she won't be disappointed or angry with me. That way, I don't have to put myself in a position that I may not be able to handle; like being confronted and overwhelmed by those uncomfortable and sometimes threatening feelings from myself and from her.*

If we don't give into the first set of fears that we encounter, and instead experience our own and the other person's feelings, perceptions, and judgments about our behavior, the next set of fears are likely to surface. One fear may be that there is something wrong with us, which then quickly is followed by a faulty judgment: *if I engaged in a stupid behavior that must mean that I am stupid.* We fail to separate our one-time behavior that was stupid with our behavior in general that is not stupid. We make *"one stupid action"* and that single incident represents the total image of who we are. We forget that we became who we are from years of being and past behaviors, not from one isolated incident. We lose perspective and objectivity. In its place, we react to our faulty judgment emotionally and start feeling inadequate, shameful, and humiliated. We get lost in despair. Once we have reached this point in the process, we have our own and the other person's feelings, thoughts, perceptions, and judgments, to deal with. This can become so overwhelming that we are taken off track and away from the responsibility process. We lose sight of the end goal. As that happens, the main goal and priority shift from taking responsibility to "getting rid" of the unpleasant feelings at all cost. This shift results in abandoning the responsibility process. We are right back to unconscious reactions and continued acting out. We have lost track of the trust that if we can sustain feeling bad for a while, those feelings will get transformed to feeling proud, self-respect, and increased peace and joy as we are taking full responsibility for our error.

Do not underestimate the power that the fears, feelings, judgments, and faulty judgments have in influencing and throwing the responsibility process off track.

Making Changes

After experiencing the possible dynamics surrounding the process of taking responsibility, it is time to delve in and *practice, practice, practice*. A suggestion: make a commitment to yourself to prioritize the end goal, to feel good about yourself and your interactions.

Taking responsibility is not an easy task! It needs to be respected and clearly understood. Once one has successfully taken responsibility, it is amazing how good one can feel. Remember *those good feelings have been earned, not given!*

Support to Stay on Track

What kind of support do you think that you need to remain on course when you are taking responsibility?

Here are some examples of skills that are worthy of further development:

- The ability to maintain perspective and receive and give reassurance.
- The ability to differentiate between an objective judgment and a faulty judgment.
- The capability to understand the other person's feelings and judgments in the context of your behavior.
- The ability to separate a one-time behavior from your whole identity and self-image.
- The capacity to allow the other person to express difficult and unpleasant feelings, and recognize that they are appropriate based upon the events that have taken place.

- The ability to experience remorse and feeling terrible about a behavior while simultaneously knowing and trusting that you are not worthless or stupid even though your behavior was inappropriate or stupid.
- Remember the following:

  o One can be smart, and still at times do something stupid or inappropriate.
  o One can be generous, and at times do something selfish and inconsiderate.
  o One can be kind, and at times do something that will hurt someone.

- Know that you are committed to showing remorse and making realistic plans to make amends.
- Have faith that the unpleasant feelings inside will not last forever.
- Trust that change is possible and realize that you are changing now!

15

Roger and Eve
Take Responsibility

The example between Roger and Eve in the Victim chapter was an illustration of what often happens when people react as victims and the responsibility process *is absent in an interaction*.

How could Eve and Roger's interaction have changed if Roger's initial behavior had been grounded in the responsibility process?

- Roger would have acknowledged his feelings in response to his boss and not suppressed them.
- Roger would have dealt constructively with his feelings directly with his boss (if he thought such a choice would have benefited him, the boss, and the company).
- Roger would have approached Eve, or someone else whom he trusted and could get support from, to share his fury, anger, powerlessness, and or disappointment that he had experienced with his boss.
- Roger would then have found ways to deal constructively with his emotions. He could have engaged in a physical activity to release some anger, whether that involved exercising, or hitting a tennis racket on a bed or pillows. Roger could have written about his experience in a journal and made sure that he didn't censor his experience. He could have discussed a strategy for how he could become more proactive in his interactions with his boss. Roger could have explored whether that would change their dynamics. He could have looked at other areas and people that he may at times feel powerless in relationships with, and start to explore strategies to reduce such occasions.

- Roger would not have set up a situation with Eve to act out his suppressed feelings, since they would no longer be suppressed, but instead, acknowledged and dealt with.

How could Eve and Roger's interaction have changed, if Eve's response to Roger's acting out would have been grounded in the responsibility process? (Presuming that Roger had not taken the steps above, but instead, created the situation with Eve described earlier).

In other words, how could Eve have responded using logic with the absence of emotionalism[45]?

1. The first step is for Eve to acknowledge her anger when it occurs, so she doesn't suppress it or act it out unconsciously.
2. The next step is to validate that her initial response was a natural and logical response to a provocation intended to infuriate (as we found out during later discussions with Roger and Eve). By doing so, Eve will indirectly give herself reassurance and counter any unconscious faulty judgments that may view her as "bad" when she feels anger. In other words, she will *accept her anger* and *subsequent experience* without it negatively effecting her self-picture; thus, supporting her attempt to stay centered and aware.
3. The third step is to slow down, instead of immediately reacting and indulging in the feeling of anger.

    a. Eve will then have a chance to experience having choices.
    b. She can start becoming curious about the reasons for Roger's behavior without demanding an immediate answer.

4. Afterward, a space has been created where she can explore her choices:

    a. She can set a boundary with Roger by not reacting with hostility to his nonverbal responses, but instead, ask him to give her verbal answers to her questions.

---

[45] Emotionalism is an openness to emotions and a display of emotions with a tendency to be easily swayed by, and engaging in exaggerated or undue display of strong feelings.

b. She can ask Roger a number of questions about, what appeared to her, to be Roger's irrational and provocative response to her reasonable request.

c. She can remain silent and wait for Roger to make another move, and allow for the potential discomfort without reacting to it.

5. When Eve is not reacting, she is containing her own as well as Roger's, emotions. When containing, she is indirectly sending a number of messages to Roger:

a. I am not going to allow you or your emotions to intimidate me.

b. I am setting a boundary around your acting out and will not support it.

c. You, your emotions, or my own emotions that were triggered in response to you, will not manipulate me.

d. I am feeling safe within myself and I trust that I have choices, and so do you.

Those messages are essential building blocks when building trust in the relationship. They act on an unconscious and very powerful level that will, in the long-term, significantly affect aspects like respect and dignity.

Once Eve has made her choice, she can move to the next step and actualize her choice. It is helpful if Eve understands she will benefit if she is able to remain logical and constructive in one of her responses. More difficulties will arise if Roger continues to throw out baits to manipulate her into a fight. Eve's emotions may be triggered several times during the course of one interaction, and that is when the challenge to remain committed and not act out will enter into the dynamics.

Depending on the depth of Roger's feeling, he may be quite invested in creating a fight with Eve. Eve must be in alignment with that reality, so she can stay centered and stay out of manipulations.

Eve (who needs to have good self-esteem and a high level of awareness when it comes to responsibility and choices in order to move to this step) can now calmly and constructively confront Roger about his behavior by asking a number of questions. Roger may defend and deny the behavior (if he is still unconscious about the acting out, or is maintaining an unhealthy position and continues to be destructive). If that happens, it will be Eve's first test to see if she can refrain from *reacting* to Roger. Instead, she can continue in a logical and unemotional fashion to give examples and make connections to the acting out, so Roger can have the opportunity to get in touch with his behavior, and make constructive, solution-oriented decisions. Roger may, after listening to Eve, connect his destructive behavior and acknowledge that he has been acting out. In optimal situations, Roger may be able to identify the feelings he has acted out like his anger and his relationship to his boss.

At this juncture, the process can move to Roger taking responsibility. Roger can show responsibility by tolerating and containing the feelings that may get triggered when Eve shares her experience.

Roger listens patiently as Eve expresses her disappointment in him for having acted out his anger with her and for having made destructive, punitive, and withholding choices. Instead of feeling threatened or defensive when he hears what Eve has to say, Roger feels appreciative that he is in alignment with reality, (knowing that he has been acting out, and accounting for it). He can experience that Eve's disappointment in him is reasonable, and as such, it aligns Roger with reality. That alignment supersedes the discomfort he may feel as a result of Eve's disappointment in him. If Roger has the capacity to prioritize the part of the experience that will support him to make future constructive choices, he will be nonreactive. This is the time when Roger can choose to apologize for his acting out (an overt act that shows he is taking responsibility for his choices and subsequent behavior). Roger and Eve can connect and achieve deeper closeness from the experience.

What was described above is a successful solution to a difficult situation. This solution is possible if the person integrates the responsibility; otherwise, the following is likely to occur:

- Roger doesn't integrate the responsibility for his acting out and choices. Therefore, the positive and good feelings coming from the experience of feeling aligned with reality don't last.
- Eve accepts Roger's apology and is moving on. She is loving and open. As Eve becomes soft and warm again, Roger is starting to experience some "bad feelings" that get connected to Eve's disappointment in him. Instead of remaining connected to his acting out, subsequent responsibility, and his apology to Eve, the "bad feelings" take over and push the responsibility issue aside.
- Roger experiences these new, "bad" feelings and he, again, starts to feel much worse inside. Roger doesn't connect and take responsibility for his acting out that lead to Eve's disappointment. Therefore, Roger starts to

focus on his experience of "bad," unpleasant feelings and inaccurately attributes them to Eve and starts to blame her for "feeling bad."

- Roger wants to stop feeling "bad" inside. He wants to punish Eve for "making" him feel so horrible because he is connecting "feeling horrible" to Eve and her disappointment in him instead of to his original acting out behavior. Roger is being victimized by his faulty thought pattern.

- Roger becomes the victim of his own feelings and thoughts but fails to realize that the responsibility ultimately lies within him. He starts to blame Eve and starts the cycle of acting out again.

- This time, Roger is acting out the resentment he is feeling toward Eve for being disappointed in him. So he attempts to cause a fight, wherein the intent is to dispose of, or dump his "rotten feelings" as quickly as possible on Eve.

- The cycle of acting out carries on.

If Roger takes responsibility, it may look like this:

- Roger continues to feel good, being aligned with reality.

- As Roger and Eve start to feel more connected to each other, Roger becomes aware of some other feelings that are surfacing for him simultaneously.

- Roger is starting to experience some "dreadful feelings" that get connected to Eve's disappointment in him.

- Since Roger has taken responsibility for his acting out, and sees that as the cause of Eve's disappointment, he feels remorseful instead of resentful toward Eve.

- Roger allows space for Eve's disappointment in him, and puts his feelings in the background.

- Curiously enough, Roger feels empowered instead of disempowered, since he connects to having choices. He can choose to continue to act out and receive the logical consequence of Eve becoming disappointed in him again. Or, he can choose to not act out and eliminate Eve being disappointed in him further.

- Roger doesn't enjoy experiencing Eve's disappointment in him. However, the overriding experience is his priority to take responsibility for his actions and choices and to make constructive choices in the future. That commitment serves as a support tool to balance the feelings out. It helps transform the "bad feelings" into remorse and a commitment to make better future choices. The experience of having choices creates freedom from victimhood.

- Roger feels empowered and respects himself for dealing with difficult feelings constructively and allows Eve to have her feelings without reacting to them.
- Roger is learning from his mistakes and choices. He is allowing himself to be human without having faulty judgment attached to it.
- Roger is realizing that as long as he is willing to change and is committed to being the best he can be, he will create more choices. Roger will most likely act out less in the future. Therefore, the fear that Eve is going to remain disappointed in him can be relieved.
- Roger is able to get perspective and accept that sometimes he, like other human beings, will be unaware and react. He doesn't have to stay that way.
- Roger has, and is continuing, to take responsibility for his behavior and that makes him experience serenity!

When someone is projecting some old feelings on you, he is a victim of the situation. What is being acted out is not a true and accurate reflection of the reality, but a state of confusion between the present and the past and between you and someone else. He concurrently is attempting (unconsciously) to manipulate you to become a victim of his experience. Therefore, it is often difficult to remain centered and nonreactive. The force of the projection is often quite overwhelming and challenging; it is crucial to accept this fact. It may take some time before you will learn to identify and catch projections when they are happening. It takes time and lots of practice to implement the behavioral changes necessary to successfully deal with projections and the feelings that come along. When someone is projecting, he is not able to take responsibility for doing so. However, if you are on the receiving end of a projection and you are able to remain logical and responsive, instead of emotional and reactive, you may be able to support the *projector*[46] (herein referred to as the person who is projecting) to become aware of what he is doing. Once the *projector* has become aware, he can take responsibility for his *continued* choices and actions. From that point on, the interaction can change from a cycle of acting out to a cycle of enlightenment.

---

[46] A projector is a person who engages in the unconscious act or process of ascribing to others his or her own ideas, impulses or emotions that are undesirable or cause anxiety.

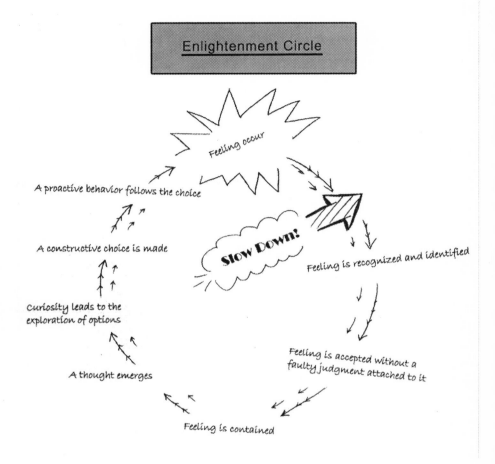

It is not always easy to identify when someone is being a victim. What follows are some examples in communication when victim stances are attempting to disguise themselves behind the notion of responsibility: (The part of the communication that contains the victim is in italics.)

- I am sorry about what I did, *but I wouldn't have done it if you hadn't provoked me!*
- I'm sorry, *but it wasn't my fault!*
- I'm sorry, *but I didn't realize you were so sensitive!*
- I apologize *if you took it the wrong way!*
- I'm sorry, *I didn't realize you couldn't take a joke!*

- I apologize that I hurt your feelings; *it is just really difficult to walk on eggshells around you all the time!*

There are many subtle forms of communication rooted in victimhood. In some of the examples above, the *but* between the apology and the second half of the statement is the clue. In each sentence the person does the following:

- Very quickly shifts the focus off herself after the apology is made
- In the second part of the apology, blames the other person for her actions
- Attempts to manipulate the other into a fight by using accusatory or inciting language in the second half of the apology

Slow Down! By now, that advice may seem redundant to you. However, it has a tremendous amount of value in discovering most of the hidden dynamics that can change your life. If you were to accept any one of the above-referenced apologies, you would indirectly be endorsing the victim in you and the victim in the other person. It is powerful when you role model how to take responsibility. It can be used as a tool to help change the dynamics of the relationship and get away from victim positions. When an apology has a victim component attached to it, it can be helpful if you first validate the positive section of the apology, instead of reacting to the victim part of the communication. For instance, if the apology sounds like this: "I am sorry about what I did, *but I wouldn't have done it if you wouldn't have provoked me!" You can respond with,* "Thank you for apologizing. *What specifically about your behavior are you sorry for?"*

By asking that question, you are gathering information and shifting the focus back to the responsibility part of the apology, instead of reacting to the victim part. If the person hasn't taken responsibility, which is indicated in the second part of the apology, it is likely that the person will have difficulties answering your question. He may react emotionally as an attempt to manipulate you into a fight. If that is the case, you will be challenged to use logic with the absence of emotionalism during the remainder of the interaction. If the person is on the fence, wavering between wanting to take responsibility and being a victim, then your question may support the person to take responsibility. To complete the interaction, it is important that you address the second part of the apology as well. Asking another question can be helpful to shift the victim stance in the second half of the apology to responsibility. An example of such question is: *When you will feel provoked by me in the future, how do you plan to deal with that differently?* That question indirectly shows the victim that he has options and choices *even* when someone else is acting in a difficult way. Hence, he has a choice to act out, then apologize; and blame, or take responsibility; and respond constructively by addressing his experience and feeling in the moment. It aligns the victim with the reality that, many times in life, one will encounter provocations and acting out; it is an unavoidable part of life.

A great way to practice can be to write your own response to the apologies using the example above as a guideline.

- I'm sorry, *but it wasn't my fault!*

  _____

- I'm sorry, *but I didn't realize you were so sensitive!*

  _____

- I apologize *if you took it the wrong way!*

  _____

- I'm sorry, I didn't realize you couldn't take a joke!

  _____

- I apologize that I hurt your feelings. *It is just really difficult to walk around eggshells with you all the time!*

  _____

Responsibility, Not an Equal Equation

When discussing the concept of responsibility, some people may express a need for both people involved in the interaction to take equal responsibility.

Be conscious that the need for that may be the following:

- A swift form of manipulation to dilute the responsibility because it may raise feelings of inadequacy if it is not pointed out how the other person is also "guilty" or "wrong"

- To shift the focus off one's own responsibility, since the unconscious deduction is that taking responsibility means admitting fault, which results in the production of feelings of discomfort
- A sign that one doesn't know how to identify behaviors that show how the other person is taking responsibility
- An attempt to regain some power that the person experienced as previously reduced
- An attempt to make the experience seem subjective, thereby diminishing the association with right and wrong

If you take responsibility, you inadvertently admit that you were wrong, or made a mistake. For many people, that evokes feelings of inadequacy and inferiority. To avoid feeling inadequate, you can divert the attention away from taking responsibility for your behavior, and instead, initiate a discussion about the subjective experience of right and wrong and good or bad behaviors. If you can convince yourself and the other person that your behavior may not have been experienced by other people as "bad," then that can help "take you off the hook." Convincing the other person can help you conclude that you might *not* have been wrong after all. The behavior that you took responsibility for that evoked feeling "rotten" about yourself may, in fact, not have been "bad" at all. So the other person's perception can now be looked upon as being less reliable, since it is subjective, and is most likely not a representation of the truth. Therefore, it has less value. Thus, "bad feelings" about yourself can be reduced or eliminated and you can be elevated back to an equal position to the other person who was confronting you about your behavior.

There are many clever and creative unconscious strategies that develop to avoid dealing with the unpleasant feelings that accompany taking responsibility for our behavior.

Unfortunately, experiencing some negative feelings about yourself when you admit that you acted wrong, hurt someone else's feelings, broke the trust, made someone disappointed, or was the cause of someone's discomfort override most other feelings. Part of the responsibility process is to sustain those negative feelings by containing them and trusting that they won't last forever.

It is reassuring to know that once you have more fully integrated taking responsibility in this manner, your needs to distract, dilute, or shift the focus to the other disappears. The "negative feelings" get transformed to feelings of self-respect, self-worth, empowerment, and hope.

There are some clear parameters universally experienced by most of the general population as *not* conducive to healthy, happy relationships. Those behaviors are often labeled as wrong or bad.

Some behaviors that fall under that category could be the following:

- Lying
- Cheating
- Stealing
- Breaking an agreement
- Not following through
- Changing a joint decision unilaterally without prior discussion or consent

There are some categories that are more subjective and therefore more difficult to identify.

Some examples are the following:

- Hurting someone's feelings by being insensitive to his or her needs
- Being aggressive and intimidating
- Seeming disrespectful
- Lacking feelings and the ability to have empathy

Those categories are often more complicated. *Is one being insensitive or is the other person projecting? Who is in alignment with what is occurring? Are both people involved in projecting?* It takes time and a number of questions to become clear and get a good reading on the situation, unless the particular behavior generating the hurt feeling or disrespect was, of course, the lying, cheating, etc.

Meet Sharon and John

Sharon experiences a negative feeling in reaction to John who broke an agreement with her. Instead of reacting, Sharon takes some time and gives some thought to what took place. Then she proactively addresses John's behavior with him in a calm, rational manner by reality-testing her perception of what had taken place. Sharon asks some reasonable questions. *"John did we have an agreement? What do you think our agreement was? Did you break our agreement?"* John answers Sharon's questions and agrees with Sharon and her perception that he had not followed through on the agreement. John said he understands that he was wrong. He also understands how that certainly can affect the trust between the two of them. John continues by apologizing for his behavior and explains the reasons behind it. He is not using the reasons as excuses, and he makes it clear that he is responsible for how he had acted and he regrets having done so.

Sharon is elated that he seems to take full responsibility for his actions. She gladly accepts his apology, and is looking forward to healing the relationship by moving on to the steps needed to build back the trust. Then, all of a sudden, John requests that Sharon state verbally that she is responsible for her experience. Sharon becomes confused and reacts by resisting.

Sharon thinks to herself, *"What about, my behavior has so far not been clearly communicating that I took, and continue to take, responsibility for my experience?"*

Sharon gets the feeling that John is backtracking from taking responsibility. She can't understand why he is not able to recognize that she took responsibility. Sharon proactively and calmly approached John about something that bothered her. By not acting out the anger and disappointment that John's breaking of the agreement provoked in Sharon, she made the choice to responsibly deal with the issue.

Sharon had not given in to any discomfort it provoked; instead, she acted logically, with the absence of emotionalism. Her behaviors showed that she had taken responsibility for her experience.

If John can shift the focus to Sharon, then John can rationalize that his behavior might *not* have been considered "as bad" by someone else. Sharon getting upset with him for breaking their agreement *was* her *subjective experience*. Hence, he might *not* be wrong after all.

When John initially took responsibility for his behavior, it had evoked feeling negative about himself. If his maneuver to shift the focus succeeds, then Sharon's complaint or criticism of his behavior is less reliable, since it is subjective and is most likely not a representation of the truth, but only her truth. Thus, it has less value and John's negative feelings about himself can be reduced or eliminated. He can be elevated back to an equal position to Sharon who made him doubt his self-worth by confronting him about his inappropriate behavior.

By getting stuck in John's need to shift the focus to Sharon, he is manipulating them into a polarized position. One solution for Sharon is to agree with John by stating that she takes full responsibility for having this experience and reassure him, *"You are right, John, this is my experience. I know that it is not*

Sam's or Ann's experience. I am fully aware that I am the one experiencing this."
By agreeing with John, as crazy as it may seem, Sharon manages to effectively
stay away from the trap to shift the subject into a prolonged diversion. Instead,
Sharon's answer helps to turn the diversion into a quick interlude that has
little or no impact on the responsibility process.

Sharon can then move on to the next step and ask John if he can give her
examples of how she has taken responsibility. When Sharon asks John that
question, she is supporting John to become aligned with the responsibility
process by not enabling him to avoid some of his negative feelings.

From the answers that John gives to Sharon's question, he will be able to
identify Sharon's behaviors. John can then recognize that Sharon has already
taken responsibility. John's request for Sharon to take responsibility can then
be recognized as having been superfluous. Sharon has gently guided John
back to the core of the issue, which is his original behavior that lead up to the
negative feelings, his responsibility, and how he plans to deal with that.

It is likely that John is trying to focus on Sharon taking responsibility as
an attempt to gain some control over the situation. It can be a way to reduce
some of his anxiety and to take some power back to create the notion of
equality. John may be trying to cover up the fact that he may not know how
to initiate the trust rebuilding process after he broke the agreement.

If the focus is on Sharon, John can avoid having to deal with additional
discomfort. He can avoid the fear of not being smart enough or good enough
that may be evoked when he doesn't know or have the answer.

John's need for Sharon to say, *"I take responsibility that it was only my
experience,"* is inappropriate when understood in the context of John being
the one who had engaged in a behavior that is universally looked upon as
unproductive, destructive, or wrong. Therefore, it is helpful *if Sharon can see
John's need to shift the focus as a signal to become more alert, so she doesn't react.*
Sharon can then become curious about the hidden dynamics behind John's
need, and experience the interaction as yet another learning opportunity.

Keep in mind; sometimes, it is appropriate for one person to take 100
percent responsibility in an interaction for her behavior while the other
person's role is to hold her accountable. For example, a person lies and the
other person confronts the behavior constructively without acting out. In that
case, the *confronter* is clearly showing that he is taking responsibility for his
actions and absence of reactive behaviors. A verbal acknowledgment of the
responsibility, unless given by the person who lied is; therefore, redundant.
When the person who lied makes a demand for the other to take responsibility
for her experience, he is out of line. *Being remorseful while simultaneously*

placing demands on the person that you have injured is inappropriate and creates confusion and contradiction.

As in the example of Roger and Eve, sometimes it is appropriate for both people to acknowledge responsibility for their acting out and participation.

As a guideline:

- Rarely, but sometimes, two people interact where one acts out and the other does not. Later, when the interaction is discussed, it is appropriate for the person who acted out to take 100 percent responsibility, apologize and show remorse for his behavior. When that is done, the person who acted out will most likely not place unsuitable demands or requests on the other person that would dilute or shift the focus off him taking responsibility

- To optimize the opportunities for a successful, continued interaction when both people have been acting out, they should take 100 percent responsibility for their behaviors, apologize, show remorse, and discuss future behaviors

Teaching how to take responsibility is one of the most precious gifts you can give to someone!

16

Next, Accountability

Accountable *and* accountability *can be described as giving satisfactory reasons or an explanation for one's behavior, being obliged to account for one's acts, being responsible, and capable of being accounted for.*

Highlighted in bold below are examples showing how we might sound when we are thinking, feeling, or behaving like a victim. Added in italics are examples of how it may sound when we are taking responsibility for the experience/feeling/thought that gets provoked, and then an example of *behavior that is based on accountability.*

A response of proactive behavior that contains accountability *in reply to an experience, thought, or feeling is responsibility carried out!*

- Someone spoke rudely to you for no reason at all, **and you left feeling horrible and powerless.**

Someone spoke rudely to you for no reason at all, *and you asked her if you had done something that had been upsetting to her. The question shows that in the moment you're committed to taking responsibility for your experience. It alerts her to her tone of voice by simultaneously giving her the benefit of the doubt that she was being rude unconsciously. Furthermore, you contain the trust that she has the ability to change, once she gently has been given the support to raise her awareness. By not withdrawing, you are respecting your feelings and being proactive in the interaction. By not accusing her, you keep an open mind that her intent is not hostile; and thereby, avoid polarizing with her. You set a boundary conveying that you will not accept being spoken to in a disrespectful or derogatory manner. You hold her accountable. More importantly, you hold yourself accountable for making constructive choices and not reacting like a victim.*

- Someone violated your boundaries, **and you are sure that there was nothing you could have done to stop her.**

Someone violated your boundaries *and you recognized the violation and the feeling it evoked inside of you. Then you asked yourself if you might have given the person some signals indicating that it was okay to violate your boundaries. You reality-tested your question by asking her what kind of relationship she would like to have with you.*

By asking that question, you begin to establish some boundaries of what is acceptable versus unacceptable behavior. You are sending the message that you are committed to being treated with respect and you, in turn, respect yourself and others.

- The deadline wasn't met, **but it wasn't your fault.**

The deadline wasn't met, *that in itself is a problem. However, you weren't going to allow that to discourage you from honestly exploring the reasons why it had happened. Instead of getting defensive, you decide to delve into the possibility that you might not have been managing your time as well as you normally do. If that were the case, you will make sure you will identify the kind of support you need to improve in that area, so that your time management will not be an issue in the future. If the reason was that you hadn't received enough backing from one of the other departments in your organization, your strategy will be to work on that issue preventing further deadline problems from occurring again. In either event, you see this as an opportunity to improve, whether it concerns communicating your needs clearly, becoming a better manager of your time, or dealing with whatever other information you might discover about yourself from the experience.*

- Someone became disappointed in your performance, **but you didn't have the right resources so you couldn't help it.**

Someone became disappointed in your performance, *and it made you feel bad. Your initial reaction was to defend yourself and start accusing and blaming the other person of having unrealistic expectations. However, instead of reacting, you slowed down and started to explore the interaction logically and objectively. You acknowledged the fact that it was reasonable that the other person was disappointed. You admitted to yourself that the work you had done had been mediocre at best. You apologized to the person. You accepted the fact that, at times, you will disappoint people and yourself. The knowledge that it doesn't happen very often helped you keep the perspective and reassured you that this experience does not have to be repeated. You then asked the other person what she wanted to do at this time. The intent with that question was to move to a problem-solving stage wherein you could explore how this kind of situation could be avoided in the future. If, in fact, the job you had been assigned to do couldn't have been done without additional resources, then that issue would need to be addressed. If you didn't have the knowledge or capabilities to do the job then maybe what needed to be explored would be the issue of how to more productively utilize your talents in a different area, or how you could gain the knowledge needed to do a better job. You didn't shy away from holding yourself accountable for the areas that were appropriate for you to take responsibility for. At the same time, you'd look ahead to prevent a similar situation from happening again.*

- Someone accused you of being self serving and not listening, **which made you angry so you withdrew.**

Someone accused you of being self serving and not listening, *which made you angry. Instead of acting out your anger, you took a deep breath and thought about your options by asking yourself some questions.*

- ○ *Was it true, had you not been listening?*
- ○ *If it wasn't true, why do you think he would have experienced you that way?*
- ○ *How could you continue the interaction at this time in a constructive fashion?*

You gave the questions above some thought, and came to the conclusion that it was your experience that you had been listening. You then continued by asking him a question. "Can you please tell me what it is about my behavior that sends you the message that I am not listening to you?" The question is a tool to bring the conversation back on track by making an effort to be specific and logical. You address one issue at a time, so that neither one of you get confused nor off track. It shows the other person that you take him seriously, and that you do listen to him, even when you might not want to hear what he has to say. It also shows that you are willing to deal with your own discomfort, take responsibility for your actions, and hold him accountable for his behavior too. By identifying specifics about your behavior, you may become aware of unconscious signals that you are sending without intending to do so. These signals may be sabotaging your interactions; and therefore, may not be in your best interest. Sometimes, the other person's perception is grounded in reality, and you are not aware of some nonverbal signs that you use. This problem is easily corrected once you become aware, and don't react defensively. Then you can have the opportunity to experience choices and the freedom to make appropriate behavioral adjustments.

The processes that are described above may, in the beginning, seem contrived and time consuming. However, the good news is that once you have changed your thought pattern and subsequent communication style and behaviors, this new way of relating can become second nature. Thus, you can save an enormous amount of time and energy that would, otherwise, be spent on getting stuck in feelings, acting them out unconsciously, and cleaning up the mess that they cause in relationships at a later time.

Accountability goes hand in hand with responsibility and is a worthwhile element in achieving freedom from victimhood. You create an opportunity to practice being accountable for your actions and holding another accountable for his actions each time you make a choice to be proactive. And instead of reacting like a victim, you confront your own issues.

Questions that may be helpful when you think about accountability:

- Do you hold yourself accountable?
- How do you hold yourself accountable?
- When do you hold yourself accountable?
- Who in your life has taught you the most about accountability?
- Do you feel confident you can hold people accountable?
- What do you do when someone is resisting being accountable?
- When do you resist being held accountable?
- Who holds you accountable?
- How do you feel, think, and behave when you are being held accountable?

Justification and Rationalization

Justification and rationalization are two wonderful tools that can be used *when one wants to maintain in a victim position.*

- *There was no point arguing. You wouldn't have been heard anyway.*

This is a way to take an "all-knowing position" that the person wouldn't listen or understand you. Then instead of addressing the issue constructively, which would have taken more effort and commitment to the responsibility process, you use that position to justify your behavior of withdrawing.

- *You didn't get what you needed, so why should you give him what he wanted.*

The above statement is an example of rationalizing withholding. Instead of dealing with the possible rejection that may come along with being vulnerable and asking for what you need, you justify the withholding behavior.

- *You tried to talk to her, but she wouldn't listen? Why should you waste your time?*

How do you know it would be a waste of your time? Or, is this yet another example of you justifying a behavior that would enable you to do what you want without having to engage in a potentially difficult or challenging discussion?

- *No one else seems to care, so why should you work so hard at this relationship.*

Taking the "easy way out," rationalizing away your lack of commitment to excellence.

- *She just makes you angry. What's the point of arguing?*

This is an example of rationalizing your passivity by connecting anger to unnecessary arguing, so you can avoid dealing with the "real issue." Hence, you preclude yourself from an opportunity to practice and learn more about what your discomfort may be about. Does it have to do with you not knowing how to deal effectively with anger and conflict?

- *It doesn't matter how hard you try things, won't change.*

This example justifies remaining a victim instead of becoming proactive. You give the excuse that things won't change so you can stop trying to be the best you can be.

Be aware of your needs to justify and rationalize.

Having a Choice

The experience of having a choice is powerful on many levels. It helps to *expand* the encounter both in relation to what happens *within you* and what happens *in relation to the other person.* One way to increase the number of choices is to change the way you communicate. Practicing changing the way you communicate will change the way you think. New thinking often leads to new behaviors.

You can start the transformation process from victim to responsibility/accountability and freedom by choosing to start changing one of the following areas:

- Thoughts
- Communication
- Behavior

Which area you begin with doesn't make a huge difference in achieving the goal. Once your communication style originates in accountability and responsibility, thoughts and behaviors with the same foundation are likely to follow.

For example, someone makes a derogatory comment. First, a feeling gets triggered. It can be anger, disappointment, fear, humiliation, shame, sadness, or pain. Second is the reaction, which encompasses behavior, thought, and communication, not necessarily in that order.

It can be challenging to distinguish which comes first as reactions happen so fast.

- *Victim Behavior:* You withdraw, look away or down.
- *Victim Communication:* "Thanks a lot. That's a really nice way to talk to me."
- *Victim Thought:* I can't believe how mean she can be, and there is nothing I can do.
- *Accountable/Responsible Behavior:* You look at the person. Remain present and proactively address the person's communication.
- *Accountable/Responsible Communication:* *"I will not continue a conversation with you as long as you keep using an abusive tone of voice and derogatory language when you speak to me. With that in mind, how do you suggest we continue this conversation? Or, "What is your intent?"*

The communication above sets boundaries by showing that you are not afraid of stating your position. When you are being specific by addressing the abusive tone and derogatory language, you contain the feelings and reality-test at the same time. Finding out what the other person's intent is, can support the process of moving forward in a positive fashion.

- *Accountable/Responsible Thought:* The person is either both unaware of her tone of voice and choice of words, or is intending to manipulate me to react.

What may be some constructive ways to deal with the situation given what you know so far? You can start with the thought, and then move on to communication and behavior. Or, you can start with the communication and move on to thought and behavior. The choice is yours, and as you practice, you may find that you are partial to one way or the other. The important point is that you stay accountable and responsible, and out of victimhood. Considering all the choices you make every day, you can really appreciate all the opportunities to practice being accountable and responsible.

Choices that we take for granted often seem small and insignificant. If you throw a piece of trash into the trash can and miss, you may choose to pick it up and put it in correctly. Another time, you may let it lay on the floor. *What makes you choose to do it one way one time and a different way the next? Does it make a difference if you miss the trash can, when you are in someone else's presence, if you are in a public place, or in your own home?*

When you are making the choice to use a rude tone of voice, does your choice have anything to do with the person you are interacting with? The time of day? Whether you are tired or not? What your relationship is with the other person, and if you have had a good or bad day?

When you make the choice to ignore someone who is speaking to you, does your choice have anything to do with your feelings toward that specific person? The task you are doing? Whether you have an interest in the topic or not? Or, if you resent the fact that you generally don't feel listened to by others?

In each situation described above, a choice can be made. Until you start to experience and become aware of these choices, you will remain a victim. You can then rationalize that you didn't choose to be rude or ignore the other person, you were simply tired or in a foul mood.

The question is, *when you are tired or in a foul mood, are you not to be held accountable for your actions?*

- Do you retain your abilities to choose when you are tired or in a foul mood?
- Does your tiredness negatively affect your interactions?
- Does it happen frequently that people get upset with you because they feel ignored by you?
- Are you using your bad mood or tiredness as an excuse for not making constructive choices that may take more energy up-front but will save time in the long run?
- If you have been told that you tend to be rude and ignore people when you are tired, and you agree that it is true, does having that awareness make a difference when you make a choice to be a victim of your tiredness?
- Do you have options available to you to deal with the situation differently when you are tired or in a foul mood, or does the choice need to be made before you get tired?

After you have answered the questions, you can make a choice. The choice may be to deal with your limitations responsibly by setting up a plan for how you will prevent yourself from being a victim of your tiredness or foul mood and allowing it to interfere in your life. You can choose to be proactive and communicate your limitations.

1. It has become clear to me that I am limited when I am tired or in a foul mood. I tend to be rude. I don't want to do that anymore. I will tell you when it happens and I'll do my best to pay attention to my tone of voice. Working on this issue is still new to me, so I may slip up. It would be helpful if you can support me by pointing out when I am rude, so that I can raise my awareness further, and change. I want to try to support us both, so that you don't get hurt, take it personally, and withdraw from me. Would you be willing to do that?
2. When I am tired or in a foul mood, I lose my focus and ignore what others have to say. I have come to realize that is a limitation of mine, so I suggest that I let you know when I am tired or in a foul mood. That way we can make sure that we don't discuss anything that is significant to you when I am tired, since you are important to me and I don't want to miss what you have to say. In addition, would you be willing to point out to me if you think I am ignoring you? I may not be aware of it all the time, and I don't want this to become a problem in our relationship.

In the previous examples you can see how the communication contains the following:

1. Choices to be proactive
2. Communication wherein you are taking responsibility for your limitations
3. Clearly defined steps that you are taking to minimize the negative effect your limitations will have on future interactions
4. Asking for support to change a negative behavior
5. By asking for support it serves two purposes:

    o   You, taking a risk by reaching out and asking directly for the other to become more actively involved in supporting you to change for the better
    o   A tool to hold the other person accountable should he choose to react as a victim when you "slip up" in the future

It is important that you create a framework of accountability that works in several directions as you are taking responsibility for your actions:

1. You hold yourself accountable for your choices and actions
2. You hold the other person accountable for his choices and actions as well

It is important that you change your relationship to your own victimhood, but also how you pay attention to, and deal with others when they act as victims.

With choices comes the task of making
tough decisions at times.

Choices are limited to you when you are a victim. You may only see one choice, to remain a victim. Choosing can create anxiety about a number of things, like a dilemma on the following:

▪   Choosing the right thing
▪   Going to have regrets later
▪   Embarking on a more difficult road than the one you're already on
▪   Making a mistake

The more unresolved and unconscious the anxiety you are holding on to, the less comfortable you'll be about making choices. Trust is another factor that will affect your willingness to make the choice to raise your awareness level. Trust is a prerequisite for being conscious of distressing situations and aware of various choices. In addition, having the ability to prioritize will greatly impact your receptivity to experience having choices.

- Is your priority to see the reality, whether it is good or bad?
- Is your priority to maintain comfort, even if that means denying what is going on around you, so that you don't have to be faced with having to make challenging choices and decisions?

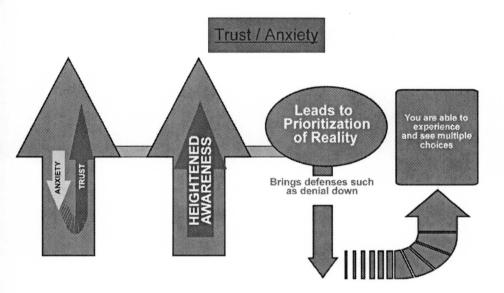

The more you trust yourself, the less anxiety you will experience. The less anxiety you experience, the easier it will be for you to raise your awareness. This awareness will make it more likely that you will be willing to prioritize facing reality including uncomfortable situations, see choices, and be able to make tough decisions.

Sometimes it is easier to "put your head in the sand" and pretend everything is okay. Another way is to "not see" the choice. By "not seeing" the choice, we can rationalize and stay in unhealthy situations that continue to hurt us. Change is scary, and choices go hand in hand with change. Choices, anxiety, change, trust, prioritization, and freedom all play a part in the hidden dynamics that affect our relationships.

It becomes easier to make the link between choices and freedom when additional opportunities are made available to us. To change a perception takes practice. It affects thought processes and communication patterns. It also affects what you do with your own and other people's feelings, and how you behave.

Therefore, you can practice the following:

- Recognize when you communicate like a victim.
- Distinguish when others communicate like victims.
- Identify behaviors that you engage in that support victim positions in others and in yourself.
- Realize when you are seeking out support that will enable you to remain in a victim role.
- Find ways to reduce reactivity.
- Change your perception.
- Learn to communicate like you already have choices whether you experience them or not.
- Be proactive not reactive.

You may already have noticed that much of the communication in this book comes from a place of seeing choices in most situations.

Choosing Not to Choose

Sometimes we trick ourselves to believe that we don't have a choice when, in fact, we made the choice to not choose, which nevertheless is a choice. Being unaware or choosing to remain unaware is also a choice.

If we were to sit down and discuss our lives and behaviors, we would find that circumstances and a variety of factors affect us and the choices we make.

But unless we have our arms tied behind our backs, we are still making the choice to do the following:

1. Act responsibly.
2. Act out irresponsibly.
3. Take no action.

Asserting Yourself and Being Proactive

When we experience having choices and are making them, we are actively working on preventing the development of resentment. It is natural to resent a person who we think hurts us or "makes us feel powerless." When we don't experience having choices and we believe it is because someone else is preventing us from having choices, we resent that other person for having the power and control.

The more proactive we are and the more assertive we are, the less need there is to be resentful.

You know you have reached a different level of evolvement when you have the experience that you can choose. Either be a victim or take responsibility!

17

Conflict: Oh No, I Got to Go!

Conflict can be described as to fight, battle, contend, be in opposition, clash on ideas, a sharp disagreement or opposition, a contest, or struggle. Struggle implies great effort.

Conflict can be an emotional disturbance resulting from a clash of opposing impulses, or from an inability to reconcile impulses with realistic or moral considerations.

Conflict, a Window of Opportunities

Why didn't our school teach us a class in conflict? Is that because we don't need to have skills to deal with conflict?

Conflict is often seen as something negative that should be steered clear of. It may be perceived as one of the following:

- A threat to intimacy and to the relationship
- A negative aspect of an interaction
- Uncomfortable
- Intimidating and scary
- Damaging
- Hurtful and painful
- Something that shouldn't happen if people love each other

Many of our experiences of conflict are unproductive and sometimes painful. The results of prolonged conflict may have been the demise of a relationship. During conflicts, there might have been a lot of yelling and screaming. And often, the problem that caused the conflict did not get resolved.

Conflict about what appears to be the same topic often reoccurs because during conflict, emotions often run high and the focus shifts away from solving the problem. Feelings are acted out irrationally, and logic is temporarily forgotten. In addition, before, during, and after a conflict, many fears get triggered.

The fear may be founded on the following premises:

- I will lose you.
- We will never be able to get over it.
- It will ruin our lives.
- We will never feel close to each other again.
- I will break down and not be able to function.
- You will force me to agree to do something I don't want to do.
- I will feel powerless.
- I can't argue with you.
- I won't win.
- You are too forceful.
- I'm never right anyway, so what is the point?

When those fears and thoughts are overpowering our ability to use reason, it is natural that we act them out by escalating the conflict. If our associations with conflict are negative, we may shy away from or try to avoid conflict. When we don't have the tools to deal effectively with conflict, it affects our self-esteem and our self-perception as a whole. *The fact is conflict is a normal part of life that cannot be avoided.* It can actually be valuable as long as it remains *issue-oriented rather than personality-oriented.* When we are able to separate the issue from the person, or from ourselves, we can better contain emotions and fears that get generated. Thus, the urge to attack the other is reduced, and we can become more objective in the interaction.

Conflict can actually be a window of opportunity, depending on how we are able to contain emotions, fears, and negative thoughts.

If we can access logic and be proactive, and if we have prepared strategies to deal with the issues involved in conflict, then it can help us do the following:

- We get closer by increasing intimacy.
- We encourage creativity.
- We achieve goals.
- We make positive changes.
- We learn and grow.
- We uncover a variety of needs.

- We establish boundaries.
- We receive and provide insight.
- We increase respect.
- We get to know ourselves and others better.
- We raise awareness.
- We clarify an issue.
- We find a solution.
- We forgive.

The dynamics of the conflict can change when a shift occurs away from the fears and negative perceptions toward the opportunities. Trust and curiosity can then be accessed.

Different Types of Conflicts

We have opportunities to experience and learn from many different forms of conflict. Many conflicts will leave a longer lasting impression on us than others. Some conflicts that may occur can be between:[47]

Individuals

- Friends
- Same-sex friends
- Opposite-sex friends
- Lovers
- Siblings
- Children
- Teenagers
- Partners
- Child and parent
- Teenager and parents

Individual and a group

- Teenager/school
- Parent/other parents

---

[47]   Lucas, *Effective Interpersonal Relationships*, 29 (see chap. 2, n.14).

Different groups

- Immediate family/extended family
- Family/another family
- One organization/another organization

Individual and an organization

- Employee/employer
- Employee/employee

The conflict will vary depending on the relationship. Some factors that affect the conflict may be the following:

- The power structure of the relationship
- The age of the individuals involved
- Self-esteem
- Fears and anxieties
- The ability to stay focused and on track
- Temperaments
- Expectations
- The ability to deal with disappointments and frustrations
- Listening skills
- Negotiation and compromising skills
- Experiences with conflict and resolution
- Trust
- Prior resentment

Sources of Conflict[48]

There can be a number of reasons for a conflict to occur. The people involved may have the following:

- Different values and beliefs
- Opposing perceptions
- Poor communication skills

---

[48]   Ibid.

- Goals and visions that do not match
- Different personal style, such as indirect or direct communication
- Contrary expectations
- A disagreement
- Inconsistencies between words and actions
- Differences in spending styles or greed
- Misused their power
- Misunderstood
- Opposing religious alliances

Being able to identify the source of the conflict can help raise the awareness. The next step is to understand the feelings, fears, needs, and thoughts that get activated. Knowing how to handle conflict constructively will enhance one's self-esteem. It will also help when it comes to intimidation.

By not shying away from conflict, we will send multiple messages such as the following:

- We can handle it.
- We are confident in our own abilities.
- We trust ourselves, and we are welcoming the learning experience.
- We believe that we can reach a solution.

Overt Agenda/Covert Agenda

Many times, we may think we know what the other person is attempting to achieve. The *overt agenda*[49] may be to want to have a discussion, while the covert agenda is to "strong arm" the other person into making an agreement. Sometimes you may not even be clear about what you want until the conflict has started. *Covert agendas*[50] can be experienced as deceitful and manipulative, as they generally are concealed or disguised under another pretense. Bringing the term covert into our consciousness can help raise the awareness when we are being subjected to someone's covert agenda.

When in doubt, ask questions about the other person's intent. If the force or direction of the interaction doesn't match your emotional reactions, it may be a sign that you are reacting to the other person's covert agenda.

---

[49]   An overt agenda is a clear plan.
[50]   A covert agenda is a hidden plan.

Polarization Equals Devastation

Polarization is a common dynamics in conflict. It is one of the reasons why conflict has such a stigma attached to it. When we are polarized we are close-minded and unmovable. It often means that we are painting ourselves, and the other, into a corner without options.

It is easy to polarize. The interest to understand is often reduced when our opinion doesn't match another's or when "we are right and the other is wrong." Instead of trying to bridge the gap that is increasing between us, we dig our heels in deeper and work harder to figure out how to convey our point of view.

Here are signs that someone is polarizing:

- Repetition
- Rigidity
- Close-mindedness
- Lack of questions asked
- Reduced interest in hearing the other
- Increased level of frustration
- Flared-up anger
- Pressure

It can be quite a challenge to become aware when we are polarized. As with other hidden dynamics, it happens fast. Therefore, one of the keys is, you guessed it, to slow down the process.

We can train ourselves to raise the awareness by asking some questions:

- Why am I feeling so frustrated right now?
- Is this conversation being productive?
- Are we getting closer to reaching a solution?
- If I don't feel like the other person understands my point of view with the information I have provided so far, what can I do differently?
- How do I need to change my behavior and communication to move this conversation along?
- Are we stuck?

Some of the questions are very similar and may seem redundant. However, they are examples of a variety of questions that can be helpful. To provide enough time and attention to raise the awareness, asking similar questions using different words is what is needed periodically. It can be thought of as a formula. *Do I need to ask myself three questions that deal with the issue of being stuck, plus two questions that focus my attention on the end goal, and one question that contains my emotions? Or, do I need to ask myself five questions that focus on my emotional reactions, three questions that deal with what I am trying to get out of the interaction and two questions that give attention to what I can do differently?*

The impulse may be to force the other to agree with us, even though that is not a constructive goal. The conflict is happening between the other and us. Yet there is also a conflict inside of us: between the impulse to react and the logical part of us that would take into consideration the actual reality and its limitations. Learning to stay out of polarized positions takes time and requires a certain amount of creativity. It is easy to be impulse-driven and repeat the same thing even if we don't receive the result we are looking for. It is not so easy to think up new and innovative ways to interact when our level of frustration has reached our ceiling. Nevertheless, our relationships can only get better once we have mastered this area.

Discomfort:
How to Learn Not to Be a Victim of It

Discomfort is something that has been discussed many times in previous chapters of this book. The frequency of the word can be seen as a metaphor for the importance it plays in our lives, and the power it has in our interactions, especially during conflicts.

Throughout a conflict, we might as well expect and accept that one of the ingredients is discomfort. If we do that up front, we will save ourselves a lot of time fighting it later.

Getting to know our relationship with discomfort will help us reach acceptance about its presence quicker. Some questions worth asking are the following:

- What does discomfort mean to me?
- When do I generally feel discomfort?
- What do I usually do when I feel discomfort?
- Do I normally recognize someone else's discomfort?
- Who in my life has taught me about discomfort?

- How badly do I want to avoid discomfort from a scale from 1-10?
- Are there times when I haven't been aware of how much discomfort I must have felt that I can look back at now and recognize?

We become victims of discomfort when we react to the pressure of it, or are intimidated by its presence. Once we have raised our awareness, we have choices.

Tools to Deal with Conflict

There are a number of tools that can be used during a conflict, such as the following:

1. Reassurance
2. Acceptance
3. Validation
4. Reality test
5. Containment
6. Staying on path
7. Staying calm
8. Identifying underlying issues
9. Intent
10. Respect
11. Limits

1. Reassurance

Reassurance often has a direct calming effect when it comes to fears and anxieties. Some examples of reassurance may be the following statements:

- I am confident we can work through our differences.
- I trust that we can use this experience to get closer to each other, once it is resolved.
- I have faith that we can get beyond the anger and frustrations that we feel now and feel close to each other again.
- I don't believe that because we don't get along right now, we will break up later.

- My intent is for us to learn more about each other and get closer.
- I am committed to our relationship, and I am willing to deal with this wholeheartedly.

2. Acceptance

We are automatically going to be more prepared to deal with challenges in our relationships if we accept that we will not feel close to each other "all the time." It is okay to be angry and not like each other at times. It is the unexpressed and unrealistic need to live in perfect harmony at *all times* that creates disappointments and frustrations.

3. Validation

Validation is an important tool to use during conflict. It can help reduce defensiveness. It can also help create comfort; hence, it works as an antidote to discomfort.

Here are some examples of validating communication:

- I understand that it must be frustrating . . .
- I agree with . . . (It may seem impossible during the heat of the conflict to find something to agree upon. Even so, the more creative you are, the more likely you will find it.)
- I appreciate your directness and as difficult as it is for me to listen to some of what you are saying, it helps me trust you more.
- I value your commitment to continuing this discussion even though it is tough right now.

4. Reality test

It cannot be stressed enough how crucial this tool can be in our lives. There are so many times that we walk around thinking we know what the other thinks, feels, and is going to do. We get in trouble from our preconceived ideas and faulty assumptions. When we do a reality test, we can find out, in the moment, whether we are misunderstanding, misinterpreting, projecting, or are in fact in alignment with reality. Therefore, we can reduce our reactivity in the moment and strengthen our capabilities to use logic.

Here are some reality-testing questions:

- What is your intent?
- Are you trying to intimidate me right now?
- What do you want from me?
- How is this conversation bringing us closer together?
- Do you want to discuss different solutions now?
- Do you think I should apologize?
- Are you willing to apologize?
- Do you think you have done anything wrong or destructive in this interaction?
- Are you angry with me?
- Are you disappointed in me?
- How do you plan to handle your disappointment?

5. Containment

To contain or to hold has been referred to throughout this book as something helpful and powerful in our interactions. There might seem to be a fine line between controlling and containing. The difference between the two is that when we are trying to control, we are trying to exercise authority over something or someone, and the force of power is implied. Containing does not involve power and authority. Instead, it implies that something is being enclosed, protected, and restrained in the moment. It can be helpful to distinguish between the two terms since subtle nuances can make a difference when hidden dynamics are at play.

How we contain something can be seen in various behaviors and communication:

- When we feel threatened, we continue to look at the other person and we do not retreat from the interaction.
- When we feel bullied, we remain calm and ask questions.
- We recognize the anger and slow down the process when we are furious instead of reacting to our impulses.
- We remain calm and present when attacked.
- We don't take on someone else's anxiety and start to act it out by switching the subject.

- We maintain perspective when our fears are intrusive.
- We do a reality test when we are insecure.
- We ask questions instead of making assumptions.

6. Staying on path and off tangents by tracking when the subject gets changed

Changing the subject during interactions happens frequently. It is seldom a deliberate act. More often, it is an automatic reaction to some unconscious emotions or thoughts. The higher the level of emotional intensity, the higher the odds are that the subject will get changed and several topics will be introduced.

Here are ways of raising our awareness about this aspect of our interactions:

- Make a conscious effort to pay attention to actions during stressful situations.
- Slow down the process and pay attention to the questions asked before reacting.
- Decide how important it is to get an answer to the question.
- Decide if the answer or that the person answers is most important.
- Be curious about the message indirectly sent when someone ignores the question.
- Accept that it is more difficult to keep the issues separated when the topic gets changed.

To confuse is part of the unconscious strategy. The confusion and the lack of focus feed the emotional reactions and undermine our ability to use logic. This is one of the reasons why conflicts often get out of control and produce a range of destructive experiences.

What are your strategies when you are dealing with someone?

- Who changes the subject?
- Who is resistant?
- Who is unwilling to stay focused?
- Who is not aware that she is not answering your questions?

7. Staying calm, realistic, and keeping an open mind

It is reasonable to expect that emotions will run high during conflict. To remain calm may be one of the more difficult goals to achieve. It is also one of the most important ones to stay committed to.

- What strategies do you have in place to remain calm during conflict?
- What kind of support do you need to stay calm?

Being realistic helps contain emotions, hence reducing the risks of being manipulated. If we have a realistic understanding of how the human mind works, there is less of a chance that we will be surprised, or caught off guard when we are met with defenses during conflict. Such understanding helps us stay open-minded and more flexible, aiding us toward conflict resolution.

8. Identifying underlying issues early on

Often the issue being discussed during a conflict may not be the real source of the conflict. It is, therefore, important to identify underlying issues. For example, you may be irritated at your significant other because he doesn't ask you about your day when he comes home from work. You may feel unimportant or taken for granted by him. Instead of discussing this issue with him, you may, over time, develop resentment. Thus, the underlying issue is his lack of attention while the conflict may be about him arriving home late for dinner.

9. Introducing intent

Unless you have skipped previous chapters, you should be quite familiar with the term intent. Introducing intent into your everyday communication can have a profound effect on your relationships. *What is your intent?* This is a simple question, yet a powerful tool. It can help to keep the conversation on track, focus our attention, heighten our awareness, and hold us accountable.

a. Clarifying intent

Clarifying the intent is a vital part of our interactions. It can help prevent misunderstandings. It can reassure us, and align us with reality.

b.   Power to change using intent

When we are caught up in the emotions of the conflict and are starting to lose perspective, shifting the focus to our intent increases the possibilities for change.

Is our intent any of the following:

- To start a fight?
- To release some anger?
- To avoid taking responsibility?
- To manipulate?
- To create intimacy?
- To understand the other person?
- To share a vision?
- To get approval?

Whatever our intent may be, once it is spoken out loud and we've taken responsibility for it, it shifts the dynamics away from the shadows of hidden dynamics into the luminosity of enlightened communication. To vent and to problem solve are two intents that are miles apart. If our intent is to vent, we will need quite a different response from the other person than if the intent is to problem solve. Sometimes we may not be aware that we want to vent. We may feel unheard as the other person is responding by giving concrete, solution-oriented suggestions. We may get disappointed and feel misunderstood. That may make us question whether the other person is really listening. As we start drawing conclusions about the other's insensitivity and lack of interest in being there for us, we may get angry. During this process, we may be perceived as resistant and difficult since the likelihood of us being receptive of any suggestions is slim to none. On another hand, if our intent is to problem solve, we might feel restless and impatient if the other person is spending too much time contemplating what has taken place.

In either situation described above, both people might genuinely believe that they were there for each other. Yet the interaction ends up as a conflict.

Neither person's intent was malevolent, yet they were so far apart that they didn't connect.

If they had been aware of the intent of the other, most likely both would have changed and become supportive to the interaction. Think about how many unfortunate, unnecessary conflicts that can be avoided simply by achieving clarity of intent.

10. Respect

Respect can be described as, "to feel or show honor, esteem, or consideration for."

Respect is a major factor that will affect our abilities to deal with conflict successfully. Without it, we will be too busy defending against some perceived deficiency or preoccupied with projecting our fears about our inadequacies unto the other person. Our contempt for the other can support a false sense of superiority. It is hard enough to contain our emotions when we feel respect for others and ourselves; with that lacking, there is nothing stopping our emotions, destructive thoughts, and fears from "taking over."

Respect helps to balance emotions and make room for logic!
Respect is earned not given!

Over time, continued *disrespectful* behavior can transform
respect and love into contempt and disgust.

A child might display behaviors that indicate he respects his parents. However, as time goes by and the ability to use critical thinking increases, the child will start to challenge and question the adults. What may have been perceived as the child's respect for his parents may, in fact, have been innocent love and learned obedient behavior motivated by the fear of retribution.

Role modeling consistency and congruency between verbal communication and behaviors become essential in building and maintaining the respect. When parents fail to create a solid foundation of respect, problems will worsen over time. Superficial expressions of respect become hollow and pointless.

The growing child will experience uncertainty and bewilderment between his wish to love and respect his parents and the negative feelings that are triggered when the parents act out and engage in disrespectful behaviors. The child is left with chaotic feelings that he hasn't learned to understand and contain. What has been learned from years of observations of the parents behavior is that it is okay to be disrespectful and act out any time the impulse to do so occurs.

Without the tools, the child will continue the erosion of respect for himself and for his parents. He will engage in the same destructive behaviors he has seen. The child turning into an adult has been deprived of an opportunity to develop self-respect and respect for others.

a. Respect for self

It starts with each individual! Unless we have self-respect, it is almost impossible to respect someone else. Respect should not be confused with being intimidated, threatened, or scared of someone. When we show respect for ourselves, it can be seen in many areas of our lives.

Respect can be shown in these areas:

- How we take care of ourselves—referring to our physical, emotional, and intellectual needs
- How we take care of our surroundings
- How we allow others to communicate with us
- How others treat us
- How assertive we are
- How we treat others

Gaining self-respect takes work. As we go through normal developmental stages, we have many chances to build our self-confidence starting in early childhood. With the right care and consideration for our own unique personality and normal human traits, we can practice making choices that will either support or undermine the building of self-respect.

We miss opportunities to gain self-respect if we are encouraged to take the "easy way out" by being catered to inappropriately or being treated like victims, avoiding responsibility. Successfully internalizing respect may be compromised without appropriate role modeling.

Once the self-respect has been integrated, it can be seen in many ways:

- Committing to being our best selves
- Making constructive choices

- Following through on our agreements
- Being responsible
- Holding ourselves accountable for our actions
- Being dependable to ourselves and others
- Exhibiting consistency
- Doing the work needed to reach our goals
- Setting and upholding high yet realistic standards for others and ourselves
- Adhering to rules and regulations without resentment and questioning the ones that need to be questioned
- Reinforcing consequences
- Acknowledging growth
- Appreciating our own value
- Treating ourselves and others as equal human beings
- Setting appropriate boundaries
- Dealing with resentment before it interferes in our lives

b. Respect for others

We may obey an authority because we would get in trouble if we didn't. That doesn't mean that we obey out of respect. When we don't respect a person, it becomes easy to engage in a number of insolent behaviors like the following:

- Using a derogatory tone of voice
- Stopping to listen
- Not answering when spoken to
- Violating boundaries
- Taking advantage of the other or the situation
- Disregarding the other's feelings, thoughts, or input
- Invalidating
- Belittling
- Intimidating
- Acting out feelings without consideration for the situation or the other

These behaviors wear down the respect for the other as well as the respect we feel for ourselves. It becomes a vicious circle that becomes difficult to overcome.

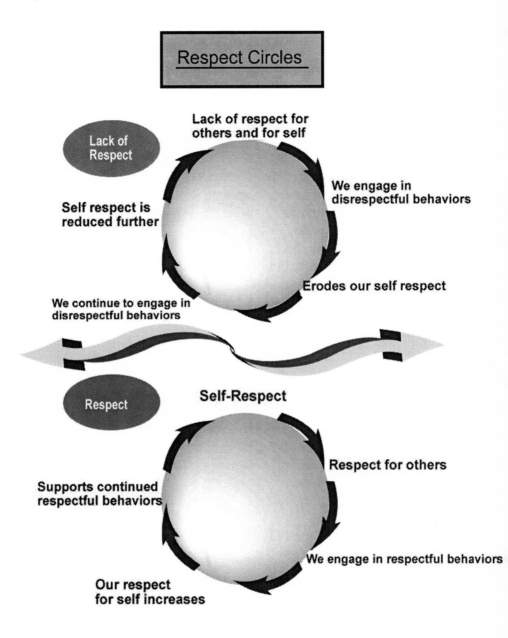

Respecting another doesn't mean that we won't challenge the other person. It also doesn't mean that we won't get angry at times, or be disappointed in the other person. When we respect one another, it can readily be seen in our behaviors toward that person. Some behaviors that fall under this category are the same as described in the self-respect section.

11. Limits

Limits need to be respected. We are being disrespectful when we push ahead when someone says she has had enough. There are a number of ways to handle a limit when someone is tired and is no longer willing to continue a discussion. One example is to find out if the person is willing to continue the discussion at a later time; and if so, schedule the discussion for later.

There are times when we are not aware of our own or other people's limits, we may still go to work even if we don't feel well. We may ignore the signs that someone is distracted and move right along sharing our information. Increasing our sensitivity to limits and boundaries will help us in our relationships.

12. Take back your power—depersonalize

There are a variety of ways we can regain power in our relationships. Some can be the following examples:

- We raise our awareness about choices; consequently, reduce the frequency of being a victim.
- We take responsibility.
- We hold people accountable.
- We set appropriate boundaries.
- We respect limits.
- We treat others and ourselves with respect.

Another powerful way that has not been explored is the ability to depersonalize.

- *How often have you been anxious or defensive because you felt that the other person seems to be blaming his or her offensive mood on you?*
- *Have you ever wondered what you might have done to someone and why he or she seems to be so cold and distant?*
- *When someone was rude or abrupt with you, have you taken it personally and been upset?*

Often, we are not aware of how we sound, that we are walking around "with a chip on our shoulder" or that we snap easily. Neither are other people. Half the time, our mood, demeanor, abruptness, or irritation have nothing to do with the person we are interacting with in the moment. Yet we seem to forget that fact when we are on the receiving end of the interaction. Hopefully, raising our overall awareness will help us become more attentive to our choices so that we are "nicer" more often, to be around.

Another idea is to take things less personally. Some ways to help us achieve depersonalization are the following:

- Let's reality test our experience more often when we are affected by someone's mood instead of withdrawing and starting to feel down, or attack, and get into an unnecessary conflict.
- Let's before we react to the other, stop and ask: Am I taking this personal right now?
- Let's remind ourselves that it is not always about us.
- Let's not be reactive; instead, be curious and listen for more information and clues to what might be going on.

a.   Modeling safety/ creating comfort

One of the more profound experiences we can have is when we are on the *giving end* of creating comfort by modeling safety. The safer we feel within ourselves, the more comfort we can give.

Modeling safety can be done through the following:

- Not avoiding conflict
- Approaching difficult topics and taking the risk that we may end up in a conflict
- Holding the trust that we can reach a positive resolution even when we feel out of control
- Holding the other accountable and not being afraid or giving up when met with resistance
- Setting appropriate boundaries in the face of threats
- Taking responsibility for our position and being willing to deal with the consequences
- Being open-minded, flexible, and humble
- Embracing the opportunity to learn and grow
- Reframing the fears of the conflict to gain insight about ourselves and the other person
- Finding the pearls in the conflict and sharing how they can bring us closer together

b.   Preemptive damage control . . . aka strategic plan

Conflict is something we have to endure in life. The more skilled we become at handling conflict, the less power it will have over us. With that in mind, it is ironic that the more trained we become, the less conflict we will have to encounter.

Preemptive damage control or PDC is an important tool to add to our toolbox. It will save us time and needless pain. PDC may consist of the following behaviors:

- Thinking about what we say before we say it
- Committing to not make threats
- Consciously picking an appropriate time and place to have a difficult conversation
- Accepting that resistance, defensiveness, and discomfort are part of the conflict, having clear strategies prepared for how to deal with each one of them, whether it is our own resistance or the other person's defensiveness
- Respecting the power of feelings. Being prepared to provide the right amount of specific type of support needed to prevent the feelings from being acted out
- Not underestimating the force of impulses. Learning to recognize the signs of an impulse before they are acted out
- Learning to identify choices
- Defining rules for ourselves ahead of time for how we shall behave when we feel angry, furious, disappointed, or irritated
- Pledging to remain issue oriented during conflicts and formulate clear strategies to be able to do so prior to entering into conflicts
- Gaining knowledge of how to be able to think objectively when under emotional stress
- Getting prepared up front to identify and confront underlying needs

We will be more self-confident if we are prepared before a conflict ensues. The less startled we become when the feelings flood us, or when the impulses fight to take over, the more choices we can make in the moment.

The more choices we can access, the more logic we can use.
The more logic we can access, the more choices we will have!

Feelings and impulses occur in human interactions. It is *what we do* with the feelings and the impulses that will make the difference.

We can choose to be Impulse Driven or Strategy Motivated!

PDC training allows us to gain back what is rightfully ours during conflicts—the right to choose before we act!

When the Conflict is Over

The work isn't done because the conflict is over. To be able to move forward without developing resentment, you need to address yours and the other person's needs. You also need to reestablish an emotional connection between the two of you.

✓ Provide and ask for feedback.

The more you communicate about what took place, how it happened, why it may have happened, and how you can prevent it from escalating and happening in a similar way again, the greater chance you will close loopholes that otherwise will go undetected and fester until a similar issue takes place again. When you ask for feedback and provide it in return, you show the other person that you care about what happened and that, being a role model, you are oriented toward being proactive and solution oriented. The following are examples of feedback in your communication:

- Identifying two things that you got out of the conflict that brought you closer to the other person
- Asking the other person to give you two examples of what she learned about herself, you, and your relationship
- Asking her to give you two suggestions of how she would like you to better handle a similar issue in the future
- Telling her that you value her and her commitment to your relationship
- Asking her to identify three needs of hers that you satisfied during or after the conflict

✓ Show your commitment to reconcile and secure a commitment from her.

A frequent fear when you are having a conflict is that the relationship will be over. That fear can be resolved once you verbalize your commitment to the relationship. As you share your commitment to reconcile the relationship, you also need to obtain a commitment from her that she shares those goals with you. This commitment is an important aspect because it helps salvage the relationship by shifting the focus from a negative to a positive objective that you both are committed to. It is important to find out what her intent is if *she is not* committed to reconciliation and resolution.

✓ Address resentment.

Discuss what she resents now that the conflict is over. Explore areas further that you suspect may still be unresolved and get closure before you end the interaction. Agreeing on how the two of you will handle negative feelings and leftover thoughts is crucial to prevent lingering resentment.

✓ Make an agreement of how you will handle conflict in the future.

Set up ground rules for how you will handle future conflicts. It is more effective to make agreements when you are calm and resolved than when you are in the midst of a conflict. When you have strategies in place, it is easier to implement them during a stressful conflict. Some ground rules that you can agree on are the following:

- Not to call each other names
- Not to use threats
- Not to use physical violence
- Not to run out of the room and slam the door
- Not to use the F Word
- Not to use other profanities
- Not to yell with the intent to intimidate or bully
- To listen

- To not interrupt
- To hold each other accountable
- To track changes of subject
- To be curious

Establishing ground rules that work for you and your relationship is an important part of functioning more effectively in your relationships. Ground rules vary depending on your values and boundaries. Negotiating ground rules can be a challenging, yet rewarding experience. It gives you an opportunity to gain more knowledge about yourself, the other person, and your relationship.

✓ Check back on the progress.

It is a good idea to check back intermittently to find out if there are issues that are accumulating that may lead to conflict. Sometimes we may solve a conflict and think that we have resolution, yet the other person is withdrawn and distant a few days later. When that happens, it is often easier, in the moment, to avoid asking questions about the behavior, hoping it will go away. In the long run, it saves time and aggravation to take the bull by the horn and find out and deal with the issues directly. Anger might surface after some time has passed, if we weren't in touch with certain needs during or immediately after the conflict. That anger might need to be discussed and shared before the person is ready to let it go, requiring additional time to reflect on the past conflict. You may think that is taking a step backward; however, to avoid resentment this is sometimes needed.

It may sound crazy to suggest that you do something constructive when you have been outraged with the other person a moment ago. However, it is a crucial step to take to help reestablish the relationship as well as help set the foundation for how comfortable and secure you will be in dealing with conflict in the future.

Assessing Your Relationship with Conflict

What kind of relationship do you have with conflict?
Which position do you take in relationship to conflict?

Defeated, Strategic, or Acted Out

Defeated	Strategic	Acted Out
Unconscious	Conscious	Unconscious/Semi-Conscious
Emotional Reaction	Cognitive Response	Emotional Reaction
Giving Up	Looking for Solutions	Committing to Sabotage
Disempowered	Empowered	False Sense of Power
Passive Position	Active Position	Active Position

Generally, we are not making a conscious choice when we take the defeated position. More commonly, it is an emotional reaction that comes from a place of hopelessness and helplessness. As such, it is grounded in passivity. Likewise, when we come from an acted-out position, we react unconsciously when our emotions are triggered. We tend to be actively destructive in this position, which is the main difference between the acted out and the defeated positions.

When we take a strategic position, we come from a place of logic and reason. We use our cognitive resources and are committed to finding solutions by evaluating options and creating strategies to deal with obstacles.

If your experiences with conflicts are negative, you will be more apt to avoid them. Your chances of success are unlikely if you feel intimidated by the thought of conflict and allow that to negatively affect you. You are at the mercy of the discomfort if you are inclined to allow your discomfort to affect your commitment in dealing with conflict. If you tend to feel more powerful after a conflict because you have been successful at bullying the other into "doing it your way," then you may be inclined to initiate conflict for the wrong reasons. If you "crave" conflict because it makes you "feel alive" then you might create more drama in your life than is necessary and productive. You may do everything in your power to stay away from conflicts if you believe that when there is a conflict it will end tragically, e.g., divorce or great loss on some other level.

Are you passive during a conflict? If so, why?

Exploring your beliefs, experiences, expectations, needs, fears, preconceived ideas, faulty judgments, and choices, or lack thereof, will help you accurately assess your relationship with conflict.

18

Feelings, the Untamed Beasts Within

Feeling *can be described as an emotion or sensitivity. A feeling when unqualified in the context refers to any subjective reaction, pleasant, or unpleasant, that one may have to a situation and/or a person, and usually connotes* an absence of reasoning.

Feelings *are generally intertwined intricately with impulses. An* impulse *can be described as an internal, sudden driving force to act without premeditation.*

Assets and Obstacles

When is a feeling an asset and when does it become an obstacle?

It usually depends on the following:

- The nature of the feeling
- The context of the situation
- The awareness of the need linked to the feeling
- The ability to contain the feeling
- The capability to access logic in the face of a feeling

Various feelings can be divided into three categories. In category number one, there are feelings such as joy and happiness. Since they are commonly associated with pleasure, we will call them the *Positive Fs*. In category number two, we can find feelings like anger, frustration, disappointment, rage, fury, envy, and jealousy. The feelings in this category will be called the *Negative Fs,* since they are frequently correlated to destructiveness. We can find pain, sadness, hurt, disappointment, and discomfort in the third category. Feelings in this category will be designated by the term *Acceptable Fs*.

As we grow up, we learn that anger can make others uncomfortable. Pain may get us attention. People may think less of us when we are envious or jealous. When we are frustrated, we should find ways to deal with it. Others may be more prone to treat us like victims when we exhibit pain or hurt than if we are angry or jealous. We may also more readily see ourselves as victims and behave as such when we experience an *Acceptable F*.

It doesn't matter which category the feeling is from. *We become victims of our feelings when the feeling "takes over" and is acted out in reactive and destructive behaviors that then impact our lives negatively.*

Generally, when we have a feeling there is an impulse to react. When there is no time and space between the behaviors that follow the feeling, the behavior often becomes reactive, and destructive.

> *The feeling is not "bad." It is* what we do with it *that can either be harmful or conducive to our relationships.*

The Outer Shell of Gain can be one of the reasons that keep us from changing our behaviors. We see only what we get in the moment when our focus is on the gain. Unfortunately, we don't realize that what we gain in the moment might have a negative impact on our relationships over a longer period of time. Some illustrations can be seen in the following diagram:

Negative Fs

	Feeling and Impulse to React	Reactive Destructive Behavior →	The Outer Shell of Gain →	Negative Expense →
CATEGORY II *Negative F's*	Anger, Rage Fury	We may intimidate. We might scream and threaten. We may break things.	We get what we want.	We alienate ourselves from others. Other people are scared of us.
	Frustration	We may give up.	The feeling is temporarily alleviated.	We may fail to reach our goals.
	Envy, Jealousy	We might bad-mouth and/or attack.	We are given a false sense of power and control.	We are not being trusted.
CATEGORY III *Acceptable F's*	Emotional Pain & Hurt	We may withdraw or lash out.	Others may give us more attention. We may feel special. We might postpone accountability.	Others may experience us as self-involved. We might end up in an unproductive conflict.
	Sadness	We might isolate. We may become depressed.	Others may give us support. Others may expect less from us.	People may feel uncomfortable around us and avoid us. We might not be able to function well in our lives.
	Disappointment	We might criticize without just cause. We may sulk and become punitive.	We support the illusion that we don't have to deal constructively with our disappointment.	We remain unconscious and victims of our disappointment.
	Discomfort	We may change the subject. We might terminate the interaction.	We get to avoid our feeling in the moment.	The original issue that caused the discomfort doesn't get resolved.

A prerequisite for enhancing our relationships and improving ourselves is the commitment and follow-through in learning how to *manage our feelings better, i.e., containing our feelings.* When we insert *Reason* and *Objectivity* in the time and the space between the feeling/impulse to react, proactive behaviors can follow. Those proactive behaviors change the negatives into positives; when that takes place, the *Outer Shell of Gain* changes into positive short-term *and* long-term gain. The long-term negative expenses vanish. See the following diagram:

Negative F's 2

CATEGORY II — Negative F's

CATEGORY III — Acceptable F's

REASON & OBJECTIVITY

Feeling	Responsive Constructive Behavior	Positive Gain
Feeling and Impulse to React		
Anger, Rage Fury	We can share our anger constructively by stating that we are angry, identify the reason and then make a suggestion for how to move forward to reach a resolution.	We can feel proud of ourselves for having dealt with a difficult situation in an intelligent and responsible way. Hence, raise our self-esteem.
Frustration	We can evaluate the situation. If it is appropriate to yell out loud, do so, while simultaneously communicate that we are frustrated.	We can feel good about having taken responsibility for our frustration by stating it clearly so the other person wasn't left not knowing what was going on with us.
Envy, Jealousy	We can acknowledge the feeling to ourselves and ask ourselves what we might need. If we need some reassurance, we can ask for it proactively.	We can feel empowered. Hence, the trust we feel for ourselves has been increased.
Emotional Pain & Hurt	We can reach out and ask for support.	Others may provide the support we need to move beyond our pain and hurt.
Sadness	We can share our experience with someone we trust.	Others may provide the support we need to move beyond our pain and hurt.
Disappointment	We can realize that we are disappointed and then express our disappointment constructively.	We can feel empowered and confident that we can handle our disappointment constructively and experience having choices.
Discomfort	We can become aware of our discomfort, and decide that we will continue to deal with the situation anyway.	We can feel more self confident and determined to reach a resolution.

Feelings like joy and happiness tend to interfere less in our relationships. Unless we are so caught up in our own emotion that we are insensitive to someone else's situation, or are expressing our joy inappropriately, people often like to be around us when we are happy. These feelings result in other positive rewards such as increasing closeness and achieving a hopeful and optimistic outlook on life.

We learn about feelings from our own experiences and from watching others as we grow up. Many of our understandings about feelings and how they affect our lives are unconscious and have never been discussed. We may have been told not to be *angry* if the time and the place weren't appropriate according to our parents. The problem was that they may have failed to tell us what we were supposed to do with that anger that was still stuck in our little bodies.

We might have been grounded after we had thrown our tennis racket across the court, when our *frustrations* got the best of us. Yet we may not have received any guidance of how to better deal with our frustrations in the future.

When we teased our little sister because we were *jealous*, our parents may have reprimanded us. At the time, it was never thought that we might have benefited from getting support to understand the feeling and receiving some reassurance. Our parents may have told us that being *envious* was bad. So, when the feeling came up again, we might have tried to hide it because we didn't want to be "bad." Yet the feeling was still there. What to do with it was unknown.

When we were five years old and told our parents that we were going to hurt someone who had been mean to us, our parents may have said that was wrong. How could we be expected to differentiate between the fact that retaliating is not the answer, and that it is wrong while our feeling is a normal response, and, as such, must be right? It is appropriate to have a reaction when someone hurts us. When our feelings and desired behavior seemed to be congruent to us, yet we were told that what we wanted to do was wrong; a natural deduction would have been that the feeling must be wrong as well. Since our feeling was so strong and we were so young (that) we couldn't separate the feeling from who we were, we concluded we were "wrong" and "bad". Maybe our parents didn't stop to find out how angry or hurt we really were. Maybe they didn't give us some alternative ways to dispose of our feelings in a constructive way. Instead, we were left with it inside. In addition, we were left feeling even more confused about what is right and wrong, good, and bad, and how our feelings play into the situation.

The messages, whether verbally given or indirectly conveyed, were often understood as certain feelings are "bad" and should be avoided. Other feelings may get us what we want whether it is attention, reassurance, or being treated special. However, rarely were we given the tools to understand our feelings and the needs linked to them.

Anger can be an obstacle or an asset. When anger is suppressed and denied, it becomes an obstacle since it keeps us in the dark, while it still controls a large portion of our actions. Anger can be used as an asset when it serves as a driving force to support us to excel. *"They think I can't make it, I'll show them."*

Reason and objectivity are needed to contain a feeling. Another component is the ability to identify the need linked to the feeling.

When we feel pain, the need linked to the feeling might be the following:

- The need to talk
- The need to get perspective
- The need to be held

When we feel anger, the need linked to the feeling might be these:

- The need to be challenged
- The need to be contained by the other person
- The need to be validated

When we feel jealous, the need linked to the feeling might be these:

- The need to reality test
- The need to be reassured
- The need to ask questions

When we respond as victims to the feeling, we tend to engage in reactive, destructive behaviors. We become empowered and can experience having choices once we realize what we need.

Feelings are not bad; they are a normal part of our every day lives. However, because we often don't have a strategy to deal effectively with our feelings, we tend to suppress, deny, and act out our feelings destructively. We fear our own feelings; and when other people express their feelings, we become uncomfortable and reactive.

Typically, specific feelings are not identified when we are communicating; creating a guessing game. The less conscious and comfortable we are with the feeling, the less control we will have over our reactions.

Disappointment might be hidden under an array of criticism. Instead of stating, *"I am disappointed in you,"* we may say, *"How could you have done that? I can't believe you would be that stupid."*

Anger might be disguised under a cloud of quiet threat. Instead of stating, *"I am really angry with you."* We might *say nothing and only give a long stern look of disapproval then turn our backs.*

Jealousy might show up as an attack. Instead of saying, *"I need some attention and reassurance from you right now,"* we might state, *"Your behavior is so rude. I can't believe I'm even going out with you."*

Emotional hurt can be concealed under sarcasm. Instead of saying, *"I want to let you know that I am hurt by what you did. I would appreciate if you would give me an explanation, and then an apology if you agree that your behavior was insensitive and hurtful,"* we might state, *"I guess I'm not important to you. How silly of me to have thought I was."*

Often, we're not even aware what the feeling is. Our behavior that follows is swift and instinctual. The fear of being vulnerable and risking humiliation if we state what we feel also supports reactive, destructive behavior. Realistically, it is riskier to continue to act out then it is to be vulnerable.

A feeling is an asset when it enhances our experience.

Developing Healthy Strategies

What can we do when we feel so angry that we are ready to explode?

If our anger is so potent that we have difficulties containing it, the responsible choice can be to take some "time out." We can use our commitment to managing our feelings better and state, *"I am so angry right now that the responsible thing for me to do is to take some time out, and then come back and continue this discussion with you later. It is important to me that we resolve this, so I would appreciate your support in me having some time out right now."* Then one can leave the interaction and go to a separate area and deal with the anger by hitting some pillows with a tennis racquet, for example. Or an old phone book can be designated to use when angry. Ripping the pages apart can often be a helpful and a constructive outlet for anger.

BIRGITTA GREGORY, PH.D.

It may sound unrealistic to be able to make a calm statement at a time when our "blood is boiling." Nevertheless, it becomes easier to do once we have practiced this new technique over a longer period of time.

The key is to keep our focus on the priority.

What is the priority?

1. *To be managed by our feelings*
2. *Or to manage our feelings*

If the anger is strong but we are able to bring in reason and logic to help *separate the issue from the feeling*, then we can make the decision to express our feeling in the moment or postpone our expression to a time that is more appropriate. To take our anger seriously, and recognize the value of creating settings, where we can release our anger is an imperative step in becoming comfortable with anger. Once we have practiced how to make choices when under emotional distress, learned how to maintain the focus on the healthy priority, and mastered the skill to put the feeling away *in the moment*, then we can continue the discussion and reach a solution. Anger that is not fully contained or stored away temporarily may interfere in the continued dialogue by spilling over in our indirect and nonverbal communication and can be as damaging as a direct outburst of anger.

The Power of Time
When We Stop and Think
"Slowing Down"

To stop and think can be profoundly effective when dealing with unruly feelings.

Sometimes we don't even have to make a complete stop if we slow down. In many parts of this book, you have read the advice, "Slow down!" It cannot be stressed enough how important this tool is to better manage our feelings.

Something natural happens when we slow down. Space is created for the following:

- Perspective
- Peace

- Curiosity
- Trust
- Self-confidence
- Solutions
- Creativity
- Learning to occur

When to Express Acceptable or Negative Fs; When Not To?

The time and the place matter! At times, we state that we "just couldn't stop ourselves from reacting." Yet, other times when we are in a public situation, we may have been able to control our feelings and not have reacted. Or maybe we at least had a less volatile reaction.

It is not a question of whether we should express the feeling or not, it is a question of whether we should express the feeling in the moment or not. Feelings need to be expressed. It is when they are suppressed, repressed, and denied that they overpower our relationships and our fears are exploited. Express the feeling freely when it can enhance the situation, and promote growth and closeness. Make a choice to postpone the expression until later, when it is likely that it will do more damage than good. It is imperative to attend to your feeling at a later time so that it doesn't get stored up somewhere in your body and cause trouble in the future.

Have you done an inventory lately of the relationship you have with your feelings?

Some questions that can be helpful to ask yourself:

- What kind of relationship do I have with my anger?
- On a scale from 1-10 (10 being the most comfortable and 1 being the least comfortable), how comfortable am I with my own anger?
- On a scale from 1-10 (10 being the most comfortable), how comfortable am I with other people's anger?
- What thoughts come up for me when I think of my own jealousy?
- When I feel hurt by someone, what do I typically do?
- How do I communicate when I am disappointed?
- Am I generally aware of my own discomfort?
- What can be some situations that may make me uncomfortable?

- If I were to take my frustrations out on someone, what would be some ways I would do that?
- Identify four ways I can improve my relationship with my feelings and raise my awareness.

Once we have a conscious relationship with our own feelings, we can improve our relationships with other people and their feelings. When a feeling is interfering, we will be more sensitive to it. Other people and our own feelings will manipulate us less frequently. Overall, we will be less reactive and more proactive.

19

The Power of Curiosity: Transforming Our Interactions

Curiosity can be described as the desire to learn and know.

Curiosity is a wonderful quality that can be seen in children. They can't get enough of it. Starting as early as they can, they curiously explore their surroundings. They embark on their excursions, eagerly touching, tasting, and feeling anything they can get their little hands on. Meanwhile, their parents run as fast as they can to catch up, at times in shear fear, hold their breath, and quickly realize that the word no will be used more than they ever could have imagined. As the children grow older, their curiosity expands. With an exciting vocabulary, they ask one question after another. They never seem to get tired of asking *"why"* as the parents finally run out of answers.

As time goes on, the child's questions begin to be more cumbersome than cute, and the parents run out of patience. *"Because I say so"* becomes a standard phrase for the exhausted parent. The more the child learns, the more curious she seems to be. At times, her curiosity is inappropriate and outright embarrassing for the parents. More often than not, the parents start to avoid the child's questions, and the delight turns into a fight.

Soon, the child has learned that asking questions can make the adults uncomfortable, embarrassed, and sometimes even angry. The child concludes that it is better to be less curious and more accommodating, less curious and more inhibited, less curious and more complacent. Curiosity is becoming something that gets the child in trouble. It is often the cause for unpleasant experiences and it produces uncomfortable feelings. Feeling like you are annoying to the people you love starts to hurt.

Whether it is at home or in school, the adults get irritated when the child asks questions that the adults clearly think are insignificant or irrelevant to the interaction.

Many unspoken yet glaring messages are sent to the growing child. There is one that stands out from the rest: *"Stop being so curious!"*

During adolescence, the roles are reversed. The parents ask questions and their inquisitiveness annoys the teenager who feels intruded upon. The once spontaneous and curious child has becomes a withdrawn and unavailable teenager.

Where did the curiosity go?

It didn't leave altogether. Some of the child's curiosity became suppressed and beaten down by the rejection and other negative responses that were given over the years. Some became redirected naturally. The parents didn't intentionally try to suppress their children's curiosity; on the contrary, so many times it was out of the wish to protect the child that the parents said "no" and "stop."

- *How can a child's endless curiosity be redirected appropriately as she moves through her various developmental stages?*
- *What kind of tools does a parent need to nurture and protect a child's curiosity?*
- *What kind of knowledge does a parent need to have about where her own curiosity went to be able to be a role model to the child once again accessing her curiosity and share the joy it brings?*

Unfortunately, the innocence, the joy, and the never-ending appetite for learning that were so remarkably connected to the child's curiosity often can't be found again. Instead, an all-knowing, close-minded, often cynical, and defensive attitude replaces it.

But it is not too late! We may have to work a little harder at finding it again, rebuilding what was once there naturally.

When we habitually interrupt to give our version or stop listening because we know what is coming, we have to stop ourselves.

Slow Down

Instead of stating that someone's statement is ludicrous, we can implement some genuine curiosity:

- What does the person mean?
- Am I missing something?

- What kinds of experiences led the person to make this conclusion?
- Did I draw the wrong conclusions; do I need to ask more questions?
- How can I learn from what was said?
- How can I grow from this interaction?
- Instead of raising our voice and attacking the person because he is acting a certain way, we can take a moment and introduce some curiosity.

There are so many opportunities throughout each day where we can practice bringing in curiosity to our lives again. When we react, we can be curious about what we can learn about ourselves from our reaction. We can make it a habit to ask a number of questions each day, to practice. It is essential that the questions and the curiosity are genuine. If our questions come from a place of sarcasm, anger, or superiority and are lacking in an authentic interest to learn, the result will be disappointing to all involved. When we forget our curiosity and feel hopeless, we must remember it took many years to lose our spontaneously curious minds. As with most areas discussed in this book, it takes dedication and practice to improve our lives.

We readily accept that we need to work hard in school to get an education. Later, we need to work hard at our job to make money. *Why would it be any different in other areas of our lives, like in our relationships? Why would we need to work any less at improving our relationships?* It is an illusion to believe that we will automatically have the talents and skills needed to be successful in our relationships without hard work and a strong commitment to learning.

Curiosity is a natural resource that each of us has. It would be a shame to waste such a valuable asset, simply by being unaware of its existence and the power it has to transform our relationships from being stuck to being liberated.

Gary and Elisabeth

Gary and Elisabeth are in the middle of an argument when Gary says, *"I am always wrong."*

"No you're not, I didn't say that. That's not what I meant," Elisabeth responds with great frustration.

"What's the point?" Gary continues as he shrugs his shoulders and looks at her indifferently.

Again, Elisabeth insists he is not always wrong. She is working so hard to convince Gary.

What happened? *Elisabeth seems defensive? Why? What happened to her curiosity about his comment? Why did Gary make the statement? Was it an indirect attempt to receive reassurance? Or maybe it was a try at diverting the attention away from the subject at hand? Did Gary feel threatened by Elisabeth? Does he, in fact, believe he is always wrong? Does Gary believe Elisabeth thinks he's always wrong? Where do they go from here?*

In the example above, notice how Gary made one comment where he managed to shift the responsibility of the interaction to Elisabeth. She, in turn, became defensive. She instantaneously took on the responsibility to make Gary feel better by assuring him that the comment *he* had made wasn't true. Elisabeth hadn't said, *"Gary, you are always wrong!"* Yet she immediately tried to convince him that she didn't think he was always wrong. *Why?* Maybe she did think he was wrong in this discussion, and felt guilty. Using curiosity instead of being reactive would have supported the two of them to stay on track. It would have been an opportunity to explore the reason and needs behind Gary's comment and find answers to the questions above.

Commonly, after spending some time arguing without getting resolution, we get frustrated, disappointed, or angry. When we don't deal with those feelings, it is often easier to make a comment that may elicit a response from the other person that will "make us feel better." The problem with that form of interaction is that the "feeling better" isn't a genuine feeling that will last. We have manipulated the other person to get our needs met, and it negatively affects the respect in the relationship. Curiosity helps us understand the real need, reason, request, or demand behind the statement. It helps us to lovingly and patiently hold each other accountable and stay on course. Curiosity helps us to stay open-minded and prepares us to explore new areas.

> When our curiosity to learn and understand is sincere,
> the joy expands, and new opportunities are presented.

Using Curiosity to Heighten Your Sensitivity

Sensitivity can be described as having or showing keen sensibilities, by being highly perceptive or responsive intellectually and emotionally, and receiving as well as responding readily and intensely to stimuli from inside ourselves and from outside objects.

Being sensitive can have many meanings. Being sensitive may mean that the person easily gets offended or hurt by others. That is not the type of sensitivity we are encouraging. The sensitivity we suggest heightening is our ability to recognize the hidden dynamics that affect the success of our relationships. Being able to perceive the feeling, recognize the faulty judgment, and identify the preconceived idea can help us achieve that. Heightening our sensitivity also means being able to translate emotional signals and utilize curiosity to transform our interactions. Example after example has shown us how we can cause others and ourselves unnecessary pain and suffering due to our lack of sensitivity. Heightened sensitivity is intimately connected to increased awareness.

Here are ways to raise awareness and heighten sensitivity:

- Make a conscious decision to pay attention to the unconscious messages that are being sent by observing body language and choice of words.
- Make a commitment to slow down. Anytime we feel frustrated, take a breath and count to ten before we move on with our agenda.
- Spend more time listening to what is being said and to what is not being said.
- Pay attention to when the other person is resistant and change our behavior accordingly.
- Track the changing of the subject and be curious about the underlying reason for doing so.

There are a number of questions that can be helpful to ask yourself from time to time:

- How would you describe someone being sensitive?
- In general, do you think you are perceptive?
- When you start to experience discomfort due to mixed messages, are you sensitive to the experience generally?
- What three steps can you take to become more sensitive and aware?
- What can be some potential drawbacks of having increased sensitivity?

With heightened sensitivity and raised awareness comes increased responsibility. For example, if we do not witness someone being hit, there is nothing we can do; whether our lack of ability to see is due to being unconscious or due to a physical impairment. However, if we do witness someone being hit, we are faced with some choices. We can look the other way and walk away without doing anything. We can continue and watch the person being beaten, do nothing about it, and then walk away. We can quickly look away and sink into denial, telling ourselves nothing happened. We can rationalize that it was none of our business; so we stay out of it, or we can intervene.

The more sensitive we become, the less we will be able to use our defenses and remain unconscious. On one hand, heightened sensitivity can bring more turmoil, pain, and stress because we see things we didn't recognize before. On the other hand, even with those consequences, it seems like our bodies can become more peaceful knowing what is going on and understanding that we have choices. The price of heightened sensitivity is well worth the cost.

20

Agreements and Follow-Through

> Agreements *can be described as the act of agreeing and being in harmony. It is an arrangement, a contract between two or more people, or with yourself.*
>
> Follow-through *can be described as "to continue and complete an action."*

Making more conscious, well-thought-through agreements and following through are behaviors that can significantly improve relationships. Purely reaching awareness without taking action can frequently be more frustrating than helpful.

We can make agreements with others. However, unless we have mastered upholding the agreements that we make with ourselves, there is a great risk that we will be less committal to others as well.

How we follow through with our agreements tells us volumes about the respect we have for ourselves. What may seem to be an insignificant agreement can turn out to have a huge effect on our self-esteem.

What messages do we send to ourselves *about* ourselves, when we nonchalantly break an agreement we made *to* ourselves?

- We are not important.
- It is not important to make agreements.
- The agreement is not important.
- What we say has no meaning.
- We don't have to follow through if we don't want to.
- We can change our minds any time we want and pretend there will be no consequences.
- The agreement didn't matter in the first place.
- We are flaky.
- We can't be trusted.

- We easily compromise our integrity.
- We don't have the ability to follow through.
- We are not capable of upholding an agreement.
- Our desires and impulses run our lives.
- We are powerless.
- We are victims of our needs in the moment.
- We are incapable of holding a vision.
- We don't want to do the work if it isn't easy and comfortable.
- We are not willing to take responsibility for our thoughts and actions.
- We will follow through next time (knowing full well that the prognosis for that is poor).
- We only honor agreements that we feel like honoring in the moment.
- An agreement can be changed anytime for any reason.
- Nobody even knew we made the agreement with ourselves, so it isn't as though we are hurting anybody when we break it.

There are so many terrific rationalizations and justifications that we can use when we break an agreement. The tragic part is that we don't realize we are breaking the trust we have for ourselves each time we break an agreement that we made with ourselves. In addition, when we break an agreement with another person, we seriously damage the trust they have in us. The messages we send to the other when we break an agreement are similar to the messages we sent ourselves. Those messages undermine the closeness and respect we feel both for ourselves and in relationship to the other.

Don't Make an Agreement

That's right; we should not make an agreement if we are under these conditions:

- Feel pressured to do so without taking full responsibility for agreeing
- Are trying to pacify someone
- Have no intention of keeping the agreement
- Give in to get out of having a discussion
- Give up because we think it doesn't matter what we say anyway
- Think that it is an unrealistic agreement
- Haven't taken the time to think through the ramifications of the agreement

- Are agreeing to avoid the discomfort of questioning the value of the agreement
- Don't know how to make and keep an agreement
- Are scared of questioning the other about his or her intentions
- Don't like the agreement but don't know how to negotiate a better one
- Are being threatened or under duress
- Assume that we have an agreement without checking in with the other to make sure we are on the same page

There are many more reasons why, at times, we should not make an agreement but do so anyway. It can be useful to take some time and explore what other reasons there might be. An agreement should be taken seriously. It needs to be respected and adhered to when made; otherwise, don't make it.

Learning How to Make Effective Agreements

There are a number of valuable questions to ask ourselves before we enter into an agreement. *Why, what, when, where, how, and with whom* should we make an agreement?

1. *Why* should I make this agreement?

    a. Will it benefit our relationship?
    b. If I do or don't make the agreement, what are the negative consequences that may occur?
    c. Will this agreement promote closeness and intimacy?

2. *What* is the purpose of the agreement?

    a. Are we making the agreement to ensure follow-through?
    b. Is an agreement going to support us?
    c. Is the type of agreement we are discussing appropriate?

3. *When* should I make the agreement?

    a. Have we had enough time to explore the pros and cons?
    b. Am I feeling pressured to make the agreement?
    c. Is time of the essence? Will it make a difference if we make the agreement now or in two hours?

4. *Where* should I make the agreement?

    a. Does the place where we make the agreement make a difference?
    b. If yes, how so?
    c. Do I respond differently if I make an agreement in a neutral place or in my home?

5. *How* should I make the agreement?

    a. Should we shake hands?
    b. Should I write a summary of my understanding of the agreement and give a copy to the other person and keep one for my records?
    c. Should I write up the agreement and request that we both sign it?

6. *Who* is this person that I am going to make the agreement with?

    a. Do I trust this person?
    b. Do I have previous experience with this person in relationship to making agreements?
    c. Based upon what I know about the person, should I make sure the agreement is made in writing, or is a verbal agreement appropriate?

It is important to get clarity on expectations when we make agreements. *What do we expect and what does the other person expect?* Expectations can be tricky. When they are unspoken, they often tend to complicate our interactions. Feelings like disappointment, anger, frustration, and discomfort can cause disruption if they aren't recognized and contained.

The Difference between an Understanding and an Agreement

Nancy and Paul have an understanding. Nancy's understanding is that it is reasonable to complete the task she has been handed by Paul in three days. Paul's understanding is that it should take no longer than two days to get it done.

Nancy and Paul don't have an agreement. However, they do have an understanding. The problem is that Nancy's understanding is quite different from Paul's and vice versa. Because Paul thinks his understanding is correct, this doesn't mean that he has any grounds to hold Nancy accountable when he shows up at her desk two days later, expecting her to have the job done, but it is not completed yet.

Paul may be disappointed in Nancy. He may be angry with her. But, unless they have discussed their understandings, clarified the differences, and worked out an agreement on how to handle the discrepancies, neither one of them has any grounds to hold the other accountable.

By not making clearly defined agreements, we are setting ourselves up for unnecessary disappointments, frustrations, and misunderstandings. Making a habit out of using more detailed and *clarifying* forms of communication can increase our effectiveness and support constructive interactions.

To transform an understanding into an agreement by reality testing can be done through the following:

- Repeating back to the other what you heard
- Asking the other to repeat back to you if you are unclear about his or her position
- Specifying the nature of the agreement and getting closure by asking something like this: *Are you willing to make an agreement with me to go to the bank and pay the bill in person by Thursday of next week?*
- Emphasizing the word agreement by using the word each time you make an agreement. Don't shy away from the term because you feel like it is too formal or sounds contrived
- Specifying some steps that will be taken to ensure follow-through of the agreement
- Following up to make sure the agreement has been fulfilled, as a measure to build trust, create continuity, and set up a framework of accountability

Negotiating and Compromising

Negotiating an agreement can be an exciting and rewarding experience. It can also be a painstakingly difficult experience. There are a number of steps that can be taken to strengthen our negotiation skills:

- Let's prepare ourselves.
- Let's gather information.
- Let's evaluate the situation.
- Let's keep our intent clean and clear.

- Let's pay attention to attempts to manipulate; whether it is our own or the other person's emotions that are the culprits.
- Let's stay centered by using logic and reason.
- Let's keep a commitment to create win-win solutions.

Asking ourselves the following questions to raise our awareness is another tool:

- Why do I think some people feel uncomfortable negotiating?
- How do I feel about the negotiation process?
- In the past, what have been my experiences in this area?
- Do I generally come away from a negotiation experience feeling good, bad, or indifferent?
- How can I take the win or lose out of the negotiation process?
- Do I often feel intimidated, challenged, curious, scared, uncomfortable, elated, or stimulated when someone approaches me to negotiate?
- What are three strengths that I bring to the negotiation table?
- What are three weaknesses that lessen my effectiveness during negotiations?
- What are some factors that may negatively affect negotiations?
- Have I had negotiation situations in the past that I think have helped my self-esteem; if so, how?

Sometimes we enter a negotiation without even knowing it. During those times, we may have felt an inordinate amount of pressure, but could not identify why. We may have left the interaction feeling taken advantage of.

Life is full of negotiations and compromises. Clarifying our intent can change the dynamics when we negotiate. Likewise, using critical thinking and recognizing our own value can have profound affect.

Following Through: Realistic Versus Overambitious Agreements

Sometimes we get so excited in the moment that we make an agreement that we later realize was overambitious. We didn't take into consideration the time involved or the amount of work that it entailed. When we agree to do something that we can't or won't follow through with, we set ourselves up for failure. This is a sure way to damage trust and let people down. When we make an agreement, it is helpful if we evaluate realistically if we are able to follow through. If the end result is breaking an agreement, we lose, whether it is due to a lack of consciousness or a lack of commitment to taking the time needed to make an intelligent, well-thought-through choice prior to making the agreement.

Sometimes we make an agreement with someone, yet realize that the chances of her following through are unlikely. The person's track record for follow-through might be poor. We might have made numerous agreements previously where a pattern of making unrealistic agreements can be seen. Again, this is a losing situation.

We can best support others and ourselves by using reason and logic when we make agreements. As much as we want the agreement, unless it is realistic, we are only setting ourselves up for disappointment later. Knowing the difference between a realistic and overambitious agreement will significantly affect the success and follow-through.

21

So Many Questions, So Little Time

If there is only one question we get to ask, let it be,
"What is your intent?"

There are so many areas in a relationship that can be explored further.
The knowledge that can be gained is immense and the questions we can ask
are endless.

In reviewing some of the concepts presented so far, they can be summarized
as follows:

- ✓ Heightening sensitivity and increasing awareness
- ✓ Being curious
- ✓ Recognizing choices
- ✓ Identifying feelings as they happen
- ✓ Slowing down the process
- ✓ Being proactive not reactive
- ✓ Capitalizing on our strengths and improving our weaknesses
- ✓ Asking for help, support when realizing limitations
- ✓ Compromising and negotiating agreements
- ✓ Being authentic
- ✓ Watching out for blame and lingering resentment
- ✓ Linking curiosity and an open mind to transformation
- ✓ Responsibility and accountability: the answers to freedom from victimhood
- ✓ Maintaining perspective and objectivity
- ✓ Becoming comfortable with feelings
- ✓ Separating fears from gut instinct
- ✓ Containing feelings and impulses to react
- ✓ Knowing our needs

- ✓ Giving reassurance
- ✓ Setting boundaries
- ✓ Staying away from power and control traps
- ✓ Becoming a role model of self-respect
- ✓ Committing to receptivity
- ✓ Recognizing the support of using logic with the absence of emotionalism
- ✓ Being alert to changes of the subject
- ✓ Separating the issue from the personality
- ✓ Steering clear of manipulations
- ✓ When in doubt use the "1-10 scale"
- ✓ Giving permission to learn and be "wrong"
- ✓ *Accepting* that change takes time
- ✓ Appreciating the value of feedback and reality testing
- ✓ Developing strategies
- ✓ Maintaining perspective
- ✓ Knowing your boundaries and reinforcing them as needed
- ✓ Interpreting situations in context not in isolation
- ✓ It takes practice and patience!

There are so many things to keep track of in relationships that, at times, it can feel quite overwhelming. That's when maintaining perspective reaches a new meaning. However long it has taken us to learn what we have learned so far, it seems reasonable to expect that new learning and behavioral changes will take some time to integrate and implement. It is unlikely that we'll do it *perfectly,* simply because we have awareness greater than before. With that in mind

be kind, be gentle, and most of all, be curious!

Communication Map in Progress

Inventory

It is valuable to assess your skills in the area of communication and review your personal characteristics when you are raising your awareness. An inventory can help crystallize factors that influence your interactions.

Communication Goals: Strengths and Weaknesses

List three goals, six strengths, and six weaknesses that you are aware of that can impact your communication.

My Goals are

1. _____
   _____
   _____
   _____

2. _____
   _____
   _____
   _____

3. _____
   _____
   _____
   _____

My Strengths are

1. _____

2. _____

3. _____

4. _____

5. _____

6. _____

My Weaknesses are

1. _____

2. _____

3. _____
   _____
   _____
   _____

4. _____
   _____
   _____
   _____

5. _____
   _____
   _____
   _____

6. _____
   _____
   _____
   _____

If you are having a difficult time identifying your strengths and weaknesses, it may be helpful to first separate your communication into a number of different subareas. The following may be some examples:

- Anxiety during presentations
- Misses or misreads nonverbal signals frequently
- Difficulties in dealing with confrontation

- _____
- _____
- _____
- _____
- _____
- _____

Quiz

Ask yourself the following questions and rate yourself on a scale from 1-10. Rate 10 if it happens often, or you agree; 1, if it rarely happens, or you don't agree; and question mark (?) if you don't understand or relate to the question.

- Are you repeatedly misunderstood?
- Do you easily get distracted?
- Do people frequently ask you for clarification?
- Do you maintain eye contact with the person you are interacting with?
- Do you check back with the person you are communicating with throughout your interaction?
- Do you explain or give reasons when you make a request?
- Do you plan what you are going to say before you approach the person?
- Do you modify your delivery depending on the person you communicate with?
- Do you ask other people for their opinions?
- Do you ask for feedback?
- Are you proactive and do state what you want?
- Do you use indirect communication most frequently?
- Do you use direct communication?
- Do you lash out when you feel offended in a conversation?
- Do you stop talking and withdraw when hurt, angry, or disappointed?
- Do you maintain your position?
- Do you look for creative ways to change your communication when you are not heard?
- Do you encourage the other person to share his or her feelings?
- Are you reactive to strong emotions?
- Do you ask a lot of questions?
- Do you follow through?
- Do you use humor in your communication?
- Do you get asked a lot of questions?
- Do you change the subject when you are uncomfortable?
- Do you intimidate others?
- Do you recognize when someone is uncomfortable?

- Do you raise your voice when you argue?
- Do you reach agreements easily?
- Are you solution oriented in your communication?
- Are you process oriented in your communication?
- Do you use inflammatory language?
- Do you attack when feeling threatened?
- Do people tell you that you seem to be in a good mood?
- Do you recognize when you're being manipulated?
- Do you feel confident in your ability to handle manipulations?
- Do you communicate defensively?
- Do you feel comfortable communicating on the phone?
- Do others intimidate you?
- Do you prefer to communicate face to face?
- Do you enjoy speaking in front of a group?
- Do you often experience disappointment in your communication?
- Do you generally resolve your conflicts quickly and positively?
- Do you enjoy listening when someone is speaking?
- Do you think that you use your body language more than the average person?
- Do you feel scared when confronted?
- Do you avoid confrontation?
- Do you initiate communication more than 65 percent in your interactions?
- Do you hold people accountable?
- Do you avoid difficult people?
- Are you successful holding people accountable?
- Are you able to repeat back what has been said more often than not?
- Do you easily get distracted?
- Do you withdraw when you feel threatened, attacked, disappointed or frustrated?
- Is it difficult for you to maintain focus in a conversation?
- Do you use abusive language?
- Do you control the conversations more than 65 percent in your interactions?
- Do you end conversations abruptly?
- Do people tell you that they can't hear you?
- Do you enjoy verbal communication?
- Do you enjoy written communication?

- Do people tell you that you don't hear what they have to say?
- Do people experience you as open and receptive?
- Do you experience curiosity often in your communication with others?
- Do you think you are judgmental?
- Do others often tell you that you seem judgmental?
- Do you admit when you are wrong?
- Are you more often than not clear about what your intent is when you communicate?
- Are you more often than not clear about the other person's intent?
- Do you get closure when you communicate?
- Are you concerned about hurting other people's feelings when you present a point?
- Do you jump to conclusions?
- Are you receptive to criticism?
- Do you interrupt frequently (6 out of 10 times in a conversation)?
- Did you enjoy answering the questions above?

Now that you have started the process of *heightened, enlightened awareness* you can create a strategic plan that works for you to continue the work. Below are some steps that may inspire your creativity.

Suggested Steps to Take

1. Become aware of your strengths and weaknesses.
2. Analyze your strengths and weaknesses.
3. Give a copy of this quiz to three of your friends and ask them to rate you, not themselves. Then ask them to give you back the completed quiz so that you can compare their experiences of you with your own.
4. Design your own personal map using communication as a tool to achieve your goals. Make a drawing of an actual map and fill in your goals and potential roadblocks.
5. Develop a strategic plan to better utilize your strengths and improve your weaknesses.
6. Make an agreement with yourself on how much time you will dedicate each week to the area of communication.
7. Reevaluate yourself three months after you have started your steps.
8. Revise your original strategic plan according to your progress.

Glossary

The descriptions in this book are derivates from *Webster's New World Dictionary: College Edition. 3rd ed.* Simon and Schuster, 1989, 1991 and the *Encarta Dictionary* associated with *Microsoft Office 2003*.

Accountability: Giving satisfactory reasons or an explanation for one's behavior; being obliged to account for one's acts; being responsible and capable of being accounted for.

Act out: To behave in a way that unconsciously expresses (often repressed) feelings, thoughts, fears, or needs. It is often an impulsive type of behavior that ignores the feelings of other people and is generally destructive, and not in the best interest of the self or others.

Agreements: The act of agreeing and being in harmony.

Anxiety: State of being uneasy, apprehensive, or worried about what may happen; state characterized by a feeling of being powerless and unable to cope with threatening events.

Boundary: A line or thing marking a limit or a border.

Conflict: (1) To fight, battle, contend; be in opposition, clash on ideas, a sharp disagreement or opposition, a contest or struggle. (2) An emotional disturbance resulting from a clash of opposing impulses or from an inability to reconcile impulses with realistic or moral considerations.

Containment: The capacity for holding, enclosing, and restraining something, someone or oneself in the moment. It does not refer to power and authority.

Context: The whole situation, background, or environment relevant to a particular event or personality.

Control: Exercising authority over, directing, commanding, holding back, curbing, or restraining.

Covert agenda: Hidden plan.

Curiosity: Desire to learn and know.

Defensiveness: Feeling under attack and being quick to justify one's actions by being ready to resist the attack or danger.

Disempower: Take or give power away.

Emotionalism: A display of emotions with a tendency to be easily swayed by emotions and engaging in exaggerated or undue display of strong feelings.

Enhancer: Something added that improves an interaction.

Faulty judgment: A judgment that is made carelessly, irresponsibly, without sufficient information or knowledge, in fear or used to compensate for fears or unaccepted or unrecognized needs.

Fear: Feeling of anxiety and agitation caused by the presence or nearness of danger, evil, pain, timidity, dread, terror, fight; feeling of uneasiness or apprehension.

Follow through: To continue and complete an action.

Fused: Unable to separate two parts form each other whether it relates to experiences or parts of an identity. To blend thoroughly by or as if by melting together: to combine.' In its participial form, it may point to the state of being combined.

Impulse: A sudden forceful inclination to act.

Influences: Something that manipulates, affects, impacts, or controls or have power over us; examples used herein: anger, disappointment, frustration, hostility, pressure, faulty judgments, rigidity, pressure; an influence that when supported correctly, can become a resource and as such, an asset in our interactions

Interpret: To explain the meaning of something by making it understandable.

Intimidate: Behavior that is making someone timid or fearful; to frighten, discourage, or suppress by threats or violence.

Intimidatee: A person who is being intimidated.

Intimidator: Tormentor, oppressor; a person who is intimidating.

Mirror back: Repeat back what was said as closely as possible to how it was said.

Nonreactive: Not be affected by some influence and act out a feeling, thought, or impulse.

Omnipotent: Having unlimited power or authority.

Oppositional-defiant behavior: An actively hostile and disobedient attitude toward something or someone, or a resistant stance against something or someone.

Overt agenda: Clear plan.

Passive-aggressive behaviors: Indirect expressions of anger, disappointment, frustration, or resentment that can be seen in behavior and communication.

Polarization: Power struggle wherein you and the other person tend to separate into diametrically opposed, often antagonistic, viewpoints.

Power: A person or thing having great influence, force or authority; the ability to do, act or affect strongly; the right to rule, determine, make decisions, and enforce obedience.

Proactive: Taking the initiative.

Projection: The unconscious act or process of ascribing to others your own ideas, impulses, or emotions that are undesirable or cause you anxiety.

Projector: A person who is engaging in the unconscious act or process of ascribing to others his or her own ideas, impulses or emotions that are undesirable or cause anxiety.

React: Emotions *run the show* and get acted out in the moment (absence of choices).

Reality test: To verify one's experience by asking questions when unsure, repeating back information, and asking the other to verify or correct one's interpretation of what the intent of the communication is.

Receptivity: Opposite of a barrier; being able and ready to take in suggestions, requests, and new ideas.

Reframe: Taking an already existing viewpoint or belief system and challenging it by adding new and different information proposing a new outlook.

Relationship: A state of being related to or connected to.

Resentment: Feeling of displeasure and indignation from a sense of being injured or offended.

Resistance: Opposing, withstanding and warding off; related to as the psychological opposition to the bringing of unconscious material to consciousness.

Respond: Logic is used with the absence of emotionalism followed by a constructive choice to act responsibly. Logic takes priority over the need for the emotion to be acted out in the moment.

Responsibility Frame: Dependable structure.

Responsibility: A condition, quality, fact, or instance of being responsible.

Trust: A firm belief or confidence in the honesty, integrity, reliability, justice to oneself, another person or thing; it can be referred to as faith and reliance.

Underlying issue: An issue that is not easily seen or noticed.

Vent: To relieve or unburden emotions/feelings via verbal expression.

Victim: Somebody who experiences misfortune and feels helpless to do anything about it. Somebody who is duped or taken advantage of, affected, or deceived by somebody or something.

Victimhood: Being harmed by or otherwise suffering from an act, condition, or circumstance and feeling helpless to do anything about it. Can be interchangeable with Victimhood and Victim stance

Victim stance: Somebody who is experiencing misfortune and is taking the position that he or she is powerless to do anything about it.

Index

Q

questions 17, 21, 22, 23, 33, 34, 35, 39,
     40, 41, 44, 47, 52, 57, 67, 74, 75,
     76, 82, 84, 87, 97, 98, 99, 101, 102,
     109, 110, 111, 114, 116, 123, 125,
     131, 133, 141, 143, 147, 148, 149,
     150, 151, 152, 153, 154, 157, 163,
     168, 169, 172, 179, 181, 184, 191,
     199, 202, 209, 217, 218, 223, 226,
     228, 230, 231, 236, 254, 264, 275,
     277, 278, 279, 290

R

rationalization 100
reactivity 55, 58, 66, 69, 75, 86, 91, 92,
     120, 122, 199, 268, 272, 276
reality test 35, 49, 52, 89, 126, 181, 182, 291
reason. *See* logic
  for understanding into agreement 287
reassurance, as a tool against conflict 249
rebellion. *See* behavior
receptivity 108
  manifestations of
reframing 127
reinforcement 25, 43, 53, 62, 152, 162, 171
relationships 17
  adult-child type 66, 90
  employer-employee type 93
  parent-child type 93
  parent-adolescent type 93
  with anger 21, 24
  with fears, judgments, and needs 85
  with power, control, and resentment 94,
     146
resentment 21, 23, 90, 93, 101, 103, 104,
     105, 137, 151, 153, 180
  avoidance of 241, 263, 264
  connection to power, control, and
     victimhood 106, 125
  felt as a victim 92, 95
  tools for dealing with 110
resistance 108, 109, 112, 114
  manifestations of 256
  tools against 113, 114

respect
  as a tool against conflict and
     emotionalism 255
  manifestations of 256
  self-respect 256
respect circles 258
responses 15, 20, 22, 27, 31, 32, 34, 47,
     52, 53, 58, 77, 91, 92, 94, 95, 98,
     119, 131, 134, 148, 155, 164, 167,
     176, 181, 194, 197, 198, 217, 218,
     230, 271, 278, 280
responsibility 201, 221
  areas of 204
  frames 188
  guidelines to 229
  inequality in 224
  inventory 202
  process 191, 196, 201, 212, 214, 216, 225
role-modeling behavior 162, 223, 255, 262
  in trust-repairing process 153
rules
  in preemptive damage control (PDC) 261
  setting up for future conflicts 263

S

self-awareness 133
self-esteem 23, 119
sensitivity 280
shame 78, 146, 148, 166, 191, 213, 235,
     279
short-term goals 137, 139, 141
skills (judgment and social) for
     development 214
slowing down 200, 217, 223, 247, 274
social groups 44
space. *See* proxemics
staying on path, as a tool against conflict 252
subjective experience 227
support 214
  in avoiding victimhood 199
  in trust-repairing process 147
suppression 21, 61, 125, 126, 195, 197,
     207, 217, 272, 275, 278
surrender 172, 185
synchronization. *See* timing, *See also* timing

CPSIA information can be obtained at www.ICGtesting.com
Printed in the USA
BVOW021116161011

273738BV00004B/19/A